For Dr. Geoffrey Walker,
With many thanks
for your hospitality. Please
do not be put off by the
title – which is awful
and not mine!

Best wishes,

William Chislett

Cambridge 2/7/98.

PORTUGAL

PORTUGAL

INVESTMENT AND GROWTH

William Chislett

Published by
Euromoney Publications
in association with
Banco Espírito Santo
Bolsa de Valores de Lisboa
ICEP – Investimentos, Comércio e Turismo de Portugal
A. M. Pereira, Sáragga Leal, Oliveira Martins, Júdice e Associados
Petrogal S.A.
SONAE Investimentos, SGPS

Published by
Euromoney Publications PLC
Nestor House, Playhouse Yard
London EC4V 5EX

ISBN 1 85564 565 3

Typeset by Julie Foster and PW Reprosharp, London
Printed in England by Clifford Press Ltd, Coventry

ACKNOWLEDGEMENTS

William Chislett was born in Oxford in 1951. He reported on Spain's 1975–78 transition to democracy for *The Times*. Between 1978 and 1984 he was based in Mexico City for the *Financial Times*, covering Mexico and Central America, before returning to Madrid in 1986 as a writer and translator. He wrote Euromoney's first book on Portugal in 1991 (*Portugal: A New Era*) and has also written books on Spain, Chile, Ecuador, Panama and Finland. Banco Central Hispano published his book *Spain: at a Turning Point* in 1994, and in 1996 *Spain: the Central Hispano Handbook*, a yearly review. In 1978 he wrote *The Spanish Media since Franco* (Index on Censorship). He is married and has two sons.

William Chislett would like to thank the following people for their help in researching the book: Belmiro de Azevedo, chairman of SONAE; António Barreto of the University of Lisbon; Scott Beaumont, Portugal country analyst of HSBC James Capel; António Castro Henriques, managing director of Banco Comercial Português; Rui Chancerelle de Machete, chairman of the Luso-American Development Foundation; Cristina Corado of the New University of Lisbon; Luis Feria, manager of Banco Cisf; Jane Fernandes, representative of the Portuguese UK Chamber of Commerce; Manuel Ferreira da Silva, managing director of Banco Português de Investimento; Elizabeth Frawley Bagley, US Ambassador to Portugal; Carlos Gaspar, adviser to the Presidency; Vítor Gaspar, head of the Bank of Portugal's research department; Marion Kaplan; Jaime de Lacerda, a director of the Portuguese Confederation of Industry; Marcos Lagoa of Barclays Bank Portugal; Kenneth Maxwell, director of the Camoes Center and a senior fellow at the Council for Foreign Relations; José Medeiros Ferreira, president of the parliamentary committee of European affairs; Trevenen Morris- Grantham of the brokers Titulo; José Luis Joló, managing director of Banco Bilbao Vizcaya in Portugal; Miguel Namorado Rosa, chief economist of Banco Comercial Português; Antonio Nogueira Leite of the New University of Lisbon; Ken Pottinger, director of the Internet service Datafile Portugal; Emanuel dos Santos, head of research, Ministry of Finance; Paul Symington, executive director of Symington Port and Madeira Shippers; Mari Vargas, vice-president, Portuguese equities of Banco Santander de Negocios; Alvaro Vasconcelos, director of the Institute of Strategic and International Studies; Manuel Villaverde Cabral of the University of Lisbon; and Peter Wise, Lisbon correspondent of the *Financial Times*. The book is written in memory of two friends, Diana Smith and Charles Hodgson, who shared a deep appreciation of Portugal.

Euromoney would like to thank A. M. Pereira, Sáragga Leal, Oliveira Martins, Júdice, Torres e Associados, who contributed Chapters 10, 14, 15 and 16.

The picture on pages 10-11 was supplied by Capstone Design. The co-publishers supplied their own pictures.

CONTENTS

1

HISTORICAL INTRODUCTION

Portugal has made great progress in the last decade in its attempt to narrow the gap in its living standards compared to the rest of Europe. Portugal's per capita GDP increased from 46 per cent of the European Union (EU) average in 1985 to 67 per cent in 1995 (see Exhibit 1.1). Anyone who has been visiting Portugal over the past 20 years cannot but be struck by the tremendous advances made in modernising the economy, improving infrastructure and consolidating democracy. The country is, however, still the second poorest EU nation after Greece.

Located in the extreme south-west of the European Union, tiny Portugal – with a population of close to 10 million – had its back turned to Europe until the "carnation" revolution of 25 April 1974 which ended 46 years of dictatorship. Portugal then was very much the impoverished man of Europe: more than one-sixth of the population over the age of 15 was illiterate; the infant mortality rate of 26 per 1,000 live births was more than double that in advanced western Europe and 850,000 Portuguese were working in France alone because there were not enough jobs at home. Child labour was common in the north of the country. Visitors to the isolated Trás-os-Montes area in the far north-east corner bordering Spain could be forgiven for believing that its abandoned villages were straight out of the Middle Ages. Per capita GDP was around US$2,000, on a par with Chile, Brazil and Argentina.

Today the illiteracy rate is much lower (although still high by EU standards); infant mortality is in line with the European norm and per capita income is around US$13,000. In 1996 Portugal was ranked 35th out of 174 countries in the UN human development index, which is a cocktail of life expectancy at birth, per capita income (measured by purchasing power parity as opposed to market exchange rates), adult literacy and the enrolment ratio in primary, secondary and tertiary education (see Exhibit 1.2).

Politically the country has veered from a right-wing dictatorship to the brink of a communist-led coup in

Exhibit 1.1

Per capita GDP convergence of selected EU countries (EU-15 = 100)

	1985	*1995*
Finland	102	92
Greece	62	63
Ireland	63	90
Portugal	46	67
Spain	70	76

Source: Eurostat, July 1996.

Exhibit 1.2

UN human development index (selected European countries)

Ranking	*Life expectancy at birth 1993*	*Adult literacy rate (%) 1993*	*Combined enrolment ratio 1993*	*Real per capita GDP (PPP 1993 US$)*
7. France	77.0	99.0	88	19,140
10. Spain	77.7	98.0	87	13,660
16. United Kingdom	76.3	99.0	83	17,230
18. Germany	76.1	99.0	79	18,840
20. Italy	77.6	97.4	70	18,160
21. Greece	77.7	93.8	78	8,950
35. Portugal	74.7	86.2	79	10,720

Source: 1996 UN Human Development Report.

November 1975. Since 1987 it has enjoyed a stable parliamentary democracy based on two alternating parties, the Social Democrats and the Socialists. The Socialists under António Guterres ended 10 years of rule by the Social Democrats in October 1995 when they won 112 of the 230 seats in the legislative elections. The Socialist Jorge Sampaio also won the presidential election in January 1996, giving Portugal a government and a presidency of the same political colour for the first time since democracy was restored in 1974.

To mark its remarkable progress, Portugal will host the 1998 World Exposition (Expo 98) which will celebrate the Age of Discoveries, when the country led western Europe into a new era of expansion, and dedicate itself to preserving the threatened oceans of the world that the country's 15th-century navigators first explored.

Break-up of the empire

Portugal's empire began with world-wide discoveries in the 15th and early 16th centuries. Subsequently Portugal lost ground to Spain, the Dutch and the British but until 1974 it retained colonies that spread from Africa (Angola, Mozambique, Guinea-Bissau and the islands of Cape Verde and São Tomé e Princip) to Asia (Macao and the island of Timor). This 20th-century empire was 22 times larger than Portugal itself.

António de Oliveira Salazar, Portugal's right-wing dictator from 1928 to 1968, used to boast that the Portuguese empire was larger than all of western Europe. To drive home the slogan that "Portugal is not a small country" the walls of classrooms, police stations and government offices displayed a map of Europe with the empire superimposed on it.

It was the wealth of Brazil's gold and iron ore mines (Brazil became independent in 1823) that made it possible for the Portuguese crown to rebuild Lisbon after the devastating 1755 earthquake – notably the city's largest square, the aptly name Praca do Comércio (Trade Square). Here, wistfully facing the river Tagus and beyond it the Atlantic Ocean, lie the government offices. Once they looked out on the trading ships and, later, heavily-laden freighters that brought back goods from the rich lodes of Africa or South America; now they look out on small, crowded ferries busily transporting commuters from one side of the Tagus to the other.

But the vast body of that empire – home, at the time of decolonisation in 1974–75, to 17 million people – was relentlessly dominated by its tiny head, a country of nine million people which insisted, in the Salazar era, that it did not have "colonies" but "overseas provinces". It was the creed of the New State – created in 1932 along corporatist lines by Dr Salazar, an economics professor, after he had spent four years reorganising Portugal's debt-ridden finances – that the distant domains in Africa and Asia, which he visited as rarely as he did any European country, were an inseparable part, however distant, of the Portuguese mainland.

The New State was never purely fascist nor aggressively capitalist. The structures of capitalism – markets, free enterprise and competition – did not exist. It was a homespun philosophy which aimed to keep Portugal cocooned from mainstream Europe.

From the outset, the empire drained Portugal of its best energies. Its brighter farmers, businessmen, administrators and younger members of aristocratic families went to Latin America or Africa to create new ventures, while artisans and tradesmen went to Africa in search of greater opportunities. Following the outbreak of wars in the African colonies in 1961, the young men who were conscripted from the countryside, and others who emigrated to Europe to avoid the draft and find work, numbered hundreds of thousands. They depleted mainland Portugal of manpower for its agriculture and its developing industries.

The centuries-long phenomenon whereby Portugal invested far more in its empire than in itself, developed better infrastructures in Africa than it did at home, and did more to encourage agriculture, mining, fishing, industry and finance in Angola or Mozambique than it did in its European territory, caused an enormous imbalance in the country's development.

The first crack in the empire occurred in 1961, in the tiny enclave of Goa on the western coast of the Indian subcontinent. Goa, along with its associated outposts at Diu and Damiao, were relics dating back to 1510 when traders bound for the East Indies needed victualling bases and forts in which to shelter. In 1954, Indian president Jawaharlal Nehru had invited Salazar to negotiate the decolonisation of these enclaves. Salazar rejected the overture, remarking in a characteristic appeal to history: "We would be giving up or selling the Portuguese of India, the lands of Alfonso d'Albuquerque and our epic achievements in the Orient, the saints of the Church, our country's martyrs. And for how much? For how much?" Salazar held on for seven years until, in the early hours of 18 December 1961, 30,000 Indian troops invaded Goa, meeting brave resistance from a garrison of 3,500 Portuguese troops. Salazar cabled the military commander: "I contemplate no truce and I wish no Portuguese to be taken prisoner. Our soldiers and sailors must conquer or die."

The loss of Goa was a shattering blow for the army; even after Salazar's death in 1970 a representative of "the province of Goa" continued to sit in Portugal's National Assembly until 1974. At about the same time as the loss of Goa, the Movement for the Liberation of Angola (MPLA) went on the attack, finding some sympathetic echoes among underground left-wing movements in Lisbon, especially among the Communists who, though outlawed, had never ceased to organise and plan for the day when the dictatorship would end. By the end of 1961, Portugal had more than 50,000 troops in Angola; three years later it was fighting in Guinea-Bissau and Mozambique. The guerrilla wars dragged on until 1974, tying down up to 200,000 troops (an astronomical figure for a country of nine million) and requiring a defence budget which absorbed at its height 40 per cent of the national budget. Under pressure of war many people were drafted who otherwise would not have joined the armed forces. It was the middle-ranking officers of this generation who concluded that they were fighting for nothing.

Salazar suffered a thrombosis in 1968 and went into a coma, dying in 1970. He was replaced by Marcello Caetano, a law professor, who was prime minister in 1968. There was a slight opening up of the political system. The Socialist leader Mário Soares (who was to be president between March 1986 and January 1996) was allowed back from exile and some political prisoners were released. But Caetano was just as adamant about a Portuguese role in Africa as Salazar. "Without Africa we would be a small nation; with Africa we are a big power," he said in April 1970.

The cost of financing the wars was increasingly at the expense of economic development at home. Caetano faced not only a debilitating war on three fronts in Africa, but growing discontent in the old Salazarist trade unions which were coming under the influence of the Communist party. In late 1973 the first oil shock hit Portugal with particular severity: inflation in 1974 was almost 23 per cent (compared to 9.8 per cent in 1973), real GDP growth dropped to 1.1 per cent, exports were 15 per cent below the 1973 level, and the country registered its first current account deficit.

The carnation revolution

In February 1974, General António de Spínola, deputy chief of staff of the armed forces, published a book on Africa – *Portugal and the future* – which caused a sensation. Caetano, writing later from his exile in Brazil, admitted: "I did not stop until the last page, which I read in the small hours of the morning. And when I closed the book I had understood that the military coup, which I could sense had been coming, was now inevitable". Spínola argued that the wars were unwinnable, and on April 25 Caetano was overthrown by a near-bloodless coup (five people died) mounted by junior officers who had earlier formed the Movimento das Forças Armadas (Armed Forces Movement, or MFA). The coup was known as the "carnation" revolution because troops put flowers in the barrels of their guns.

Nationalisation

The only organised political force was the underground Communist party which wasted no time in filling the power vacuum. It had sympathisers in the MFA which soon split between conservative force, middle-of-the-road liberals who wished to encourage national consensus and the extreme left which pushed for revolution. Álvaro Cunhal, the Stalinist leader now in his 80s, and the only west European Communist leader to have praised the Soviet invasion of Czechoslovakia in 1968, returned from exile (he had escaped from the fortress prison at Peniche in 1960).

The MFA grew more radical. A coup by Spínola, then president, was foiled in March 1975 and he went into exile. A new government was formed and the Supreme Revolutionary Council nationalised all banks save three foreign ones. Because of the close links between the banks and industry, 53 per cent of Portugal's gross fixed capital formation passed into the state's hands at a stroke. The state became the owner of brewery, cigarette, petrochemical, cement, steel, shipbuilding, water, insurance, television and radio companies. Workers took over control of many companies in the name of social equality and the large estates in the Alentejo were occupied by landless peasants goaded on by the Communist party. At the height of the left's purges over 2,000 people were in jail for political reasons, considerably more than at the time the dictatorship was overthrown.

In the heady aftermath of decolonisation and nationalisation it appeared that Portugal would jump straight from a form of fascism to something close to communism. This was just what the Communist party hoped for on Nato's south-western flank (Portugal was a founder member in 1949 even though Nato's preamble laid down the principles of "democracy, individual liberty and the rule of law.") But it had not counted on the innate common sense of the Portuguese.

Parliamentary democracy

Ignoring the calls of radical MFA officers to cast blank votes and thus reject civilian politicians, 92 per cent of the electorate went to the polls on 25 April 1975, in the first free general election for more than 50 years, to elect a Constituent Assembly to draw up a new constitution. The Socialists emerged as the largest party. In November, the moderate military led by Colonel (later President) António Ramalho Eanes forestalled a left-wing coup and purged the armed forces of its radical elements. This action, and the calling of parliamentary elections, ushered in democracy and a string of weak governments. Mário Soares became Prime Minister. Between January 1976 and July 1987, Portugal had 10 governments, ranging from two minority Socialist administrations to the non-party appointee governments of President Eanes and Social Democrat/Centre Democrat coalitions. Six provisional governments swiftly came and went between 1974 and parliamentary democracy.

Decolonisation reduced military costs enormously, but it resulted in the loss of preferential access to oil, sugar and coffee at a time when the prices of these commodities rocketed. It also brought home a flood of people from the former colonies. By the time Angola achieved independence on 11 November 1975, around 600,000 Portuguese citizens had returned, increasing the population of mainland Portugal by 6 per cent. The combination of decolonisation and nationalisation set against the background of a deteriorating economy was an explosive mixture. Somehow the state had to find funds for the new army of employees installed by politically inspired overmanning in the new public enterprises and by one government after another bringing its clientele into the civil service, where they obtained lifelong tenure even after their sponsors had left office.

By the late 1970s, there were 650,000 state employees in a labour force of 4.2 million. Governments were driven to selling or mortgaging Salazar's gold reserves as their last line of defence against bankruptcy. By 1978, when Mário Soares' government made the first application for Portugal to join the EC, only half of its gold reserves were free, and total gold and foreign exchange reserves covered three-and-a-half months of imports, a very low level by European standards. The International Monetary Fund (IMF), the US and the EC came to the rescue, and the IMF seal of approval for an austerity programme acted as the launching pad for a US$800 million syndicated loan which was the start of a new relationship between Portugal and the international banking community. The country had to tighten its belt, but no loss-making state-owned companies were closed. The 1976 constitution did not allow the "conquests of the working class" to be denationalised.

When the IMF's austerity programme ended, the state began another bout of spending it could not afford – not least on extravagant projects such as the Sines petro-chemical complex. The budget deficit reached a massive 15 per cent of GDP in 1982, the current account deficit 13.5 per cent and foreign debt 72 per cent. Once again the IMF saved Portugal. When the Socialists came to power again in mid-1983 they found foreign currency reserves covering two weeks of imports. To bridge the gap they mortgaged US$300 million of gold reserves to secure an emergency loan from the Bank for International Settlements and embarked on another austerity programme.

EU membership

Signed in the beautiful cloisters of the monastery-cathedral of São Jerónimo, built to celebrate Portugal's maritime brilliance, the 1985 Treaty of Accession to the EC marked the burial of the isolationist Salazar dictum of a Portugal "proudly alone." After 500 years of living with its back to Europe, Portugal came face to face with the continent.

European Union integration has provided a unique opportunity for Portugal to shake off some of its structural problems and upgrade its infrastructure using funds from the Community Support Framework. Huge inflows of EU aid, estimated at its height to account for at least one percentage point of annual GDP growth, have changed the face of Portugal in many areas.

The 1987 elections were a watershed in post-1974 politics because they produced Portugal's first government with an absolute majority. The Social Democrats led by Anibal Cavaco Silva, a Bank of Portugal economist and technocrat who had been finance minister in an earlier coalition government, won 50.2 per cent of the vote and 148 of the parliament's 250 seats. Weary of political bickering and see-saw governments, voters gave Portugal the stability it needed to enact constitutional reforms, begin to restructure the economy, and create a modern state. On 1 June 1989, after two years of negotiations, constitutional changes paved the way for privatisation and the unravelling of the tangled web of land collectivisation.

Economic overview

One of the most impressive results of Portugal's integration into the EU has been the sharp fall in consumer price inflation from 19.3 per cent in 1985 to 3.1 per cent in

Exhibit 1.3
Inflation, 1990–96 (% change)

	1990	*1991*	*1992*	*1993*	*1994*	*1995*	*1996*
Portugal	13.4	11.4	8.9	6.5	5.2	4.1	3.1
European Union	6.1	5.1	4.2	3.5	3.1	3	2.5
Differential	7.3	6.3	4.7	3	2.1	1.1	0.6

Source: INE and Eurostat.

1996, when the differential relative to the EU average stood at an historically low 0.6 percentage points (see Exhibit 1.3).

The fight against inflation has been sustained by the escudo's stability, favourable external price trends and moderate growth in unit labour costs, as a result of both wage restraint and robust productivity growth. A key role was played by the adoption of exchange rate stability as a goal of monetary policy, after the escudo joined the exchange-rate mechanism (ERM) of the European Monetary System in April 1992.

Until mid-1993, Portugal's ERM membership was accompanied by periodic pressures on the exchange rate, as illustrated by the high volatility of the spot exchange rate and, occasionally, by forward exchange rates approaching the lower boundary of the fluctuation band. The Bank of Portugal countered these pressures, which were linked to wider turbulence affecting other European currencies as well as to the weakness of the Spanish peseta, through a combination of interventions in the foreign exchange markets, increases in its intervention rates and realignments of the escudo parity in the ERM (November 1992 and May 1993). Since the widening of the ERM fluctuation band to 15 per cent either side, the escudo has traded within the old 2.25 per cent narrow band at close to its central rate of 102.5/Dm.

Portugal, which like all peripheral markets is vulnerable to sharp changes, has gained exchange rate credibility (volatility has sharply declined) and succeeded to some extent in uncoupling the escudo's fortunes from those of the peseta. Portugal and Spain (Portugal's second largest market and main source of imports) tend to be lumped together and viewed from abroad as one country. In March 1995, the central parity of the escudo was devalued by 3.5 per cent, half the size of the peseta's devaluation.

Economic growth over the past decade has been well above the average for the EU-15 (see Exhibit 1.4) in most years, with the notable exception of 1993 when Portugal was in recession.

Unemployment has risen (to some 7 per cent from 4.1 per cent in 1992) but in 1997 it was still below the cyclical peak of 8.5 per cent in 1984 and much lower than the EU average of 11 per cent. The jobless rate, which does not take into account considerable underemployment, is strikingly lower than in neighbouring Spain (21 per cent), partly because of less rigid labour market conditions. The Portuguese concern to hold onto a job is eloquently expressed by the fact that it is not uncommon for people to work for nothing when their company goes through hard times. This is said to be unique in Europe.

Exhibit 1.4

Real GDP growth in Portugal and the EU-15 (%), 1987–96

	Portugal	*EU*
1987	5.5	2.8
1988	5.8	4.2
1989	5.7	3.5
1990	4.3	2.9
1991	2.1	1.6
1992	1.1	1
1993	1.2	-0.6
1994	0.8	2.8
1995	2.4	2.4
1996	3.0	1.6

Source: INE and the European Commission.

Almost all the jobs lost have been in traditional sectors, particularly textiles and clothing which are struggling against competition from lower cost producers in Asia and eastern Europe. Employment-shedding in the textile sector is likely to continue with the phasing out of the MFA agreement reached under the Uruguay Round.

While jobs are being lost in these sectors, new ones have been created in the rapidly emerging motor industry. The AutoEuropa joint venture plant of Ford and Volkswagen at Palmela, inaugurated in April 1995, will employ about 10,000 people, directly in the factory and indirectly in companies supplying parts, when it reaches full capacity (100,000 vehicles a year). Exports of the Ford Galaxy and the Volkswagen Sharan multipurpose vehicles accounted for about 10 per cent of Portugal's total merchandise exports in 1996. Siemens, the German electronics and electrical engineering group, chose Portugal in 1996 from 26 competing countries as the site for its US$380 million memory-chip plant that will create 750 jobs.

Despite a strengthening of the real effective exchange rate, exports have stood up well. They grew by around 8 per cent in real terms in 1996 and 11 per cent in 1995. Exporters have held their prices steady, improved productivity and taken a squeeze on profit margins. The current account registered a deficit in 1996 equivalent to 2.3 per cent of GDP in 1996 (–0.2 per cent in 1995 and –1.7 per cent in 1994). International reserves at the end of 1996 stood at US$21.3 billion (equivalent to 7–8 months' imports). Although labour costs have risen, Portuguese wages are still far below those of their major EU partners (just over one quarter of the EU average in 1996 in the manufacturing sector), but they are substantially higher than the aggressive new competitors in central Europe (Czech Republic, Poland and Hungary) with ambitions to join the EU.

Portugal has made a tremendous leap forward in its standard of living over the past 25 years (the number of cars per 1,000 inhabitants has quadrupled to 260, close to two-thirds the EU average), but the country's overall competitiveness has been gradually declining. The country fell from 32nd position in 1995 to 36th in 1996 in the world ranking of the 45 most competitive countries drawn up by the IMD (see Exhibit 1.5), a Swiss management school. It was overtaken by the Czech Republic and by Colombia. The IMD defines competitiveness as "the ability of a country to create added value and thus increase national wealth by managing assets and processes, attractiveness and aggressiveness, globality and proximity, and by integrating these relationships into an economic and social model."

Its slippage reflects both the greater advances made by thrusting countries such

Exhibit 1.5

World competitiveness: Portugal's ranking out of 46 countries at each level of criteria aggregation, 1993–96

	1996	*1995*	*1994*	*1993*
Domestic economic strength	42	36	35	33
Internationalisation	32	26	24	25
Government	32	29	25	24
Finance	29	28	34	32
Infrastructure	39	37	32	31
Management	41	34	36	38
Science and technology	36	41	44	44
People	32	29	26	31
Assets	36	30	29	32
Processes	36	35	34	35
Attractiveness	29	29	27	28
Aggressiveness	39	36	36	37
Overall ranking	36	32	30	32

Source: IMD World Competitiveness Yearbook 1996.

as the Czech Republic as well as Portugal's structural deficiencies, particularly the poor quality of its education system.

The Socialists, as market-oriented as the hard-nosed Social Democrats, are determined to ensure that Portugal qualifies for the first round of European monetary union in 1999. Portugal is enjoying its strongest period of growth since the mid-1980s, when it joined the European Community. The economy was growing at 3–4 per cent in 1997, inflation was running at below 3 per cent, its lowest level since the 1960s, exports were buoyant and foreign investment plans were increasing. The numbers are good; if the country is excluded from round one it will be, unfairly, for political reasons.

2

INFRASTRUCTURE AND RESOURCES

Close to 10 million people occupy an area of 92,100 square kilometres in the extreme south-west of Europe. In addition to the mainland territory, Portugal comprises the autonomous island regions of Madeira and the Azores in the Atlantic Ocean, and the enclave of Macao on the Chinese mainland. Macao will be handed over to China in 1999.

Despite being a small country (Portugal accounts for less than 4 per cent of the EU's territory), its citizens are not cramped for space, apart from overcrowded Lisbon and Oporto on the Atlantic coast. Population density averages 107 inhabitants per square kilometre (close to 800 in Lisbon), on a par with France but far from the EU average of 146. More than one-third of the population lives in towns of over 10,000 inhabitants. The largest cities are the capital Lisbon (2.5 million) and Oporto (1 million) in the north, including their suburbs. Other major cities are Coimbra and Braga, both of them in the north. The population of the Azores and Madeira together is less than half a million.

Portugal is roughly divided into three parts by two main rivers, the Douro and the Tagus, which flow from Spain to reach the Atlantic coast cities of Oporto and Lisbon respectively. To the north of the Tagus Portugal is relatively mountainous, with an average height of about 1,200 feet and numerous peaks of 3,500 feet or more. By contrast, the average for southern Portugal is no more than 700 feet, and there is very little land above 1,500 feet. The area to the south of the Tagus is a long flat plain, quite dry in the summer, separated from the south coast – the Algarve plain – by another range of mountains which rise to 1,800 feet. Madeira is a mountainous island and the nine islands of the Azores are volcanic.

The climate is Mediterranean in the south and temperate in the north. The warmest month is August, with average daily maximum and minimum temperatures of 28° and 17°C) and the coldest month is January (14° and 8°C)

The country reverted to the same time zone as Britain and Ireland in 1996 after four years of alignment with the rest of continental Europe. Moving back to Greenwich Mean Time (GMT) ended an unpopular "dark age" that forced most of the country to travel to school and to work before dawn. The previous government turned the clocks forward by an hour in 1992 to equate business timetables with Spain, Germany and France, Portugal's main trading partners, but the measure took a toll on the country's health and peace of mind.

Traditionally most Portuguese have lived close to the ocean and the most important frontier has thus been the open boundary of the Atlantic, and not that with Spain. A poignant verse by Fernando Pessoa (1888–1935), one of the country's greatest poets, captures the human consequences both of Portugal's voyages of exploration in the 15th and 16th centuries, when colonies were established, and of the massive migration during this century:

> "Oh salted sea, how much of your salt
> Comes from Portugal's tears.
> Because we dared to sail so many mothers have wept,
> So many sons have prayed in vain.
> So many brides have gone unwed
> To make you our own, oh sea."

Portuguese commonwealth

Portugal and its colonies set up a Portuguese-speaking commonwealth in 1996 (see map). Angola, Brazil, Cape Verde, Guinea-Bissau, Mozambique, São Tomé e Príncipe and Portugal created the Community of Portuguese Speaking Countries (CPLP). Almost 200 million people share a common language. The purpose of the CPLP is to assert as a group a wider diplomatic and cultural influence and not to set up any special trading or currency zone. The group helped Portugal win a seat on the UN Security Council in 1997 for two years.

The threat to Portugal's influence in its former colonies was made clear in 1995 when Mozambique became a full member of the English-speaking Commonwealth. The West African nations of Guinea-Bissau and São Tomé e Príncipe have also moved closer to La Francophonie, the French-language community of almost 50 countries.

The group also made a common diplomatic effort on East Timor, a Portuguese colony until Indonesia annexed it in 1975. Portugal has long called for self-determination in the former colony and persistently denounced the human rights violations committed by Indonesian soldiers in East Timor. The jubilation in Lisbon was palpable in October 1996 when the Nobel peace prize was awarded to Bishop Carlos Belo of East Timor and José Ramos Horta, a human rights activist, for their efforts to find a peaceful solution to the conflict that has claimed more than 200,000 lives, about one-third of the country's pre-invasion population according to Amnesty International. Expresso, the weekly newspaper, appeared the next day with a front page photograph of an Indonesian minister making a rude gesture at an anti-Indonesia demonstration several years earlier, and the Lisbon town hall plastered the city with posters congratulating the Nobel prize-winners.

Regionalisation

Portugal is one of the few EU countries not to have devolved any significant power over the last 20 years (with the exception of the Atlantic islands of Madeira and the Azores), although its 1976 constitution states that elected administrations should be created to

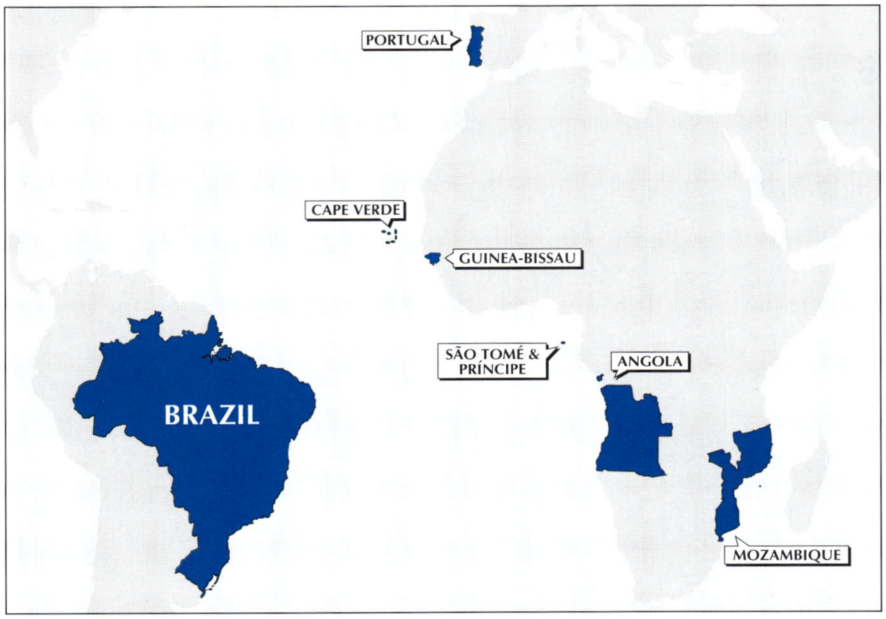

Left. The Community of Portuguese Speaking Countries. Right: the regional administrations proposed in the draft law of May 1996, but subject to a referendum.

further the "direct and active" participation of citizens in political life.

More than 20 years later, Portugal remains one of only three EU countries, with Greece and Ireland, not to have devolved some political power to its regions. The government is responsible for 93 per cent of total public spending and the municipalities 7 per cent compared with 58 per cent in Spain by the central government, 15 per cent by the municipalities and 27 per cent by the regions.

There is particular resentment in the north (see next section), the hub of Portugal's private enterprise, over the imbalance in the development of this part of the country compared with Lisbon, the seat of government, in the south. Professor Pedro Arrija estimates that the north makes an annual net transfer to the south of more than US$3 billion as a result of relatively higher tax contributions and a lower level of public services. This is one reason why per capita GDP in the north (87 per cent of the national average) trails behind that of Lisbon (129 per cent). The investment in the 1998 World Exposition (Expo 98) will accentuate the balance.

For administrative purposes, Portugal is divided into 18 districts and two autonomous regions (Madeira and the Azores). They, in turn, are divided into municipalities which are then subdivided into boroughs. Each district has a local government. Each municipality is administered through a *Câmara Municipal* (town council) headed by a *presidente* (mayor). The district governors are appointed by the government; the mayors are elected.

When the Socialists, who are four seats short of an overall majority in parliament, pushed through a draft law in May 1996 to create regional administrations with the support of the communists, thereby fulfilling a promise they made when they were in the opposition, Social Democrat (PSD) deputies stormed out of the parliament. The PSD subsequently convinced the prime minister, António Guterrez, to hold a referendum on what has become an emotional issue.

Portugal, unlike Spain, has no clearly defined regional identities or differences and everyone speaks the same language. According to a self-disparaging Portuguese saying, "Portugal is Lisbon, the rest is just scenery".

Pressure for regionalisation comes from a few powerful local politicians in the Socialist party in the north of the country (and to a lesser extent among the Social Democrats) particularly from Fernando Gomes, the Socialist Mayor of Oporto. As consensus is the watchword of Socialist Prime Minister António Guterres – after the rather arrogant style of the Social Democrat Anibal Cavaco Silva, the prime minister for the previous 10 years – the government heeded the call for a referendum on the issue by the Social Democrats (generally opposed to regionalisation).

The regionalisation issue cuts across party lines; even supporters are divided over how many regions should be created. It is by no means certain that the government would win a referendum with an overwhelming majority. Any move towards regionalisation is unlikely before 1998.

Regionalisation could be used as a way to decentralise the bureaucracy, but unless carefully controlled and limited it would generate another level of bureaucracy which Portugal – faced with enough red tape already, in addition to budgetary constraints and many other more pressing priorities, such as education – can ill afford. It would also favour the creation of regional political "barons": the Social Democrat Alberto João Jardim, head of Madeira's regional government since 1978, was re-elected for the sixth consecutive term in October 1996. The press have dubbed him the "last Mohican" as he is all that is left of the Social Democrats' hold on power.

The Socialists envisage regional assemblies with limited powers that would be able to raise taxes and would have some control over health, education, roads and administration of EU regional incentives. The example of the autonomous islands of the Azores and Madeira is not a good one to follow; the finances of both are parlous. The government is wary of going down the same expensive road as Spain with its 17 autonomous regions vying with one another for a greater share of the national pie.

The north of Portugal

Although there are no regions in the generally accepted sense of the word, the north-south divide runs so deep that there are almost two Portugals. "Oporto works, Coimbra sings and Lisbon enjoys itself" is a popular saying in the northern city of Oporto, the country's hub of private enterprise. Northerners like to recall that Lisbon may have witnessed the great maritime adventures of the 15th and 16th centuries from the banks of the Tagus, but Henry the Navigator was from Oporto. The history of Portugal also has its roots in the north: the kingdom was proclaimed in Guimaraes in the 12th century, its name being derived from "Porto Gal" – originally Portus Galia, the gate of Galicia (Spain's north-western region bordering with Portugal).

With a closely packed population of around four million, the north accounts for about three-quarters of Portugal's manufacturing firms and, until the launch of the AutoEuropa Ford Volkswagen car plant in Palmela in the south in 1995, as much as three-fifths of its exports (largely textiles and clothing, shoes and wood and cork products). AutoEuropa accounted for close to 10 per cent of total exports in 1996. The work ethic is generally stronger in the north. Many of the leading groups in the north were built up by self-made men. Belmiro de Azevedo, head of SONAE, the largest private sector group, is the son of a carpenter and Américo Amorim, who runs the world's largest cork group, served his apprenticeship as a salesman travelling third class by train through the Soviet Union and eastern Europe.

The north itself is further divided between: the area of Oporto, the scene of many of Portugal's innovations in business, politics and culture in the last 200 years; the factory towns of the Minho (Braga, Famalicao, Fafe and Santo Tirso) where workers divide their time between industrial labour and small-scale farming, especially the white grapes for *vinho verde*; the area of relative industrial development around Guarda, in the north-east near the Spanish border, where motor companies in particular built assembly lines in the 1970s; and the semi-deserted rural area of Trás-os-Montes (literally, behind the mountains) in the far north-east up the river Douro, which was almost cut off from the modern world until post-1974 governments strove to open up the underdeveloped interior, building new roads and schools and extending electricity.

The harsher climate, the fragmentation of its land into unproductive *minifundia* (small plots) and the virtual non-existence of jobs outside archaic agriculture meant that the north and north-east were traditional exporters of labour to the African colonies in the 1930s, 1940s and 1950s, and to France, Belgium, Britain, and Germany in the 1960s. It was no coincidence that Portugal's huge European migratory movement coincided with the 1961–74 wars in the African colonies. Soldiers were largely conscripted from poor rural families in the north (traditionally northerners have bigger families than those in the south of Portugal), and the men left behind tended to migrate. Not until decolonisation did Lisbon stop looking outwards and begin to look to developing the interior, greatly aided by EU funds.

Communications with Bragança, ancient capital of Trás-os-Montes, have been considerably eased by the new highway superseding the old N15 to Vila Real and Oporto, and the journey from Oporto to Spain has been made much quicker by the motorway from Aveiro to Vilar Formoso.

It was the north which resisted the Communist take-overs of 1975: in one well-known case workers blocked the factory gates and would not let the left's commissars through until they had agreed to reinstate management and renounce their take-over plans. Because businessmen in the north spread their risks, and did not form oligopolistic groups like the Lisbon-based entrepreneurs (such as the de Mello, Champalimaud and Espírito Santo families – all of whom have since re-emerged with their old and new businesses) they largely escaped the 1975 nationalisations. Significantly, the first choice for re-privatisation in 1989 was Unicer, one of the very few northern companies to have been nationalised (one other was the Oporto-based Banco Português do Atlântico). Unicer was taken over because it was mostly owned by Lisbon-based capital. Unicer continued to operate like a private commercial company after it was nationalised and became the jewel in the state's crown. Its privatisation – and indeed many others – was handled by Banco Português de Investimento (BPI), the first of the new private Portuguese banks to be set up in the late 1980s, with its headquarters in Oporto. Since then BPI has acquired two of the privatised banks and today is Portugal's fourth largest banking group.

The north is the area which has best adapted to the pace of modernisation brought by EU membership. One reason for its greater sophistication and capitalist spirit is undoubtedly the constant flow since the mid-1970s of emigrants returning from Europe, and importing new living standards, although the flow has now slowed to a trickle.

Political scene

For the first time since democracy was restored in 1974, Portugal has a government and a presidency of the same political colour. The Socialists led by António Guterres ousted the centre-right Social Democrats of Aníbal Cavaco Silva from 10 years in power in the October 1995 general election; in January 1996 the equally long serving Socialist president Mário Soares was replaced by Jorge Sampaio, but the Socialists fell four seats short of an outright parliamentary majority (see Exhibit 2.1).

The Socialists need the support of one of the three opposition parties to pass legislation on a case-by-case basis, but they can only be voted out of power by the Social Democrats, the conservative Popular Party and the Communists joining forces, something that is most unlikely to happen. The Socialists and the Social Democrats together have 86 per cent of the seats in the unicameral *Assembleia da República* and 78 per cent of the vote.

The revolutionary troublemaker of 1974–75 has become almost a model of democratic stability, establishing a two-party system along the lines of other EU countries like Britain and Spain. It is easy to forget that Portugal has come a long way in a short time; its transition to democracy only two decades ago was quite unique in Cold War Europe: the right- wing dictatorship was overthrown by a *coup d'état* and this was then followed by a communist attempt at taking over. Furthermore, these events took place against a background of decolonisation.

Henry Kissinger then at the State Department was convinced that Portugal was all but lost to the West. He told Soares, then foreign minister, in 1974 that he would be the Portuguese Aleksandr Kerensky because he worked with communists in the government.[1] Soares said: "But I don't want to be Kerensky." And Kissinger replied; "Neither did Kerensky." In a sense, both were right. Unable to tame the Portuguese Revolution, the communists did not stay in power long and the socialists took over: for the first time, "Kerensky" won and the "Bolsheviks" lost.

Exhibit 2.1
Seats in parliament and % of the vote

	Seats		*% of vote*	
	1995	*1991*	*1995*	*1991*
Socialists	112	72	42.9	29.1
Social Democrats	88	135	34	50
Communists	15	17	8.6	8.8
Popular Party	15	5	9.1	4.4

Source: Portuguese government.

The electorate was tired of the Social Democrats in 1995 as they had been in government for too long (since 1979 in coalition government and on their own between 1985 and 1995). The consequences were predictable: confusion between the party and the state, too many "jobs for the boys" and a rising tide of sleaze (large in Portuguese terms, but

[1] Anecdote recounted by Carlos Gaspar, adviser to the Presidency, at a seminar on Portugal at a Camoes Centre/Tinker Foundation conference in New York on 19 October 1994.

small compared with Spain, Italy and France). The cohabitation between the avuncular Soares, now the grand old man of Portuguese democracy, and the aloof Cavaco Silva, a Social Democrat, became strained. The normally diplomatic Soares lost his cool and called the government "a dictatorship of the majority" in November 1995 shortly before stepping down as president.

The Socialists, heavily defeated in the 1991 and 1987 elections, regenerated themselves during their long period in opposition. A new generation, many of whom were too young to play an active role in the first years after the 1974 revolution, replaced the old guard. Almost all the party's leading members and ministers today are, like Guterres, in their 40s. Guterres had never served in a government until he became prime minister, devoting his energies to reorganising the party machinery which he still controls as secretary general.

In his youth he was close to left-wing Catholic movements and after a period of aggressive capitalism in Portuguese terms – when the economy was stabilised and structural reforms begun under the Social Democrats – Guterres has gently introduced a more socially conscious element into government. His style of government is also more consensus-seeking than that of the confrontational Cavaco Silva; he brought into his cabinet non-party members and independents. The Socialists and the Social Democrats agreed in February 1997 on constitutional reforms, allowing referendums for certain issues and reforming the electoral law, which will reduce the number of deputies in parliament. The Socialists, however, are as market-oriented as the Social Democrats and are determined to do everything that is necessary to make the grade for the first round of European monetary union in 1999. Guterres, in opposition, was rather sceptical about the benefits of Emu but no sooner had he taken office than he was converted to the cause.

As fellow Socialists Sampaio and Guterres are working together much more closely than Soares and Cavaco Silva. The president has no executive power under Portugal's "semi-presidentialist" system but plays an important role as a political arbiter, with powers to veto legislation as well as to dissolve parliament and appoint governments to resolve political crises.

Guterres also enjoys a warmer relationship with Helmut Kohl than Cavaco Silva did. Kohl's closest ally in the Iberian peninsular was Felipe González, Spain's 1983–96 prime minister, until he was replaced by the conservative José María Aznar. Although Aznar's Popular Party is closer to Kohl ideologically, the social Christian element brought into the Portuguese Socialists by Guterres and a better personal chemistry look like making him Kohl's man in the Iberian peninsular.

After a year in office the Socialists were more popular than when they won the election, faring well in opinion polls. This raised the possibility of an early election so that the Socialists could win an outright majority.

Out of office and without Cavaco Silva as their leader the Social Democrats have disintegrated. Cavaco Silva stepped down as party leader in 1995 and ran for the presidency against Sampaio, losing narrowly with 46 per cent of the vote. He will probably run again in 2001. Marcelo Rebelo de Sousa, a university professor, replaced Fernando Nogueira as party leader in March 1996. Nogueira had only lasted a year. The Social Democrats are a weak opposition: one of the party's problems is that after so many years in power it is finding it difficult to forge a suitable role as the main opposition party. Robelo de Sousa is also constrained by his friendship since boyhood with Guterres.

The first hurdle that Rebelo de Sousa has to surmount is to do well in the December 1997 municipal elections. The Socialists control most towns including the cities of Lisbon and Oporto. With the next general election not due until 1999, it is by no means certain that Rebelo de Sousa will stay the course. One person who could push for the party leadership closer to the next general election is José Manuel Durao Barroso, a former foreign minister.

Popular Party (PP), tapping a deepening vein of Euro-scepticism, more than doubled its share of the vote in the 1995 general election to 9.1 per cent, winning three times as many seats (15). But it too was in a state of disarray. Manuel Monteiro, the PP's 34-year-old leader, resigned in October 1996 after he was challenged by a younger firebrand.

The PP is a revamping of the Centre Social Democrats (CDS), whose one-time leader Diego Freitas do Amaral (a former president of the General Assembly of the United Nations) is a lone shot for the presidency in 2001. He narrowly lost to Soares in the March 1986 presidential election.

Portugal's Communists, the most hardline in Europe, also have 15 seats. They are strong in rural areas like the Alentejo and the industrialised Setúbal. Carlos Carvalhas replaced Alvaro Cunhal, the historic leader imprisoned during the Salazar dictatorship, as secretary-general in 1992, but he lived under his shadow until Cunhal stepped down as the party's president in 1996 when he was 83. Cunhal's retirement has made it easier to forge a more modern leftist party.

Unwittingly and rather ironically, given the CIA's role in staving off a communist take-over in 1975, the Communists were rehabilitated in 1994 by the US ambassador to Portugal, Elizabeth Frawley Bragley, a Democratic political appointee, when she took up her post. As the Communists had more seats in parliament than the PP, she naturally included them on her list of visits to political parties soon after she arrived. She was met at the party's headquarters by a barrage of press photographers to record the historic meeting – the first time, unknown to her, that a US ambassador had met with the Communists since 1975. What was normal for her in the post-Cold War world was front page news in the Portuguese press and provoked angry phone calls.

With such a weak opposition and no obvious issues upon which to latch unless the all-party consensus (excluding the Communists) on European monetary union is broken, the Socialists look like having a relatively easy ride in government and could be in power, like the Social Democrats, for a decade.

Social changes

Portugal has undergone profound changes over the past 30 years[2] in population, health and education services and the social security system (see Exhibit 2.2).

The population has not grown very much between 1960 (8.8 million) and today (almost 10 million), but this hides the fact that it declined sharply during the 1960s due to emigration and then rose in the 1970s and 1980s, because of the return of

[2] This section draws on the pioneering study *A Situação Social em Portugal, 1960–95* (Instituto de Ciências Sociais, University of Lisbon) prepared by António Barreto.

people from the colonies and a drop in emigration. Almost 1.8 million people emigrated, mostly to Europe, but also, on a smaller scale to the United States, Canada, South Africa and Venezuela. Many people from the north visited Paris before Lisbon or even before they saw the sea; transport to France was more regular than to Oporto or Lisbon. In 1975 up to 600,000 people returned (7 per cent of the population). Portugal absorbed the *retornados* without trauma, a remarkable achievement.

Exhibit 2.2
Selected social indicators

	1960	*1994*
Fertility rate	3.2	1.4
Emigration[1]	511,000	5,500
Life expectancy	63.5	74.7
Jobs in agriculture (% of total)	44.4	11
Illiteracy rate (%)	33.1	11[2]
Population in towns of over 10,000 (%)	22.6	33.1[2]
Health spending (% of GDP)	0.9	5

[1] 1960–65 and 1990–94.
[2] 1991 census.

Source: A Situação Social em Portugal, 1960–95.

While death rates have remained stable, birth rates have dropped by more than 50 per cent. The population is expected to remain virtually stagnant until at least the year 2010 because of the low birth rate and increased life expectancy. The average fertility rate of 1.4 children per woman is one of the lowest in Europe after Spain's 1.2, and is well below the generational replacement rate of 2.1 children, which was last registered in the early 1980s. The sharp decline in the birth rate, in line with the general European trend, is shrinking the under-15 age group (18 per cent of the population in 1996), while the relative share of the over-65 age group in the total population is rising (14 per cent in 1996). By the year 2010, according to government projections, the over-65 age group will account for a larger share of the population (17.6 per cent) than the under-15 age group (16.7 per cent). This change is occurring more quickly in Portugal than in most other EU countries.

Portugal stopped being a country which voted with its feet in the mid-1980s when, perhaps for the first time in its history, the number of incoming workers outnumbered those leaving.

The flow of people from rural areas to the coastal towns, mainly the areas of greater Lisbon and Oporto, continues. Between 1981 and 1991, the last two census years, the population of 204 municipalities decreased and that of 101 increased, all of the latter near the coast. The three largest cities – Lisbon, Oporto and Setúbal – account for 44 per cent of the population, the highest such percentage among EU countries. The coastal areas are expected to account for 70 per cent of the population by the year 2000.

While Lisbon and Oporto's metropolitan areas have per capita income levels similar to those of the EU average, per head GDP in the Alentejo in the south is less than 50 per cent of the EU average. Regional disparities are higher in Portugal than in most other EU countries. Lisbon has climbed in the prosperity league table of European cities in the past 10 years. Its gross value-added is forecast to expand by an average 3.4 per cent a year up to the year 2000, according to the European Economic

Exhibit 2.3

Gross value added growth of selected European cities (% per year)

Berlin	3.5
Brussels	1.8
Dublin	4
Helsinki	3.2
Lisbon	3.4
London	3
Madrid	3.2
Stockholm	2.2

Source: European Economic Research and Advisory Consortium.

Research and Advisory Consortium (see Exhibit 2.3), the fastest growth after Dublin and Berlin.

There have also been significant changes in the structure of employment. Twenty years ago agriculture still employed more than 25 per cent of the labour force. Today it is about 11 per cent. Services have steadily grown in importance (to 56 per cent) and industry accounts for 33 per cent. The female participation rate (women workers as a percentage of the labour force) has almost tripled in 30 years to more than 43 per cent. Today there are more female university students and civil servants than male.

Public health services now cover 100 per cent of the population. The considerable improvements in infant mortality and life expectancy rates are certainly due to the wider availability of the health services. Infant mortality has dropped sharply from 80 per thousand in 1960 to around 9 per thousand today. The Portuguese live, on average, 11 more years than they did in 1960.

Public expenditure on health increased from 0.9 per cent of GDP in 1960 to close to 5 per cent today, compared with an EU average of 6.5 per cent.

Education

Portugal has made considerable progress in improving its education system, but the gap *vis-à-vis* most other OECD countries is still substantial. This shortcoming is a major deficiency in a country which traditionally has relied on labour-intensive methods of production and is now shifting towards greater value-added production that requires a higher-skilled workforce. Education is an increased priority area for the government (it is one of the few areas where spending is increasing substantially in real terms), although the scope for meaningful change is limited because of budgetary restrictions.

The country has paid a high price for not investing more in its children. António de Oliveira Salazar, the dictator who ruled Portugal from 1928 to 1968, mistrusted education because of its "corrupting influence", and after the dictatorship ended in 1974 students suffered from poor quality teachers. The vicious circle of poorly qualified teachers instructing students who then become teachers themselves remains today.

Although Portugal was one of the first countries to introduce compulsory primary education in the 19th century, the illiteracy rate in 1986, when the country joined the EC, was still 15 per cent among those over 15 years old. Furthermore, the average length of education for the labour force was 4.5 years (7.6 years in the EC as a whole); just under 70 per cent of workers had only primary education, and 30 per cent had received no vocational training.

Earlier post-Salazar governments made well-meaning but largely ineffectual efforts to improve education and training, but it was not until 1987, when the Social Democrat government of Anibal Cavaco Silva (who received his degree from a British university) came to power and the country enjoyed political stability, that education became an absolute priority, helped by funds from the Community Support Framework.

The aim of reducing Europe's highest illiteracy rate to 10 per cent by 1992 was more or less achieved as progress was made in raising the proportion of children in pre-school, primary and secondary education. Primary school attendance is nearly 100 per cent for the first time in Portugal's history. Today illiteracy (still the highest rate in the EU) is limited almost exclusively to the adult population (and perhaps some young immigrants). An education ministry report in 1995 found that 47 per cent of adult Portuguese have little or no ability to read or do arithmetic.

The targets for lowering the very high drop out rates, however, were missed: 36 per cent of students aged 12–15 still drop out.

Although the funds dedicated to education every year have grown rapidly over the last decade (to 5.5 per cent of GDP, in line with the EU average), average spending per student is still low (55 per cent of the OECD average). Portugal is still producing, in the words of an OECD report,[3] (3) "large numbers of people with a low level of educational attainment, offering few opportunities for effective adult education and vocational training."

The low level of attainment was underscored by a survey conducted in 1996 among 13–14-year-olds in 45 countries on their level of mathematics. The study by the TIMSS International Study Centre put Portugal towards the bottom with a score of 454, well below the average of 513. Singapore was top with 643. The OECD's analysis pointed out that:

- a large proportion of the teenage population failed to complete basic education, remaining exposed to serious risks after entry into the labour market; in addition, the system was under-performing in terms of school achievements, especially in mathematics and sciences;
- despite the extension of the education system, school attendance above the lower secondary education level remained below that of most other OECD countries;
- notwithstanding efforts to diversify streams at the secondary education level, the largest proportion of students attended courses providing general rather than vocational education. At the higher education level, the largest participation was in courses with little link to the needs of enterprises; and
- vocational training has been traditionally marked by the dominant role of the state and little development of training within firms.

The number of students at universities and polytechnics has increased from 53,000 in 1970 to more than 255,000 today. There are now 25 universities compared with four in 1974, and 15 polytechnics. Half the number of students do not complete

[3] 1995 OECD report on Portugal.

their studies and 80 per cent of those that do take almost seven years to finish courses that generally last five years.

The government has made pre-school education its priority and aims to increase the percentage of five-year-olds in school to 90 per cent by 1999 from 30 per cent in 1996. (The Social Democrats set a target of 75 per cent by 1992 and were wide of the mark.) Education expenditure increased in 1997 for the third year running in real terms and represented 18.8 per cent of the total budget, up from close to 17 per cent in 1995.

One of the toughest challenges facing the education ministry is to make schools more attractive in order to reduce the drop out rate among 12–15-year-olds. Physical education facilities stopped being built in 1981 in order to speed up the opening of new schools and are only now being built again. A pilot scheme was started in 1996 to give more personal tutoring to students deemed to be borderline cases for completing basic education.

Universities have serious funding problems, which is hardly surprising given the ludicrously low tuition fees. Students paid Esc1,200 a year between 1944 and 1992 when the Social Democrat government raised the fee to Esc55,000, despite fierce protests by students, and to Esc89,000 for the 1996 academic year. The Socialists suspended the law soon after winning the general election in October 1995 and put the fee back to Esc1,200 (US$7). A new framework was still being studied in 1977. The new fee is likely to be between Esc55,000 and Esc89,000, if the government does not cave in to student pressure, and support is to be provided for poor families. University education can be a considerable burden because of the added expense of accommodation and food.

The quality of teachers in general and university ones in particular leaves a great deal to be desired. The disparity between pay in state and private universities is considerable, though the former tend to attract the brighter students. A lecturer teaching six hours a week at a state university would typically earn around Esc95,000 a month compared to Esc220,000 for an eight hour week at a private university.

One of the very few bright spots in the education profile is the widespread knowledge of foreign languages. The Portuguese are excellent linguists; a high proportion speak French and English. Emigration and the fact that films are not dubbed on TV or in the cinema play an important role in acquiring language skills.

Social security

Improvements in social security (pensions, health care, elderly support, children's benefits, maternity assistance, unemployment and other related benefits) have been considerable, but, like other OECD countries, growth in welfare spending is outpacing contributions, accentuated by deteriorating demographic trends.

The crux of the problem today is that social aspirations are probably on a par with those in other EU countries but the economy's ability to meet them is not.

Welfare benefits were made universal after the 1974 revolution with the creation of the non-contributory scheme for people not covered by the general contributory scheme. This provides minimum protection for individuals and families whose monthly income is below a certain limit and a "social pension" for old-age and invalidity. Coverage of benefits was expanded during the 1980s and in 1993–95 the Social Democrats introduced a number of policy reforms, including a rise in the retirement age for women (65 from 1999) and a change in the pension formula.

The total number of pensioners has increased from 108,000 in 1960 to more than 2.6 million today. The profound change is dramatically underlined by the ratio between the working population and pensioners: today, there are 1.7 workers per pensioner compared with 30.7 in 1960. The size of pensions, however, is very small – average Esc437,000 (US$2,833) a year – and the lack of qualified people and institutions to care for the elderly is obvious. Similarly, the number of beneficiaries and the levels of unemployment benefits are low.

The unfunded government liability is estimated to be about 160 per cent of GDP, compared with 70 per cent in the UK. Aware of the need for reforms, a government-appointed commission was preparing a White Paper on social security to be published not later than June 1997. Two broad sets of issues are involved.[4] The first is one of financial sustainability, in so far as steps need to be taken to ensure that the funding of pension commitments does not result in an unacceptable increase in taxation or borrowing. This has particular relevance for the development of non-wage labour costs. The second relates to the structure of benefits and contributions.

Social security outlays grew to close to 12 per cent of GDP in 1996, up from 8.4 per cent in 1986 (see Exhibit 2.4), but this was still 3.5 points below the OECD average. Most of the rise came from higher spending under the general system covering private sector workers (2.3 million pension beneficiaries and 4.3 million contributors). There is a separate system for public sector employees and a special regime applies to the banking sector.

There are large contribution arrears (2.6 per cent of GDP in 1994) in the private sector and financial reserves are not large enough to protect the system against growing spending pressure. In the public sector, employees' contributions only covered 45 per cent of social expenditure in 1995, the remainder being financed by the government (1.5 per cent of GDP).

While pension payments for agricultural workers and beneficiaries under the non-contributory scheme are low (34 per cent of the minimum wage), the OECD noted in its 1996 report on Portugal that pension provisions in the general contributory scheme differ from the European norm in several respects:

- The accrual factor (2 per cent) and the maximum percentage of assessed income (80 per cent) are still higher than in most European countries. A worker in the general system, with 40 years of contributions and constant earnings growth over his career, receives a pension equal to 75 per cent of the salary in his last year of service.
- The reference period for calculating pensions (the highest 10-year average income of the last 15 years) results in looser ties between the present value of benefits and contributions than in other countries where pensions are assessed over career earnings or contributions.

[4] See the chapter in the 1996 OECD report on Portugal.

Exhibit 2.4

Social Security outlays (% of GDP)

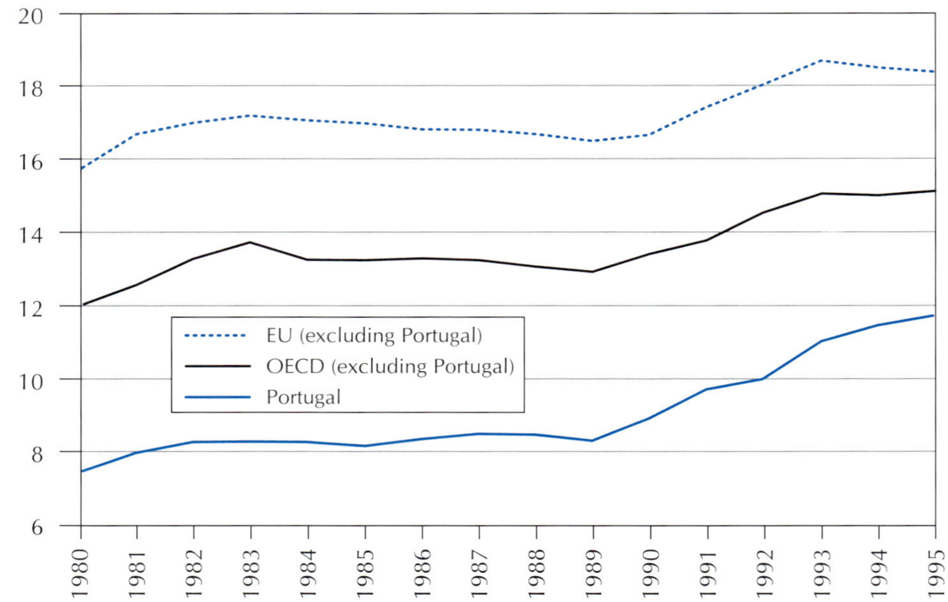

Source: OECD.

- Pension adjustments reflect a higher degree of policy discretion compared with other countries, due to the absence of a formal indexation mechanism.

On the contribution side, the rate in 1996 of 34.75 per cent for dependent employment (23.75 per cent for employers and 11 per cent for employees) is relatively high; contributions also finance social welfare programmes, whereas in other European countries general tax revenues are used for this purpose. This imposes a high tax on labour and coupled with the weak link between contributions and benefits could be encouraging evasion.

OECD projections show a sharpening of demographic trends up to the year 2050 (see Exhibit 2.5) when the population over the age of 60 will rise to 33 per cent from the current 20 per cent. The ratio of the retired age population to the working population is forecast to reach 52 per cent in 2050, double today's rate. Pension spending would more than double to 16 per cent of GDP and without further reforms the gap between expenditure and contributions would reach 8.5 per cent of GDP in 2035.

Obviously this situation cannot be sustained indefinitely. The options (see Exhibit 2.6) for reforming the pay-as-you-go pension system are: (i) to reduce the accrual rate and link pensions to lifetime earnings; (ii) to raise the retirement age, and (iii) to reduce privileges granted to specific groups of workers, in particular, the highly preferential pension formula applying to public employees hired before September 1993. A combination of different measures is needed.

Exhibit 2.5

Population projections and elderly dependency ratios

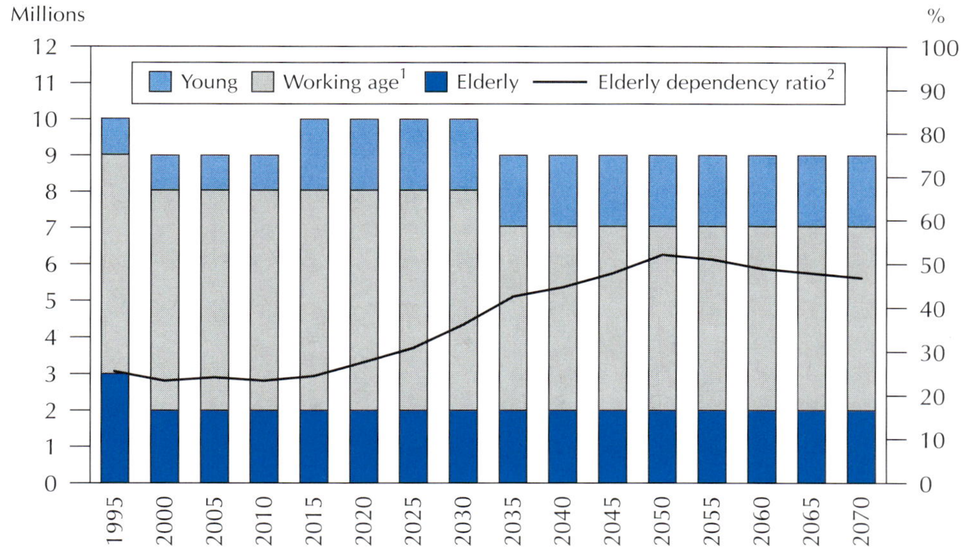

[1] Defined as from age 20 until the scheduled retirement ages for public pensions in Portugal.
[2] The ratio of the retired age population to the working-age population.
Source: OECD.

Exhibit 2.6

Pension policy options: alternative equilibrium contribution rates (%)

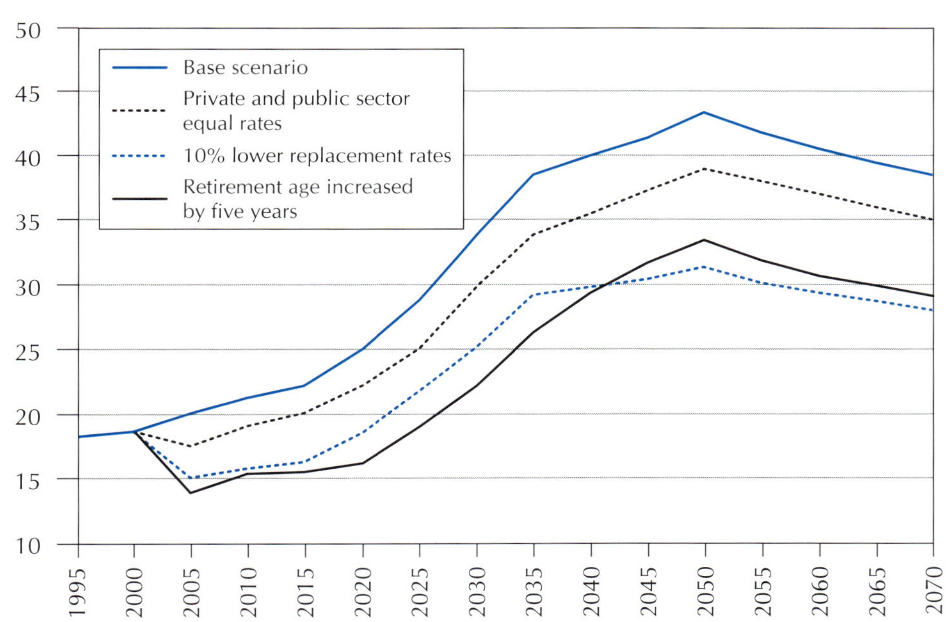

Source: OECD.

The most radical option would be a Chile-style mandatory fully-funded system. Spain has ruled out such a reform and it is highly unlikely that Portugal would take this route. Greater importance, however, could be given to optional private pension funds (over and above the obligatory state system) which have grown strongly since they were introduced in 1987. Funds under management amounted to Esc1.6 trillion at the end of 1996 (9.9 per cent of GDP, compared with 3.9 per cent in Spain).

Taxation

Portugal's tax burden has risen to 34 per cent of GDP from 29 per cent in 1985, the steepest rise in the OECD after Greece and Italy. Tax evasion, however, remains high and the present government is clamping down more strongly than the Social Democrats did. A significant part of budgetary consolidation depends on success in the fight against tax evasion rather than cutting expenditure.

The average self-employed doctor or lawyer, according to their tax declarations, earned less than a waitress or a construction worker in 1995 and close to 90 per cent of total value-added tax revenue came from only 300 big companies. An estimated 70 per cent of companies declare a loss. The underground economy is estimated to represent at least 15 per cent of GDP.

Under the government's reforms companies suspected of under-declaring will be obliged to pay taxes on the earnings for businesses of a similar size in the same sector. The self-employed who declare an income lower than the minimum national wage (less than US$250 a month) are to be taxed at the average rate of their peers. Employers' organisations back the crackdown but, in return, are pressing for greater protection for taxpayers: it takes, for example, 3–5 years for an appeal against a tax ruling to be resolved because of the congested courts, and meanwhile the money has to be paid or a bank guarantee produced.

The government has taken a stick-and-carrot approach. Under the Mateus Plan, named after Economy Minister Augusto Mateus, the government is helping ailing but viable companies to recover if they first clear their tax and social security debts. In return the state provides companies with a partial guarantee of loans from banks. This enables banks to lend money at interest rates that are considerably below the level these companies have had to pay in the past. Interest on the loans is paid at a spread of no more than 2 per cent over the Lisbor rate. This means a rate of about 6–8 per cent, considerably more attractive. In some cases companies were paying more in interest on loans than on wages.

By 31 January 1997, the deadline for registering for debt repayment, more than 185,000 businesses and individuals had signed up to clear their debts. Debtors have eight years to clear the slate – without incurring fines or interest payments. Up to Esc120 billion is forecast to be recovered in 1997 alone, which will make a significant contribution to the effort to cut the budget deficit. The government claims that as much as Esc1.5 trillion (US$9 billion) could be recovered, more than half the total debt that has accumulated over the decades.

The aim is to increase total tax revenues through better enforcement procedures and without increasing personal tax rates. As is usually the case in such situations, it is wage earners who suffer the most from increased taxes, as they are taxed at source. Portugal's top marginal tax rate is 40 per cent (on income of over Esc6.1 million, US$35,400) Corporate tax, however, was reduced to 34 per cent from 36 per cent as of July 1997 (37.6 per cent including the local taxes element, down from 39.6 per cent).

The government is spending more on improving tax collection systems. In 1996 Portugal still did not have cross-checking between corporate tax and VAT payments, and the quality and frequency of inspections is low. In some respects, however, the system is more sophisticated than in other EU countries as payments can be made through ATMs.

Infrastructure and EU funds

EU funds have enabled Portugal to upgrade its infrastructure in a way that was unthinkable 20 years ago. Net transfers, however, peaked in 1996 at Esc622.4 billion and are diminishing (see Exhibit 2.7).

The country received an estimated US$23.5 billion in EU funds between 1985 and 1996, most of it to finance infrastructure improvements, and in the 1994–2000 period it will invest a further US$18 billion, with around one-third being funded by the EU. Funds currently account for some 3 per cent of GDP a year. Portugal will get another facelift, with new motorways, a second bridge over the Tagus, a rail link on the existing bridge, expansion of the Lisbon underground and construction of the Oporto light railway system. Such investment will spur economic growth, accounting for almost 1 per cent of GDP expansion, for a few years.

Exhibit 2.7

Transfers between Portugal and the EU, 1993–97 (Esc billion)

	1993	*1994*	*1995*	*1996*	*1997*
Transfers from Portugal to the EU	**163.1**	**247.5**	**170.5**	**174.6**	**211.3**
Tariffs	35.4	40.0	40.3	27.2	30.5
VAT contribution	98.8	142.6	102.0	103.4	100.4
GDP contribution	28.8	64.4	28.0	53.8	80.2
Others	0.1	0.5	0.2	-9.8	0.2
Transfers from the EU to Portugal	**619.7**	**507.9**	**661.1**	**837.0**	**758.0**
EAOGF – Guarantee	86.4	139.7	138.5	134.2	137.0
Structural funds	500.4	321.4	434.9	612.1	530.3
FEDER	286.0	218.1	299.2	424.3	322.3
EAOGF – Orientation	62.1	49.6	55.3	64.2	69.3
ESF	152.8	53.7	80.4	123.6	138.7
PEDIP	10.8	5.6	–	–	–
Cohesion fund	15.7	33.7	82.5	80.0	85.0
Others	5.9	7.5	5.2	10.7	5.7
Net transfers	**456.6**	**260.4**	**490.7**	**662.4**	**546.7**

Source: Banco Comercial Português.

AECOPS, the national construction association, estimates that the Portuguese construction sector will benefit from an average annual increase in investment of 6.1 per cent between 1996 and 1998. Portugal has one of the highest levels of per capita annual cement consumption in Europe (791 kg in 1995 against an EU average of 453 kg).

In addition to EU and government funds, the private sector is expected to be more involved in housing and motorways. Portugal's housing shortage is estimated at around 600,000 houses or more than 20 per cent of the existing stock. There have been legislative changes to encourage property renovation and residential dwelling construction. The government is also encouraging the private sector to build a series of small motorways through Portugal to operate under a shadow- tolling system.

Energy

The country's high dependence on imported oil began to be reduced in 1997 when it received natural gas from the European–Algerian pipeline. Until then Portugal was the only EU country not consuming natural gas, which it is estimated will account for 8–10 per cent of the country's primary energy consumption by the year 2000. Spain began receiving gas through the same 1,400 km pipeline from the Algerian Sahara in November 1996; the two countries will be linked by 2000, creating a circular supply system.

The 2,500 km pipeline runs from Hassi R'Mel in the Algerian desert through Morocco, across the Straits of Gibraltar to Cordoba in southern Spain, into Portugal and then northwards along the Atlantic coast. An extension linking northern Portugal to northern Spain was expected to be completed by June 1997. Portugal is now wholly reliant for its gas on a country that is in a virtual state of civil war, but the government believes that whatever happens in Algeria no administration there would ever put gas exports at risk because of their importance to the economy. In addition to the 2.5 billion cubic metres of gas it will eventually recieve from Algeria every year, Transgás, the state company responsible for the US$1.3 billion investment, planned to diversify its sources with an annual 500 million cubic metre purchase of Nigerian gas, starting in 1999. Natural gas will bring significant gains in competitiveness to industries such as ceramics.

The biggest consumer in Portugal is Turbugás, a consortium led by Powergen, the UK electricity company, which is building a 990MW natural gas-fired power plant near Oporto.

The national power company, Electricidade de Portugal (EDP), up to 30 per cent of which was expected to be privatised in a first share offering in 1997, was restructured in 1994. The group consists of: Companhia Portugesa de Produção, a production company; Rede Eléctrica Nacional, a high-tension transmission company to manage the national grid; four regional distribution companies; 10 specialist service companies and the holding company EDP. The restructuring has improved efficiency and profitability.

The state is to retain majority control of EDP indefinitely, limiting private ownership to 49 per cent.

Water

Drinking water supply and distribution are being reorganised and hydroelectric capacity expanded. The government's ambitious goal is to ensure that virtually all households are connected to the public water supply by 1999. The EU will contribute up to 85 per cent of the cost. New reservoirs, water treatment plants, pumping stations and pipelines are being built.

In Portugal the municipal authorities are still responsible for providing utilities including drinking water. The only exception is Lisbon, where drinking water was distributed by Companhia das Aguas de Lisboa until 1974 when EPAL took over the concession. Under reforms made in 1993 and 1994 51 per cent of EPAL was transferred to a new state-controlled company, IPE, and EPAL became the model for four new water companies, serving the densely populated Oporto and Algarve areas.

Shortly after taking office the government halted work on a controversial hydroelectric dam across the Côa river in north-east Portugal to save the world's largest collection of Stone Age engravings. The Social Democrats had agreed the dam's construction by Electricidade de Portugal, the power company. Only 50 engravings were found at first, but the site attained world-wide importance and triggered an international campaign when it was discovered that more than a thousand roughly engraved Ice Age animals had been carved on rock along the threatened valley. More than US$29 million had already been spent on the dam.

The government, however, is determined to go ahead with the huge Alqueva dam on the Guadiana river close to the Spanish frontier – something that has been planned, without success, for the last 36 years. The 250 sq. km reservoir would be the largest man-made lake in Europe, providing a strategic source of water for the impoverished Alentejo, a region cyclically hit by drought, and for the built-up Algarve tourist region on Portugal's southern coast.

Water management is a sensitive issue between Portugal and Spain and inflames nationalist sentiment.[5] It is the greatest source of disputes between the two countries; the Food and Agricultural Organisation (FAO) believes the border could be the first flash point within Europe in a clash over water resources.

The two countries share three major river basins. Spain is particularly prone to drought and has one of the highest levels of per capita water consumption in the world; the 1991–95 drought was the worst this century and decimated crops and caused severe water shortages throughout southern Spain. The rivers Spain wants to tap for a planned network of dams and canals to divert water from its lush, verdant north to its dry south feed into Portugal. Drought and Spanish consumption cut the Duero's flow into Portugal by 25 per cent in the 20 years before the last drought ended, according to studies by Portugal's Laboratory of Civil Engineering. Abundant rain during 1996 radically transformed the situation in both countries, but the problem remains.

In response to formal complaints from the last Lisbon government, Madrid now informs its neighbour regularly of its intentions. The problem is a complex one as the Spanish government has to balance the interests of farmers and industrialists, and the north and south of the country, with those of Portugal. Spain. however, is not to blame for all of Portugal's water problems. Waste is also rampant. For every litre of water consumed in Oporto, for example, it is estimated that another litre is lost through

[5] See *The Wall Street Journal* (European edition) of 26 October 1995.

leakage. Moreover, irrigation systems along the Tagus are far less efficient on the Portuguese side than in Spain.

Telecommunications

Portugal is to liberalise all telecommunications services by 2000, two years after most EU countries but three years ahead of the 2003 deadline set for the country. A second national operator will be established, ending Portugal Telecom's monopoly control of infrastructure and basic telephone services. Cellular telephones, paging, cable television and data services have already been liberalised but Portugal Telecom (PT), the only operator for fixed-link telephones and leased lines, still controls about 90 per cent of the overall market.

Electricidade de Portugal, the national power company, and Caminhos de Ferro Portugueses, the state railway, will form the core of the new fixed-line operator.

Portugal Telecom (51 per cent owned by the state in 1996) is rapidly building up its fixed- line network.[6] The penetration rate increased to 38.5 lines per 100 people in 1995 from 24 in 1990 and is projected to reach 46 per 100 by the year 2000, although this will still be below the EU average for 1994.

The quality of service is also being substantially improved; digitalisation of lines was 80 per cent in 1996 and looks set to reach 100 per cent in 1999. This is a higher rate than Spain's Telefónica and Deutsche Telecom. Digitalisation ensures better quality speech with fewer failed and interrupted calls and should allow for faster introduction of new advanced services. PT is also preparing for competition by reducing the prices of trunk and international calls and increasing the prices of local calls, installation and rental charges. Portugal's local calls have been among the cheapest in Europe and its international and inter-city calls among the most expensive.

Portugal was a latecomer to the European cellular market but it is catching up fast. Its first mobile network was launched in 1989 by Portugal Telecom's subsidiary, Telecomuniçãoes Móveis Nacionais (TMN), and was based on an analogue network technology. This network never found favour in Portugal, due to high tariffs and handset prices, as well as limited network capacity, and it took almost four years for it to peak at only 31,000 subscribers. The number stood at less than 15,000 in 1996 and the network is expected to be closed down around the turn of the century.

TMN and its rival Telecel (owned by AirTouch, an internationally diversified cellular company; Telepri, a joint holding company of the Espiríto Santo financial group and the Amorim Group, the world's largest cork producer; and Eurofan, a telecommunications equipment manufacturer) launched GSM networks in October 1992 only a few months after the first European GSM networks started operating in Germany. By the end of 1993 Portugal had broken the 1 per cent penetration barrier and in 1996 it was 6.7 per cent, compared with an EU average of 8 per cent. The rate is estimated to read 9 per cent in 1997.

The telecommunications market is regulated by the Instituto das Comuniçãoes de Portugal (ICP), which is part of the Ministry of Communications. The Office for General Competition and Prices (part of the Economy Ministry) regulates the pricing issues of telecommunications services.

[6] This section draws on reports by Salomon Brothers (6 November 1996) and HSBC James Capel (1 May 1996).

Of the 656,500 mobile phone subscribers at the end of 1996, Telecel had 331,400. Although Portugal will bring forward the liberalisation of its telephony market to 1998, the European Commission rejected the government's request to delay ending Portugal Telecom's monopoly over telecommunications networks. It ruled in early 1997 that competitors to Portugal Telecom should be allowed to operate some services over their own networks as of July and that GSM mobile phone operators be permitted to use "alternative infrastructure" immediately.

As part of the sweeping realignment of global telecom alliances Portugal Telecom reached a share swap agreement with Spain's Telefónica in April 1997. Under the deal, aimed at developing joint ventures in the Iberian peninsula and Latin America, Telefónica was to acquire 3.5 per cent of PT and the Portuguese operator 1 per cent of Telefónica. The accord came hard on the heels of PT's decision to choose Concert, the alliance between British Telecommunications (BT) and MCI of the US, as its strategic partner, and just before Telefónica pulled out of Unisource, the European telecoms alliance, in which AT&T, the largest US carier, is present, in order to also join Concert.

PT and Brazil's Telebras, the state-owned operator, have an alliance known as Aliança Atlântica. Telefónica heads a consortium that controls a regional operator in Brazil and also has significant operations in Argentina, Chile, Peru and Venezuela. MCI has made strategic investments in Mexico.

Telefónica's 3.5 per cent stake in PT was to be reserved for a global share offer of the Portuguese operator later in 1997 that would reduce state ownership to 25 per cent. Under the agreement, telephone calls between Spain and Portugal are to become regional rather than international, a step that reflects the growing integration of the economies. BT was to acquire 1 per cent of PT and MCI 0.5 per cent.

TV Cabo, Portugal Telecom's wholly owned subsidiary, is building blanket cable television coverage. It received its first licences for so-called "interventions" (franchise areas with around 2,000 homes in each) in May 1994. Commercial service was launched at the end of 1994. It is the only operator.

Labour market

Portugal's unemployment rate is higher now than in the recent past but at 7–8 per cent it is still well below the OECD average (see Exhibit 2.8), and strikingly lower than Spain's 21 per cent. Hiring and firing is more flexible and much less restrictive than in Spain, though this is not to say Portugal does not have other structural problems in the labour field.

Underemployment is high, particularly in rural areas, as is long-term and youth unemployment (49 per cent and more than 15 per cent, respectively). The OECD said in its 1996 report on Portugal that the main challenge lies in creating conditions where the "output of the education and training system matches the demand for skills." The OECD observed that there is a shift away from traditional labour-intensive sectors such as textiles/clothing and shoes and some mismatch in skills is emerging, as suggested by the parallel rise of vacancies and unemployment.

As well as a low jobless level, Portugal also stands out because of high participa-

Exhibit 2.8

Rate of unemployment, 1970–96 (%)

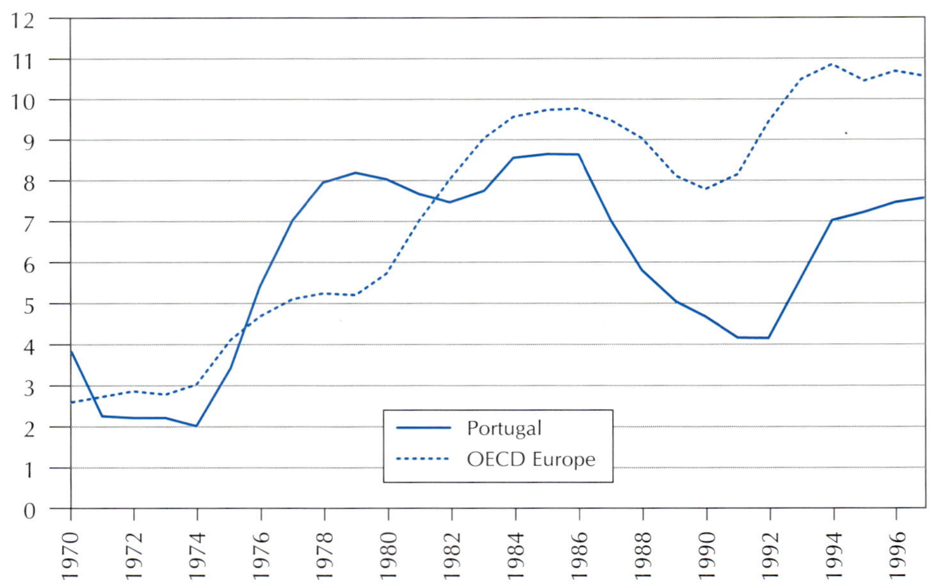

Source: OECD.

tion rates, which have traditionally exceeded the European averages. The participation rate (the proportion of the working-age population who are part of the labour force) in 1996 was more than 67 per cent (50 per cent in Spain).

Both factors are quite remarkable when it is remembered that Portugal's population increased by around one million between 1973 and 1980 because of the return of Portuguese nationals from former colonies and a reduction in emigration. The unemployment rate during this period shot from 2.2 per cent to 8 per cent, and since then it has never risen higher than 9 per cent.

Firing restrictions were last eased in 1991 by the Social Democrats through a wider range of admissible lay-off reasons, the possibility of collective lay-offs and easier resolution of severance pay disagreements. Although employers complain that the rules are still stringent by international comparison, and the Socialist government will probably not make any significant changes, the fact of the matter is that firms are generally able to get around the restrictions. Companies have tended to circumvent regulations by relying on short-term contracts or adopting the *recibo verde* (green receipt) method which involves no contractual arrangement. Under this system – named after the colour of receipt books – anyone wishing to hire someone simply issues a bill for their services which can be ended whenever they want. The practice is used in the public sector, although it is illegal.

Small firms, the great majority in Portugal, and particularly those who do not pay taxes and social security contributions, have found it easy not to comply with firing regulations. Action is rarely taken against them. Larger firms, however, especially

Exhibit 2.9

Cost of individual dismissals in the European Union

	Average cost of a justified dismissal (number of days' salary)	*Maximum payment of an unjustified dismissal (number of days' salary)*
Belgium	154	180
Denmark	91	273
Finland	91	600*
France	119	450
Germany	91	540
Greece	203	720
Ireland	56	728
Italy	315	420
Luxembourg	–	360
Netherlands	77	–
Portugal	70	600*
Spain	231	1,260
Sweden	105	960*
United Kingdom	147	360

* For a worker with 30 years seniority.

Source: Spanish Economy Ministry (October 1995).

Exhibit 2.10

Labour costs in manufacturing (DM per hour in 1995*)

Germany (West)	45.5
Switzerland	42.7
Belgium	38.3
Norway	36.9
Austria	36.8
Denmark	36.5
Finland	36.2
Netherlands	35.5
Japan	35.5
Luxembourg	33.8
Sweden	31.1
Germany (East)	29.8
France	29.0
US	25.1
Italy	24.6
Canada	23.4
Spain	22.3
Australia	22
United Kingdom	–
Ireland	20.6
Greece	12.9
Portugal	9.2

* Some of the figures are provisional. The exchange rate used for conversion to DMs is the 1995 average for each currency.

Source: IWD.

where trade unions are active (eg, banks) have to abide by the book. The average cost of a justified dismissal in 1995 was 70 days' salary and the maximum payment for an unjustified dismissal was 600 days (see Exhibit 2.9).

Spending on unemployment benefits and on job promotion programmes is low by international comparisons (around 2 per cent of GDP). Much of the spending on active labour market programmes is financed by EU funds.

Nominal wage growth is much more sensitive than in most EU countries to the employment situation. Such is the Portuguese concern for job security that wage cuts or below inflation increases are quite common in private firms going through financial difficulties, and in some cases people work for nothing, building up wage arrears that are often not paid off. The Portuguese work the second longest number of hours a year (1,882 in 1995 compared with 1,772 in Spain) among the 19 most industrialised countries, after the United States

Social security contribution rates for dependent employment are close to the EU average (23.75 per cent for the employer and 11 per cent for the employee in 1997) but overall labour costs are still by far the lowest (see Exhibit 2.10).

Under the 1996 social pact between the government, trade unions and employers – the first since 1992 – the working week of 44 hours was reduced to 40 during 1997, more flexible working time and job demarcations were introduced and non–contractual work curbed. The maximum period for unemployment benefits for people aged between 45 and 54 was extended to 15 months for those with exhausted benefits and 30 months in other cases. A minimum income scheme was also established for the poorest with no job prospects. The national minimum wage was Esc56,700 (US$329) in 1997 (received by an estimated 140,000 people).

The communist-dominated Confederação Geral de Trabalhadores Portugueses-Intersindical Nacional (CGTP) refused to sign the pact, but it was subscribed to by the União Geral de Trabalhadores (UGT) which is allied to the Socialists.

Unionisation is around 30 per cent in Portugal, but close to 80 per cent of workers are covered by collective bargaining agreements (see Exhibit 2.11).

Exhibit 2.11

Unionisation and collective bargaining coverage (%)

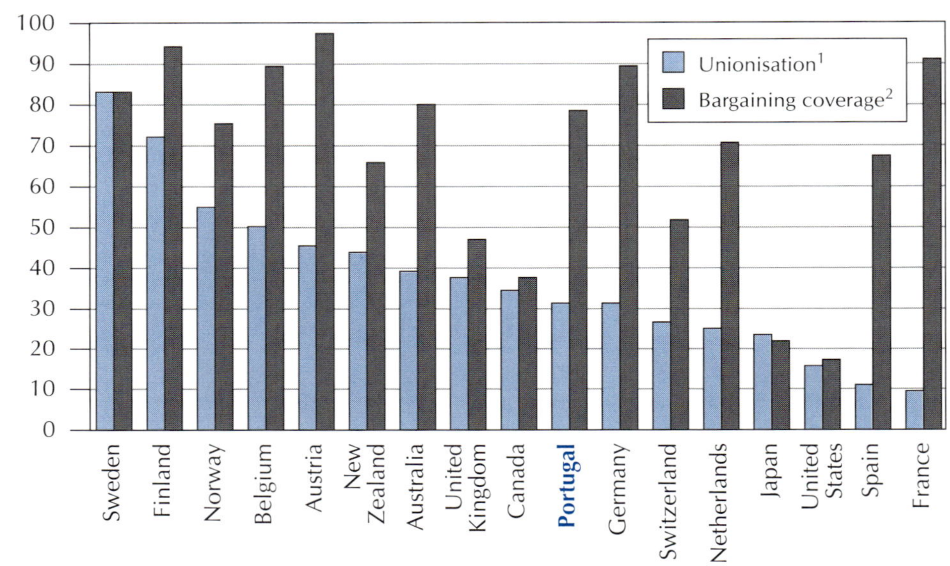

[1] Number of trade union members as a percentage of wage and salary earners.
[2] The number of workers covered by collective agreements as a percentage of wage and salary earners.

Source: OECD, *Employment Outlook*, July 1994.

3

ECONOMIC MANAGEMENT AND EUROPEAN MONETARY UNION

The government's resolve to participate in European monetary union (Emu) from the outset was underlined in an unusual way at the Madrid European Union summit which baptised the new single currency, the euro. In the same way that the New Testament declared that "Thou art Peter, and upon this rock I will build my church," António Guterres, the prime minister, proposed the dictum: "Thou art euro, and upon which euro we will build Europe's future."

Guterres had just won the October 1995 general election and he wasted no time in using the forum to let the world know that Portugal was deeply committed to Emu. The remark raised eyebrows because Portugal is not the first country that springs to mind as a founding member of Emu, due to be launched in 1999. The country's progress on the convergence front, however, has been such that there has been a significant change in the markets' perception of Portugal's chances of making it into the first round. The 10-year yield gap with Germany (a key yardstick of Portugal's risk premium and of its Emu prospects) was down to 89 basis points (bp) in April 1997 from 380 bp at the end of 1995. The reduction in the Bank of Portugal's key rates was accompanied by a more than proportional fall in short-term market rates, underscoring the greater probability of the escudo joining the euro in 1999.

As a small country on the south-western periphery of Europe, the government believes that if it fails to qualify it will miss an historic opportunity to form part of a strong area of economic stability that will provide sustained growth in investment and better job prospects, as well as being at the centre of the decision-making process. Life inside Emu would be more comfortable than being left out in the cold. Failure to be part of the first group – expected to include most countries – could undermine the stability of the Portuguese economy and make it more difficult to join Emu at a later stage.

The Portuguese economy stands to benefit considerably from joining Emu. According to the theory of optimum currency zones (Emu meets the conditions for a common currency) the potential benefits depend on the degree of openness of an economy (exports and imports measured against GDP). Portugal's intra-EU trade represented 40.2 per cent of GDP in 1995, compared with 24.4 per cent for Spain, 24 per cent for Germany and 21.2 per cent for France. It would thus stand to gain proportionately more from trade and investment flows than these countries. The theory of optimum currency areas refers to a group of nations that link their currencies through permanently fixed exchange rates, and the conditions that would make such an area optimum. The formation of an optimum currency area is most likely to be beneficial when the following conditions exist: the more mobile resources (mainly capital and labour) there are among the various member nations, the greater are their structural similarities and the more willing they are to closely coordinate their fiscal, monetary and other policies.

The cost of Emu membership is the loss of the exchange rate as an instrument to offset external shocks. There are two kinds of shocks: symmetric (ie, one affecting all Emu countries with the same intensity) and asymmetric (ie, one affecting countries in varying degrees). If the shock were symmetric then the exchange rate of the common currency, in this case the euro, could be modified to offset the upset. In this case the loss of a national currency would imply no loss of economic policy capacity. If the shock were asymmetric then the loss of the exchange rate would represent a cost if there were no other factors within Emu to offset the shock: price and wage flexibility, labour mobility between member countries or a centralised budget which acts as an automatic stabiliser. In the event that these three factors were insufficient, loss of the exchange rate would represent a higher cost.

Portugal's costs are only those linked to the probability of suffering an asymmetric shock which, in turn, depends on the degree of similarity between the economies comprising Emu. The more similar they are the lower is the probability of asymmetric shocks. By calculating the coefficient of correlation between Portugal's GDP growth and that of the EU-5 (Germany, France, the Netherlands, Belgium and Luxembourg) over a long period one can evaluate whether the Portuguese economy is one that has been traditionally characterised by asymmetric shocks: the closer to one the less asymmetric shocks have been suffered. Portugal's coefficient between 1974 and 1996 was 0.67 (Spain's was 0.66) and 0.8 between 1986 (when Portugal joined the EC) and 1996, which shows that its economic cycles have become increasingly closer to those of the EU hard core.

The political cost of being excluded from Emu would also be high, particularly as Guterres has staked so much on Portugal making the grade. Indeed, the prime minister believes his government could fall if Portugal is excluded from the first round, as this could prove to be the spark that brings together an opposition largely in disarray.

Trends are generally positive and Portugal has achieved convergence with a far better track record for currency stability than Spain, which has undergone significant devaluation. Economic growth is steady (around 3 per cent in 1997), inflation is low, public finances are largely on track, external accounts are broadly stable, and international reserves remain high. Portugal met the interest rate and exchange rate requirements in 1996, and in 1997 was moving towards the other three criteria (inflation, budget deficit and public debt).

The JP Morgan Emu calculator of 14 April 1997 gave Portugal a 79 per cent chance of forming part of the first round in 1999, compared with 75 per cent for Spain, 58 per cent for Italy and 41 per cent for the UK. The probabilities are calculated from the interest swaps market, in which investors swap floating rate interest payments for an investment for fixed-rate ones. The bank compares the post-1999 or 2002 swap spread to Germany with the spread they expect to see if Emu expectations were

Exhibit 3.1

Fulfilment of the EU convergence criteria, 1995 and July 1996 (%)

(Figures in bold indicate convergence)

	*July 1996** *Inflation*	*Interest rates*	*1995* *Deficit/GDP*		*Debt/GDP*		*No. of criteria fulfilled, 1995*
Reference	**1.2**[1]	**6.9**[3]					
Maximum	2.7[2]	**8.9**[4]	**3.0**[5]		**60.0**[6]		
Germany	**1.6**	**6.4**	3.6	–	**58.1**	–	3
France	**2.1**	**6.8**	5.0	—	**51.2**	–	3
Italy	5.0	10.7	7.2	—	125.1	—	0
United Kingdom	3.0	**7.9**	6.0	—	64.0	–	2
Spain	3.9	9.9	6.1	—	65.7	–	0
Netherlands	**1.8**	**6.4**	3.4	–	79.0	–	2
Belgium	**1.7**	**6.8**	4.5	—	133.7	—	2
Denmark	**2.0**	**7.5**	**1.4**	—	71.9	—	3
Greece	8.6		9.2	—	111.6	–	0
Portugal	3.3	9.9	5.4	—	71.4	–	0
Ireland	**2.2**	**7.7**	**2.4**	–	85.1	—	3
Luxembourg	**1.4**	**6.8**	**+0.3**	—	**5.9**	=	**4**
Austria	**1.8**	**6.6**	6.2	–	69.4	–	2
Sweden	**1.9**	**8.8**	8.1	–	79.9	–	2
Finland	**0.6**	**7.5**	5.6	—	59.6	=	3

* Average of the last 12 months.

1 Average 12-month CPI of the three countries with the lowest inflation.

2 Average 12-month CPI of the three countries with the lowest inflation plus 1.5 points.

3 Average long-term interest rates of the three countries with the lowest inflation.

4 Average long-term interest rates of the three countries with the lowest inflation plus 2 points.

5 General government deficit: maximum allowed is 3% of GDP. –/— means an increase/decline over 1994.

6 Public debt ratio: maximum allowed is 60% of GDP. –/— means an increase/decline over 1994.

Source: Datastream, European Commission forecasts (May 1996) for the deficit and public debt (except real figures for Germany). Prepared by Banco Central Hispano.

to fall to zero. The markets assume that if Emu happens, Germany will be part of it, so Germany always has a probability equal to the highest value of any other country.

Inflation

Portugal has done very well in the last few years in reducing inflation, largely due to exchange rate stability. Consumer price inflation on a 12-month moving average basis, the method used for the Emu requirement, was headed towards 2.25–2.5 per cent in 1997, down from 3.1 per cent in 1996 (a 25-year low) and 4.1 per cent in 1995. This would meet the Emu requirement of a maximum limit of 1.5 percentage points above the average of the three EU members with the lowest inflation (around 1.5 per cent).

The inflation of tradable goods in 1996 was close to that of core EU countries, but non-tradable goods have not performed so well. This inflation is greatly dependent on salary increases in the services sector, which is generally close to the figure for the economy as a whole. A new price basket was due to be adopted for the consumer price index in 1997, reflecting the changes which have taken place since the current basket was introduced in 1991. The new basket would give greater weight to non-tradable goods and reduce that of food, but as the main problem with Portuguese inflation convergence is non-tradable goods, the basket was postponed until 1998.

Reducing inflation continues to depend on a stable exchange rate and wage restraint. The public sector wage rise agreed with the unions for 1997 was 3 per cent, down from 4.25 per cent in 1996. This was good news for the government, although it was at the top end of its parameter; unions in the private sector asked for a 3.5 per cent increase. The Bank of Portugal has supported a cautious decline in interest rates and intervened in the foreign exchange markets when necessary to keep the escudo within 3 per cent of its central rate against the Deutschmark.

Interest rates

Under this condition, long-term interest rates should be within two percentage points of the average of the three members with the lowest rates. By fulfilling the inflation, budget deficit and public debt requirements, Portugal's interest rates would automatically meet the convergence criterion.

Exchange rate stability and the progress made on the inflation front have enabled the Bank of Portugal to gradually reduce intervention rates, in line with the downward trend in Europe. The liquidity injection rate stood at 6.5 per cent in 1997, down from 8.55 per cent at the end of 1995, and the absorption rate at 6.2 per cent (8 per cent).

Budget deficit

The general government deficit target was 2.9 per cent of GDP in 1997, just below the magic 3 per cent requirement and down from 4 per cent in 1996 (see Exhibit 3.2) when the deficit undershot the original target for the third consecutive year. This provided a sound platform for reaching the 1997 goal.

The government aimed to do this without raising taxes or cutting social spending; total revenue was forecast to increase to 45.9 per cent of GDP from 45.3 per cent in 1996, thanks to higher economic growth and greater tax collection efforts (see Chapter 2), while spending would be kept at 48.8 per cent of GDP. The targeted increase in corporate

Exhibit 3.2

Budgetary indicators, 1995–97 (% of GDP)

	1997[f]	*1996*	*1995*
Gen. government deficit	2.9	4.0	4.9
Primary balance	1.5	0.9	0.7
Current balance	0.7	-0.4	-1.2
Current revenues	42.4	41.6	39.6
Current spending	41.7	42.0	40.8
Capital balance	-3.6	-3.6	-3.7
Public debt	68.5	70.7	71.5

[f] Forecast.

Source: Ministry of Finance.

Exhibit 3.3

Structure of the primary balance, 1989–97 (%)

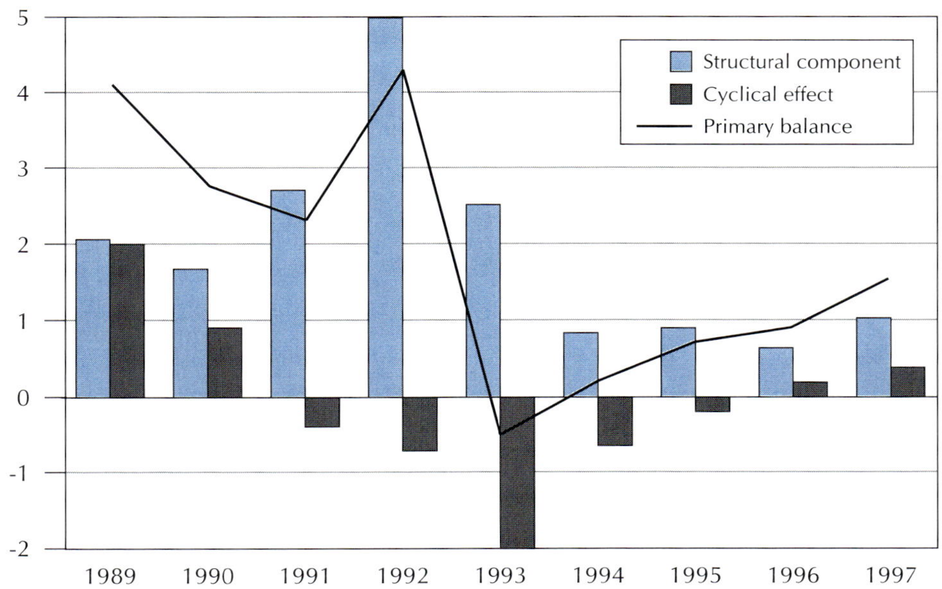

Source: Banco Comercial Português.

income tax receipts of 15.8 per cent after 31.1 per cent in 1996 was regarded as a difficult target to meet.

The upturn in the economy since 1993 (ie, the cyclical effect), rather than expenditure cuts, is largely responsible for the improvement in the primary balance (net of debt interest payments) to around 1.5 per cent of GDP in 1997 (see Exhibit 3.3). The structural component of the primary balance has not changed significantly since 1994, showing the unchanged nature of budgetary policy. The non-implementation of structural reforms makes public finances very sensitive to fluctuations in the economic cycle.

Although its bureaucracy is more bloated than Spain's (27 per cent of salaried workers were civil servants or worked for state companies in 1995), the government did not resort to the drastic measure of a wage freeze in the public

Exhibit 3.4

Structure of public spending, 1995–97 (% of total)

	1997	*1996*	*1995*
Defence	5.2	6.4	6.3
Foreign affairs	0.9	0.9	0.8
Finance	31.7	32.4	37.8
Internal administration	4.0	3.9	3.8
Justice	1.4	1.4	1.4
Economy	1.1	1.0	1.2
Agriculture	2.0	2.2	2.2
Education	18.8	18.2	16.9
Health	13.7	13.7	13.6
Training & employment	0.2	0.2	0.2
Social Security	7.5	6.9	3.7
Environment	0.8	0.9	0.7
Culture	0.5	0.5	0.3
Science & technology	0.3	0.3	0.2

Source: Ministry of Finance.

sector in order to curb the budget deficit. Staff costs were budgeted to grow 8.5 per cent in 1997.

The leeway for cutting welfare expenditure is slim as Portugal still lags behind most of Europe on social spending (see Chapter 2). Education, reflecting the government's priorities, is one of the few areas where spending is growing in real terms. Expenditure accounted for a projected 18.8 per cent of total public spending in 1997, up from 16.9 per cent in 1995 (see Exhibit 3.4).

Public debt

Public debt reached around 68 per cent of GDP in 1997, higher than the Emu requirement of 60 per cent but fulfilling the condition because it was on a downward trend. The use of privatisation receipts to lower the public sector borrowing requirement is playing a crucial role in public debt reduction.

Privatisation

The size of Portugal's public sector has been reduced steadily since 1989 through an on-going privatisation programme. State-owned companies accounted for less than 10 per cent of GDP at the end of 1996 and below 3 per cent of total employment, down from 19.4 per cent and 6.4 per cent respectively in 1988.

Before the 1974 revolution, most of the heavy industries and the financial system were controlled by a few families. As in Spain, much of industry was owned by the banks which in many cases acted more like holding companies than classical banks. The relationship between banking and industry, characterised by privileged lending and lack of market criteria for investments, was incestuous. This situation was compounded by the 1975 nationalisations which swept 53 per cent of fixed investment into the state's hands. The state became the owner overnight of brewery, cigarette, petrochemical, cement, steel, shipbuilding, water, insurance, television and radio companies. A succession of governments, motivated by political rather than managerial criteria, nominated (and constantly changed) the top and many of the middle management in public enterprises, with dire consequences for planning, efficiency and public and foreign debt.

The government began to re-privatise in 1989 when a law was passed that allowed for the privatisation of up to 49 per cent of state-owned companies. A year later the constitution was changed to allow 100 per cent privatisation. The process started (see Exhibit 3.5) with the partial sale of a brewery (Unicer), followed by a bank (Banco Totta & Açores) and two insurance companies (Tranquilidade and Aliança Seguradora).

In the 1989–95 period banks and insurance companies accounted for 60 per cent of the revenue obtained. By 1996 privatisation of the insurance sector was virtually complete and privately-owned commercial banks accounted for more than two-thirds of total bank deposits compared with 16 per cent in 1989. Privatisation of the banking sector was concluded by selling the state's 80.5 per cent stake in Banco Fomento e Exterior in a competitive public tender to Banco Português de Investimento and the

Exhibit 3.5

Major privatisations, 1989–96

Enterprise	*Tranche*	*Date*	*Method*	*Percentage sold*	*Total revenue (Esc billion)*	*Sector*
Unicer	1	26/04/89	Public offer	49.00	9.4	Brewery
Banco Totta e Açores	1	10/07/89	Public offer	49.00	28.6	Banking
Aliança Seguradora	1	02/10/89	Public offer	49.00	7.1	Insurance
Tranquilidade	1	04/12/89	Public offer	49.00	25.8	Insurance
Unicer	2	28/06/90	Public offer	51.00	13.3	Brewery
Banco Totta e Açores	2	31/07/90	Public offer	31.00	22.4	Banking
Transinsular		06/08/90	Public offer	51.10	1.8	Insurance
Tranquilidade	2	09/10/90	Public offer	51.00	18.9	Insurance
Centralcer		12/11/90	Public offer	100.00	34.6	Brewery
Banco Português do Atlântico	1	11/12/90	Public offer	33.00	49.8	Banking
Sociedade Financeira Portuguesa		06/05/91	Public offer	100.00	16.1	Finance
Aliança Seguradora	2	29/05/91	Public offer	51.00	6.8	Insurance
Bonança	1	25/06/91	Public offer	60.00	18.8	Insurance
Banco Espírito Santo & CL	1	09/07/91	Public offer	40.00	60.9	Banking
Banco Fonsecas & Burnay	1	27/08/91	Public tender	80.00	36.1	Banking
Banco Espírito Santo & CL	2	25/02/92	Public offer	60.00	89.0	Banking
Mundial Confiança		14/04/92	Public offer	100.00	33.4	Insurance
Banco Português do Atlântico	2	25/05/92	Public offer	17.64	50.6	Banking
Petrogal	1	04/06/92	Public tender	25.00	40.8	Oil
Banco Fonsecas & Burnay	2	20/07/92	Public offer	20.00	9.0	Banking
Império		17/11/92	Public offer	100.00	25.5	Insurance
Banif		23/11/92	Public offer	16.01	5.3	Banking
CPP		02/12/92	Public offer	100.00	40.8	Banking
Bonança	2	09/12/92	Public offer	15.00	4.3	Insurance
UBP	1	03/02/93	Public offer	61.11	24.4	Banking
Banco Português do Atlântico	3	07/07/93	Public offer	17.50	32.4	Banking
Banco Português do Atlântico	4	25/03/94	Direct sale	7.50	15.4	Banking
CMP	1	31/05/94	Public tender	80.00	31.8	Cement
SECIL	1	31/05/94	Public tender	51.00	31.2	Cement
Cimpor	1	04/07/94	Public offer	20.00	39.6	Cement
BPSM	1	16/11/94	Public tender	80.00	37.3	Banking
Bonança	3	12/12/94	Public offer	25.00	6.6	Insurance
Banco de Fomento e Exterior	1	27/12/94	Public offer	19.50	19.4	Banking
Banco Português do Atlântico	5	24/03/95	Direct sale	24.40	75.1	Banking
BPSM	2	28/03/95	Public offer	20.00	6.8	Banking
CMP	2	29/05/95	Public offer	20.00	7.8	Cement
SECIL	2	29/05/95	Public offer	7.90	4.7	Cement
Portugal Telecom	1	01/06/95	Public offer	14.49	74.9	Telecommunication
Portugal Telecom	1	01/06/95	Direct sale	12.77	67.9	Telecommunication
Portucel Ind	1	27/06/95	Public offer	12.10	10.4	Pulp and paper
Portucel Ind	1	27/06/95	Direct sale	32.20	29.1	Pulp and paper
UBP	2	11/07/95	Direct sale	20.00	7.5	Banking
Petrogal	2	31/07/95	Public tender	20.00	40.0	Oil
CNP	1	24/04/96	Direct sale	99.00	12.7	Oil
Portugal Telecom	2	11/06/96	Public offer	6.66	42.7	Telecommunication

Exhibit 3.5 *continued*

Major privatisations, 1989–96 *continued*

Enterprise	*Tranche*	*Date*	*Method*	*Percentage sold*	*Total revenue (Esc billion)*	*Sector*
Portugal Telecom	2	11/06/96	Direct sale	15.10	103.7	Telecommunication
Banco de Fomento e Exterior	2	28/08/96	Public tender	65.00	136.0	Banking
Cimpor	2	15/10/96	Public offer	20.47	50.2	Cement
Cimpor	2	15/10/96	Direct sale	24.53	65.3	Cement
CNP	2	18/10/96	Public offer	1.00	0.1	Oil
Banco Totta e Açores	3	19/11/96	Public offer	3.06	4.5	Banking
Banco Totta e Açores	3	19/11/96	Direct sale	10.14	16.0	Banking
Tabaqueira		19/12/96	Public tender	65.00	33.2	Tobacco

Source: Data supplied by the Portuguese authorities.

remaining 13.2 per cent of Banco Totta & Açores was floated on the stock market. Caixa Geral de Depositos, the largest banking group, is expected to remain state-owned.

Privatisation proceeds (see Exhibit 3.6) totalled US$11.5 billion between 1989 and 1996, making Portugal the industrialised world's third largest privatising country after Britain and New Zealand, according to the OECD. A significant proportion of the receipts has been used for public debt retirement. Portuguese wits joke that thanks to the communist party, which was a strong force behind the nationalisations, the country was able to meet the Emu public debt requirement; without the re-privatisations the government would have been hard pressed to find the funds to cut the level of its debt.

The Socialists accelerated the privatisation programme after they took office in October 1995, focusing on industry and services, including steel, shipbuilding, oil, chemicals, mining, gas, pulp and tobacco as well as airport management and motorway construction and operation. The largest sales in 1996, when a record US$3 billion

Exhibit 3.6

Privatisation proceeds, 1989–97 (US$ million)

	1989	*1990*	*1991*	*1992*	*1993*	*1994*	*1995*	*1996*	*1997*[e]
Total proceeds	500.9	1,189.5	1,197.4	2,322.7	500.0	1,133.8	2,423.9	3,011.0	3,044.9
State proceeds	362.6	215.4	753.0	1,637.2	413.6	565.3	888.8	2,471.0	2,496.8
Debt redemption	284.5	503.0	505.3	1,480.9	319.1	180.8	818.8	1,893.4	1,997.5
as % of GDP	0.5	0.7	0.7	1.6	0.4	0.2	0.8	1.8	1.9
as % of public debt	0.8	1.1	1.0	2.6	0.6	0.3	1.2	2.7	2.9

[e] Estimate.

Source: Ministry of Finance and Banco de Portugal.

was obtained, were a second tranche of 22 per cent of Portugal Telecom and a second tranche of 45 per cent of Cimpor, the largest cement producer, floated on the stock market.

Although the programme is an aggressive one, the government is keeping controlling stakes in some privatised companies such as Portugal Telecom and EDP (51 per cent in each). Under pressure from the European Commission the government removed the limits on EU investors acquiring privatised companies. The previous government had set some case-by-case restrictions on foreign holdings which led to complaints of illegality in Brussels.

Proceeds from privatisation in 1997 are estimated at Esc410 billion. The programme also extended to the transport system and included the partial sale of Brisa, the motorway monopoly, 90 per cent controlled by the state in 1996; Ana, the airport authority, and TAP Air Portugal, the national airline.

Caminho de Ferro Portugueses (CFP), the state railway monopoly, was split into two state-owned companies, one to manage track and other infrastructure, the other to run trains. Management concessions would be granted to private-sector groups to operate some suburban and regional lines. Build, operate and transfer contracts for light suburban railways, or metros, would also be put out to tender in some areas. Companies such as cement or chemical groups would be able to submit proposals to run their own trains over the state-owned railway.

Privatisations have had an enormous impact on Portugal's small stock market, lifting market capitalisation and trading volumes and moving the Lisbon stock market closer to the levels of a developed European market (see Chapter 11).

Proceeds from privatisations in 1997 (see Exhibit 3.7) were expected to be higher than 1996's US$3 billion. The biggest privatisation to date, scheduled for June, is the initial public offering of Electricidade de Portugal (EDP), the electrical utility. Up to 49 per cent was authorised to be sold in a deal that could be worth as much as US$4 billion, the equivalent of Portugal's general government deficit in 1996. The first offering, however, was expected to be kept to about 30 per cent, enabling the government to reap the benefit of any subsequent price rise for a second tranche.

Exhibit 3.7

Privatisations, 1997–99

Electricidade de Portugal–IPO	1997
Portugal Telecom – 3rd tranche	1997
ANA (airport management) – 1st tranche	1998
Petrogal (oil) – last tranche	1998
Portucel (pulp)	1998
Brisa (motorways) – 2nd tranche	1999
EDP – 2nd tranche	1999
Tabaqueira (tobacco) – 2nd and 3rd tranches	1999
Gas de Portugal	1998/99

Source: Ministry of Finance.

Spain's three biggest electricity producers – Endesa, Iberdrola and Unión Fenosa – planned to seek holdings in EDP when it was privatised. This was expected to produce cross-holdings in the Iberian electricity sector aimed mainly at expanding business through acquisitions in Latin America. EDP and Spain's state-controlled Endesa were part of an international consortium that acquired a controlling stake in 1996 in Cerj, the electricity company in the Brazilian state of Rio de Janeiro.

Saudi Aramco, the big Saudi oil producer, planned to take up to 35 per cent of the Petrogal oil group where the state holds 55 per cent.

The Spanish question

Portugal's fundamentals are better than Spain's. Given the very close economic links between the two countries, however, some quarters are questioning the wisdom of going into Emu without Spain, in the event that Portugal's neighbour fails to qualify for the first round. Anibal Cavaco Silva, the former prime minister, believes it would be "totally unrealistic" to join if Spain's entry was delayed.

Such is the government's resolve to participate in Emu from the outset that its official position is that Portugal's entry should be decided on the economy's own merits, regardless of whether Spain is admitted. There is a strong degree of national pride over the issue; Portugal lay under Spanish dominance between 1580 and 1640 and entry before Spain would give the Portuguese a rare opportunity to cock a snoop at their neighbours. The government, however, would prefer both countries to adopt the euro together. What lies behind its determination is a feeling that Portugal is economically better qualified than any other southern European candidate and should not be excluded on political grounds alone if Spain fails to make the grade. The worst case scenario for Lisbon is that both countries are left out and Spain resorts to competitive devaluations, though such moves are unlikely as they would reduce Madrid's chances of joining Emu at a later stage.

After the restoration of Portuguese independence, the two countries turned inwards and lived back-to-back for more than 300 years until they both entered the European Community in 1986 and came face to face. Spain's King Juan Carlos – who spent part of his childhood in Portugal where his father was in exile during the Franco years – played an important part in the improvement of mutual understanding in the Iberian peninsula. Nevertheless, a great deal of mistrust remains between the two countries, expressed in a still popular Portuguese saying: "Spain produces neither good wine nor good marriages."

EC membership opened the door for an economic invasion of Portugal by Spain. The country is Portugal's main source of imports and its second largest export market. Spain exports more to Portugal than to the whole of Latin America and runs a hefty trade surplus with its neighbour. Exports grew at an annual average rate of 16 per cent between 1985 and 1992, compared with overall yearly growth of 7.25 per cent, while Portugal's exports to Spain expanded 10.6 per cent a year (5.8 per cent average growth). Spain's exports to Portugal surpassed Pta1 trillion (US$7.8 billion) for the first time in 1996. At the same time, Spanish banks and companies have also invested heavily in Portugal.

It is the imbalance in investment, more than in trade, which worries Portugal, though there is nothing it can do about it. More Spanish investment goes "next door" than to any other country, except, recently, Mexico and Peru because of large one-off investments by Spanish banks and multinationals such as Telefónica and RepSol. Statistics, however, do not separate out the investments made through Spanish subsidiaries by non-Spanish firms, which have long treated Iberia as a single economic unit. The increasingly strong Spanish presence is a sensitive issue as it plays on Portuguese fears that they are being swallowed up by their economically more powerful neighbour (see Exhibit 3.8). For Spanish firms, tiny Portugal (roughly the size of Andalusia) is a natural extension of their domestic market and the Spanish presence there has anticipated the European single market. The Spanish–Portuguese border was one of the first to do away with regular controls. Portuguese supermarkets, for example, turn to Spain for some of their supplies that, although available at home, are inefficiently produced or marketed.

Exhibit 3.8

Comparative indicators, Spain–Portugal

	Portugal	*Spain*
Population (millions)	9.9	39.1
GDP (US$ billions)	127	557
Exports (% of GDP)	21	22
Imports (% of GDP)	29	22

Source: OECD.

There are over 3,000 Spanish companies in Portugal, most of them small, compared with less than 400 in 1989. Portugal has around 200 companies in Spain. Spain is estimated to have invested more than Pta500 billion in Portugal between 1992 and 1995.

The largest Spanish investment was the purchase by Banco Bilbao Vizcaya (BBV) of Lloyds Bank in Portugal in 1991. Lloyds had been in Portugal for 128 years and was known simply as *o banco inglês*, the English bank. For a bank from Portugal's oldest ally to decide to pull out was a bad enough blow for the government. Selling it to Portugal's historical enemy par excellence was tantamount to being stabbed in the back by your best friend.

Other big Spanish banks – the assets of BBV (parent bank) alone represent around 60 per cent of the combined assets of the Portuguese banking system – have also moved into the financial sector. Banco Santander owns Banco de Comércio e Indústria (BCI) and is a strong player in the stock market through Banco Santander de Negócios, its investment banking arm. Banco Central Hispano has 20 per cent of Banco Comercial Português, the most aggressive bank.

4

THE BANK OF PORTUGAL AND MONETARY POLICY

The Bank of Portugal is formally independent from the government, although its autonomy has occasionally been called into question. Monetary policy is focused on price stability via exchange rate targeting, especially against the peseta and the Deutschmark. As a very open economy, currency stability plays a vital role in capping import-induced inflation.

Since the widening of the exchange-rate mechanism (ERM) bands to ±15 per cent in August 1993, the escudo has traded within a narrow range close to its central parity of 102.5/Dm. Exchange rate credibility has increased, as evidenced by the last devaluation in March 1995 when the escudo was devalued by only 3.5 per cent compared with the Spanish peseta's 7 per cent.

The central bank uses three instruments to steer monetary policy: an overnight credit facility whose emergency lending rate sets the ceiling for short-term money market rates; a facility for swift absorption of liquidity whose absorption rate sets the floor for money market rates; and repurchase agreements (repos). The repo rate is usually halfway between the two and variable (only rarely is it fixed) and thus the key one to follow.

Repos are conducted at the beginning of each reserve requirement maintenance period and expire either on the first day of the following period (regular repos) or within the reserve period. Until July 1994, regular repos were issued at pre-announced rates subject to a quantity ceiling, with suspensions in periods of extreme pressure in the foreign exchange market. Since then the Bank of Portugal has conducted regular repos at variable rates unless it wants to give a clear signal concerning changes in monetary conditions, in which case it has resumed the announcement of repo rates. The Bank decided to change its policy because of the unwarranted interest attracted by changes in the rate on previous occasions, which undermined its role in exchange-rate management.

Use of variable repos has given the Bank a better indicator of demand pressure in the money market, while avoiding the disruptions which were previously associated with the suspension of repos at times of exchange market turbulence.

A new reserve requirement system for banks was launched in November 1994 when the ratio was lowered to 2 per cent (non-remunerated), in line with other EU countries, from 17 per cent (partially remunerated). The liquidity released by the reduction of the ratio was sterilised through certificates of deposits issued by the Bank of Portugal. These securities cannot be traded with the public, but they are negotiable between institutions subject to minimum reserve requirements and between such institutions and the Bank.

Two types of certificate of deposit were issued: series A, non-interest bearing with two and three year maturities; and series B, with maturities ranging from four to 10 years and interest rates set quarterly according to market conditions.

The reserve base was also redefined. Deposits and other liabilities of international branches (but not overseas branches) located in Madeira and Santa Maria islands offshore centres, liabilities against the government and investments in escudos by non-residents were included in the reserve base. Treasury bills, CLIPs and repurchase agreements sold outright to the public as well as foreign currency deposits and other foreign currency liabilities *vis-á-vis* emigrants were excluded.

By regulating the money market with a system of official rates to stem speculative runs and making interest rate moves in line with those of the Bundesbank, the Bank of Portugal has kept the escudo stable. The repo rate (also known as the liquidity injection rate) was down to 6.5 per cent in 1997, the absorption rate 6.3 per cent and the emergency lending rate 8.3 per cent. Such a favourable monetary background was emphasised by Portugal also boasting the lowest bond yield in southern Europe during the last quarter of 1996.

Maintaining the escudo's stability will continue to be the cornerstone of monetary policy. Currency stability, declining inflation and a lower budget deficit have considerably narrowed Portugal's 10-year yield gap with Germany, which in April 1997 was down to 89 bp from 380 bp at the end of 1995.

The money market

[1] This section and the next one draw on a report by Banco Santander de Negocios Portugal.

Portugal's two interbank markets are being gradually integrated.[1] The interbank money market (MMI) is a regulated market in which authorised financial institutions exchange funds represented by the balances of their sight deposit accounts at the Bank of Portugal or dematerialised securities entered in the securities account at the central bank. These operations, the maturity of which cannot exceed one year, are designed to balance the surplus of, and need for, primary money between banks obliged to set aside minimum cash reserves. The Bank of Portugal uses the other market, the interbank securities market (MIT), to mop up and inject liquidity, through the sale and purchase of certain types of securities to and from authorised institutions.

Operations conducted by MMI participants are processed via the market telephone system (SISTEM) which consists of an IT application and a set of telephone links between the Bank of Portugal and authorised participating institutions.

In the liquidity injection operations carried out by the Bank of Portugal, institutions that are non-member associates of the Lisbon Stock Exchange may sell fixed-rate coupon treasury bonds with repurchase agreements to the Bank of Portugal. Treasury bills may also be used in the liquidity injection or absorption operations.

Swaps and FRAs

The market for these products is fairly well developed in Portugal. FRAs cannot be traded via SISTEM, and there is no regulatory framework for this market. Institutions, however, operate in accordance with the rules of the international money market, though they may agree among themselves to other types of contracts. Standard contracts fall due on the third Wednesday of the months of the March, June, September and December cycle and may not have a duration of more than one year. The interest rate implicit in the agreement is the Lisfra rate of the Monday (or last business day) immediately prior to maturity, the interest arising from the operation being exchanged on the date of maturity.

The Lisfra rate is the overall average resulting from the calculation of the arithmetic mean of the individual bid and ask rates taken from a sample of eight of the largest banks, excluding the two highest and two lowest interest rates.

Short-term currency swaps (up to one year) now account for a considerable portion of the volume traded on the Portuguese money market; interest rate swaps, however, still account for a small part of the transactions.

5

TRADE

As a nation of with a long history of trading it is not surprising that the Portuguese economy is one of the most open in Europe (as measured by the ratio of trade to GDP). Total trade in goods and services amounts to more than 50 per cent of GDP, one of the highest ratios in the European Union.

Portugal imports around half of its food, four-fifths of its energy, most of its capital goods and, since joining the EU in 1986, an increasing amount of its consumer goods. The country has consistently run a trade deficit. The main export sectors are both traditional ones – particularly textiles, clothing, shoes and wine – and relatively new ones, especially the motor industry (see Exhibit 5.1) The start-up of the Ford and Volkswagen joint production plant, a project with a very big impact for a small country like Portugal, has quickly changed the structure of exports. Machinery and transport equipment accounted for 36.2 per cent of total exports in 1996, up from 31.1 per cent in 1995.

Merchandise exports grew from US$5.6 billion in 1986 to US$23.8 billion in 1996, while imports expanded from US$7.1 billion to US$34.1 billion. The trade deficit reached a hefty 9.6 per cent of GDP, and the current account deficit tripled to 2.3 per cent of GDP. Today, the EU absorbs more than 80 per cent of exports (around one-third in 1960) and supplies more than 70 per cent of imports. Sales to Europe first burgeoned after Portugal joined EFTA in 1962; they gathered momentum with its Trade Agreement with the EC in 1972. This led to diversification away from the traditional, rigid basket of port wine, sardines and olives towards a range of manufactured goods including threads and textiles and subsequently clothing, footwear, components for electronic equipment and machine tools. Export growth in clothing was so pronounced that Portugal was sometimes labelled a "pyjama republic".

When Portugal joined EFTA, its colonies – particularly the two richest, Angola and Mozambique – were not allowed to trade with anyone but the motherland: they absorbed 25 per cent of Portugal's exports and many Portuguese manufacturers, shielded from domestic competition by high tariff and technical barriers, coasted on their exports to the captive African colonies' markets. When tariff barriers collapsed, with the dismantling of EFTA links and the lead-up to EC accession, many manufacturers were faced with questions of quality and prompt delivery dates for the first time.

Decolonisation in 1975 and the ensuing political and economic chaos whittled Portuguese exports to Angola, the main market, down to 2.5 per cent of the total in 1989. The principal markets today are Germany, France and Spain.

Exhibit 5.1

Foreign trade figures

	1995		1996	
Principal exports	*Esc billion*	*% of total*	*Esc billion*	*% of total*
Textiles, clothing and shoes	1,068.9	31.3	1,102.2	30.0
Machinery and transport equipment	1,063.2	31.1	1,331.5	36.2
Chemicals and petroleum products	348.5	10.2	321.5	8.7
Food, beverages and tobacco	215.4	6.3	234.3	6.4
Paper and publishing	215.4	6.3	176.1	4.8
Wood and cork	193.5	5.7	205.4	5.6
Minerals and ores	145.8	4.3	144.8	3.9
Other items	163.3	4.8	161.8	4.4
Total (including other)	**3,414.0**	**100.0**	**3,677.5**	**100.0**
Principal imports	*Esc billion*	*% of total*	*Esc billion*	*% of total*
Machinery and transport equipment	1,885.5	38.6	2,171.2	41.2
Chemicals and petroleum products	797.6	16.3	843.7	16.0
Textiles, clothing and shoes	534.4	10.9	555.7	10.6
Food, beverages and tobacco	345.7	7.1	360.4	6.8
Combustible fuels	292.2	6.0	291.1	5.5
Base metals	268.4	5.5	234.8	4.5
Paper and publishing	146.4	3.0	149.4	2.8
Other items	619.4	12.7	659.1	12.5
Total (including other)	**4,889.6**	**100.0**	**5,265.4**	**100.0**
Main destinations of exports	*Esc billion*	*% of total*	*Esc billion*	*% of total*
Germany	738.4	21.6	781.0	21.2
Spain	503.0	14.7	523.5	14.2
France	477.4	14.0	519.3	14.1
United Kingdom	375.5	11.0	396.2	10.8
The Netherlands	179.4	5.3	179.7	4.9
United States	158.1	4.6	167.7	4.6
EU	2,733.9	80.1	2,940.5	80.0
EFTA	104.2	3.1	99.6	2.7
Total (including other)	**3,414.5**	**100.0**	**3,677.5**	**100.0**
Main origins of imports	*Esc billion*	*% of total*	*Esc billion*	*% of total*
Spain	1,015.8	20.8	1,181.8	22.4
Germany	703.8	14.4	815.5	15.5
France	583.4	11.9	583.5	11.1
Italy	410.4	8.4	435.7	8.3
United Kingdom	323.9	6.6	354.1	6.7
The Netherlands	220.6	4.5	233.3	4.4
EU	3,614.6	73.9	3,982.7	75.6
EFTA	142.1	2.9	125.1	2.4
Total (including other)	**4,889.6**	**100.0**	**5,265.4**	**100.0**

Source: INE.

Exhibit 5.2

Competitive positions, 1989–97 (%), 1991 = 100

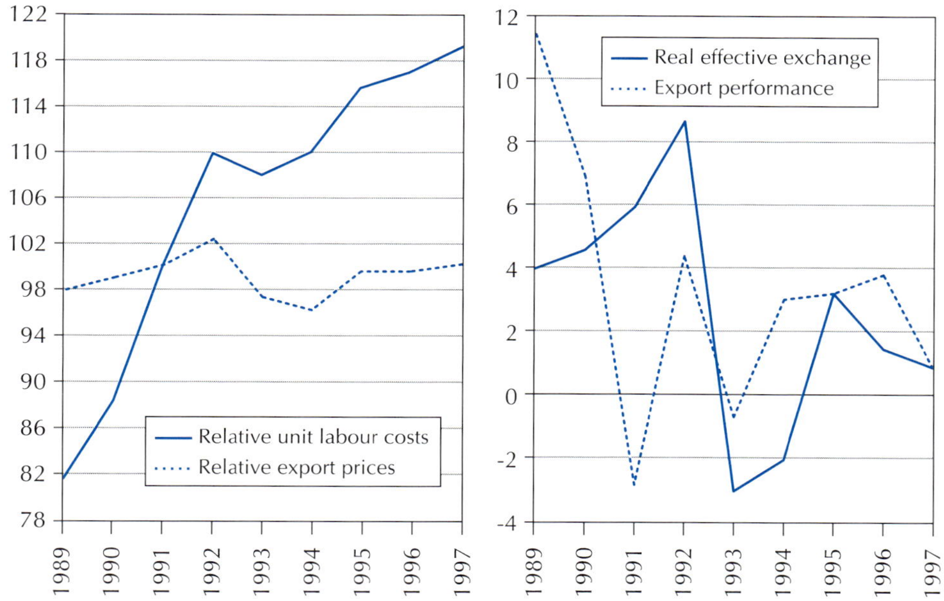

Source: Banco Comercial Português.

Free access to the main European markets, a competitive exchange rate (broadly stable in nominal effective terms, but appreciated in real terms as inflation has exceeded, albeit by little in recent years, that of its EU partners), greater productive capacity and higher productivity have helped to boost exports – which have been the driving force behind the recovery since the 1993 recession. Despite the escudo's appreciation and a deterioration in unit labour costs, exports have held up, though the pace of growth has ebbed (see Exhibit 5.2).

AutoEuropa

The impact of the huge AutoEuropa plant on exports has been considerable. The US$2.5 billion joint venture between Ford and Volkswagen to produce multipurpose vehicles (MPVs) – the Ford Galaxy and the Volkswagen Sharan – accounted for around 10 per cent of total exports in 1996 and its relative share will continue to grow. AutoEuropa hopes to enjoy a 3 per cent share of the European market by the year 2000.

Ford and Volkswagen were attracted not just by Portugal's much lower labour costs, but also by the country's base of efficient workers, suppliers and infrastructure. A total of 52 Portuguese companies supply AutoEuropa and another 110 sub-suppliers are involved. The state-of-the art plant at Palmela incorporates the latest developments in automation and computerised production control. In the body shop, for example, 173 robots apply 60 per cent of 4,600 welding spots automatically.

Exports of cars and transport equipment account for close to 30 per cent of total exports (18 per cent in the late 1980s), while the relative share of shoes and textiles has dropped to around 30 per cent from 40 per cent.

Portugal's low labour costs are a key factor in maintaining a competitive position, but the gap is inevitably narrowing as part of a general pressure for better living standards. Productivity and infrastructure in the broadest sense (ie, the quality of education and not just of the roads) is assuming an increasing importance. Portugal's competitive advantage is narrowing against central European countries (the Czech Republic, Hungary and Poland), all of which are likely at some stage to form part of an enlarged European Union (see Exhibit 5.3).

A warning was sounded when Portugal was overtaken by the Czech Republic in the 1996 ranking of the 45 most competitive countries drawn up by the IMD, a Swiss management school.

Furthermore, these countries may be a threat to Portugal's historically high transfers from Brussels. The changing situation is graphically illustrated by the fact that whereas Portugal was a place favoured by Germany for outward processing trade (OPT) in the textile industry – cloth and even buttons were sent and finished clothing made – today countries like Poland are increasingly taking this business away from Portugal, which, in turn, is using its former colony, Cabo Verde, for the same purpose.

Clothing and textiles

This troubled industry is struggling against the phasing out of the Multi-Fibre Arrangement (MFA) reached under the Uruguay Round. The number of jobs has declined to below 130,000 from a peak of 158,000 in 1990.

Textile companies, most of them very small, are concentrated around the northern cities of Oporto and Braga. Leading companies include Coelima, Portugal's largest manufacturer of bed linen, which has a significant percentage of the US luxury bed linen market.

Low labour costs (less than US$2 an hour compared with US$14 in some northern European countries), long working hours, cheap cotton from the former Portuguese colonies and protectionism led to a steady expansion of the textile industry between the 1930s and the 1950s, followed by major growth after Portugal joined EFTA in 1960 and after it gained better access to the EC with its 1972 Trade Agreement. When Portugal entered the EC in 1986, her new partners ceased to enforce the quotas on textile imports that had constrained Portuguese manufacturers over the previous decade. The industry continued to thrive, and became a dominant force in western Europe, retaining its EFTA markets while adding those of the EC and fighting for a foothold in the United States in spite of severe limitations.

The phasing out of the MFA agreement has triggered a surge in textile imports in Europe from low-cost Asian producers who are undercutting Portugal. At the same time lower wages in countries such as Poland and Hungary has made them more attractive than Portugal for outward processing trade (OPT). Portugal (and Greece) are the closest competitors to central and eastern European countries and hence stand to lose the most. (Spain's textiles are of a higher quality.)

Exhibit 5.3

Country rankings of Portugal's main European competitors

	Portugal 1994	Portugal 1995	Spain	Italy	Greece	Czech Republic	Hungary	Poland
Domestic economy	31	42	33	28	39	34	43	40
Internationalisation	22	32	25	21	35	34	30	42
Government	26	32	35	45	42	34	40	43
Finance	28	29	25	27	39	33	43	44
Infrastructure	26	39	23	29	41	35	24	45
Management	37	41	33	26	43	39	38	37
Science and technology	39	35	30	24	39	43	36	37
People	26	32	26	25	29	28	33	30
Credit rating	21	24	18	20	42	29	50	51

Source: IMD World Competitiveness Yearbook 1996.

An on-going restructuring process is taking place, but there is still a great deal of structural weakness. With some very notable exceptions, such as Texteis Manuel Gonçalves, over-manning (usually low-paid, low-skilled female labour) is still common. Reliance on cheap labour and labour-intensive production has discouraged efforts to modernise factories and prolonged the life of antiquated production and management methods.

The emphasis in the better companies is now on anticipating and setting trends in styles and design, and sub-contractors are trying to add value. The CITEX training and design centre near Oporto is helping the industry to adjust to tougher times.

Shoes

The Portuguese footwear industry has been on the march for more than 20 years (see Exhibit 5.4). Exports rose from 5.7 million pairs in 1974 to 85.3 million in 1996, of which more than 93 per cent were leather. Growth, however, has levelled off. Portugal is the second largest exporter of leather footwear in the EU, with a market share of around 11 per cent. The 1,100 companies employ 48,000 people and account for around 9 per cent of total exports.

The success of the footwear industry, which is concentrated around São João de Madeira in the north, is underscored by Campeão Português, a leading concern, which sells casual, sporting and safety shoes. Campeão sells ski boots to Norway,

Exhibit 5.4

Footwear exports, 1982–96 (US$ billions)

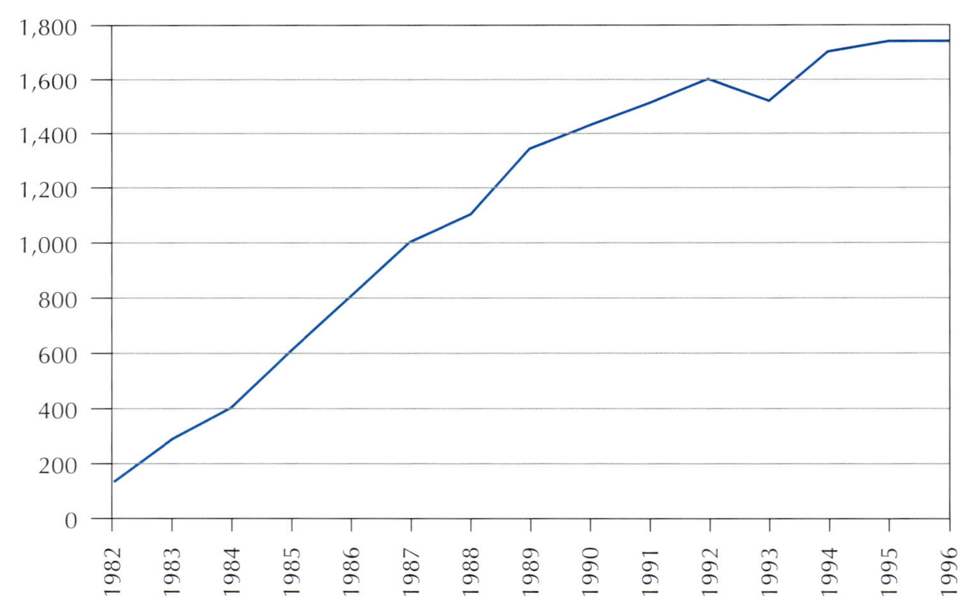

Source: APICCAPS.

rubber-soled safety shoes to the Middle East, and makes the Le Coq sportif range for the French company.

Portugal's costs are low compared to the rest of Europe, but they are much higher than south-east Asian producers such as Taiwan, against whom Portuguese producers cannot hope to compete in the big cheap shoes market (Portugal imported 23.5 million pairs in 1996 compared with 204,410 in 1983). The drive in the quality end of the market is focusing on reducing the delivery time and introducing state-of-the art technology to boost productivity (2,136 pairs of shoes a year per worker in 1992 compared with an EC average of 3,514).

A particularly innovative invention is the water jet cut system for synthetics, first developed by France and then upgraded by leading companies in Portugal, and ink-jet stitch marking. Electronic catalogues are also being increasingly used.

Ceramics

Ceramics have been an art in Portugal since at least the 15th century. Based around Aveiro and Coimbra in the north, companies have been investing heavily in higher-priced decorative tiles for export, while other firms have diversified into products like clay and porcelain ovenware.

The Cerexport group (Cerexport, Faianças da Capôa and Porcelanas Quinta Nova) is the industry leader. Cerexport has been gradually reducing production of clay ovenware and increasing output of porcelain, whose margins are higher, while Faianças de Capôa has confined production to high-quality glazed earthenware under the Vista brand name. Cerexport is expected to merge with Vista Alegre whose china is well known abroad.

Port wine

Port, one of the world's greatest wines, is a particularly Portuguese product which dates back to the very earliest days of trade between Britain and Portugal. The oldest British port company, Warre's, was founded in 1670. The industry is still centred around the northern city of Oporto, from which the wine gets its name.

The industry has gone through a rough patch but is now back on an even keel. Overproduction in 1989–91 (see Exhibit 5.5) caused by the Casa do Douro, the wine growers association, breaking agreed ceilings produced a slump in prices and brought the industry to the brink of disaster. Shippers rallied together and bought up excess stocks, releasing them very gradually onto the world market and actual production was cut back so that it was lower than the authorised output between 1992 and 1994, although it had crept up again by 1996. Under pressure from the government, a new entity to control production and exports, known as CIRDD, came into force in 1996.

Wine production quotas are calculated every year by the Port Wine Institute using the previous year's exports as a reference and passed onto the Casa do Douro to implement among individual growers. In 1989 and 1990 the Casa do Douro distributed growing rights far in excess of the quota, causing havoc in the trade when the excess production began to come onto the market. The Casa, which was also respon-

Exhibit 5.5

Port production and sales (in pipes of 550 litres)

	Authorised production	*Actual production*	*World sales*	*Difference*
1989	183,333	216,825	147,387	69,438
1990	145,402	193,194	146,969	46,225
1991	139,080	147,456	141,742	5,714
1992	107,471	101,333	141,346	-40,013
1993	113,793	108,184	155,296	-47,112
1994	139,080	136,818	154,842	-18,024
1995	161,207	163,528	167,968	-4,440
1996[e]	164,368	164,368	165,000	-632
Total	**1,153,734**	**1,231,706**	**1,220,550**	**11,156**

[e] Estimate.

Source: Port Wine Institute.

sible for classifying vineyards and controlling stocks in the port-growing Douro region, was suspected of abusing what is effectively a system of patronage. Those who suffered the most at the end of the day were the growers, for whom life was tough in the years when production was cut right back in order to reduce the excess stocks. Prices for farmers dropped by 23 per cent in 1991–92. No action was taken against the Casa's leaders, not even by its members.

To the consternation of shippers, the Casa added salt to the wounds by acquiring a 40 per cent stake in one of Portugal's oldest and most venerable shipping houses, the Real Companhia Velha (RCV). Shippers protested that the Casa could not be both referee and player and tried to prevent the sale going through. The Casa's finances were in a parlous state in 1996 and the sale shrouded in mystery as the Casa had reportedly still not taken possession of its shareholding, although it had paid for it.

The CIRDD, whose president is government-appointed, took over some of the Casa's regulatory powers. It is made up of six representatives from the Casa and the same number from the Port Wine Institute. Shippers hope that the new inter-professional body will smooth the traditionally uneasy relations between themselves and the growers.

Despite the problems, the industry's quality image has not suffered and port has held its own more successfully than Spain's sherry industry. Shippers, working with squeezed margins, have made great efforts to modernise labelling and bottling. The government stopped shipment of port in bulk in July 1996 (vintage port has been bottled in Portugal since 1970) in order to achieve fuller control over bottling and hence ensure quality. Bulk sales accounted for 23 per cent of total port exports in 1995. There was evidence of fraud by some importers who were mixing the port with other wines. The industry generally welcomed the move as it enhanced quality control (bottling requirements at source in Oporto are strict), but the large bulk shippers stand to lose business because large retailers in countries like Belgium and the

Netherlands have tended to switch to other fortified wines rather than import bottled port. This might produce a collapse in lower-priced port sales.

As part of the quality drive, some companies, notably Symington Port and Madeira Shippers, the largest company, which owns Warre's, Graham's, Dow's and Quinta do Vesúvio, are very successfully selling premium qualities such as late-bottled vintage (a blend of the best wines of a single year but not a "declared" vintage), 10- and 20-year old port and port aged in wood. Premium products account for around 9 per cent of total port exports.

Although long associated with Britain, and still regarded as a bastion of Britishness within Portugal (along with the Oporto Cricket and Lawn Tennis Club), the port industry long ago ceased to be in the hands of British families. Apart from Symington (the family first came to Oporto in 1882 but its members still consider themselves British and have UK passports), the wineries huddled around the Vila Nova da Gaia quayside are largely in the hands of multinationals. Six of the 10 largest companies belong to big groups. Allied Domecq owns Cockburn and IDV owns Croft.

Wine

Portugal is best known for its port wine (the 1992 Fonseca Vintage Port was ranked fourth in the 1995 world top 100 drawn up by *The Wine Spectator*), but the country is also carving a niche for itself in the world of bargain table wines.

Portugal relies on native grape varieties for the bulk of its table wines; there are only a smattering of transplanted varieties such as Cabernet Sauvignon and Chardonnay. The best wines today are fresh and fruity, in marked contrast to the sometimes woody and even tired flavours of the old-style wines. Two of the main marketing forces behind *vinho verde* and *rosé* are the Guedes family of Oporto, whose Mateus *rosé* wines are marketed world-wide under the Sogrape name, and JM Fonseca of Setúbal near Lisbon, whose *rosé* wines are mainly sold under the name of Lancers.

The demarcated Douro region has considerable potential. Labels such as Sogrape's Esteva, Miguel Champalimaud's Quinta do Couto and Eduardo Serpa's Quinta do Pacheca are becoming increasingly known abroad. Other promising regions include the Alentejo.

The Wine Spectator, the bible for wine drinkers, gave 10 Portuguese wines a score of more than 84 (out of 100) in a ranking of bargain values published in October 1996 (see Exhibit 5.6).

Portugal would be hardly affected by the proposed EU wine reform which has been stalled since 1994 because of fierce resistance from much larger producers like Spain. The reform aims to balance production (which is broadly stable) and consumption (which is declining) through adjustment programmes to reduce the EU "wine lake". Portugal would have a reference production of 9.85 million hectolitres, which would be the basis for determining the quantities of wine to be distilled. This amount was not reached in 1996, and it is unlikely that Portugal will exceed the EU-set distilling limit in the future. National wine stocks have been depleted by low output for a number of years.

Exhibit 5.6

Portuguese wine values

	Score	*Price*
Quinta de Abrigada Alenquer 1992	87	US$8
Sogrape Dao Duque de Viseu 1992	87	US$9
Manuel Salvador Pereira Vinho Verde Alvarinho Dom Salvador 1994	85	US$10
Cooperativa Reguengos de Monsaraz Reguengos 1994	85	US$5
Sogrape Alentejo Vinha do Monte 1992	85	US$9
Sogrape Douro Reserva 1992	85	US$10
Quinta de Mato Miranda Ribatejo 1992	84	US$5.5
Caves Dom Teodósio Dao Cardeal 1991	84	US$6.5
Caves Velhas Bucelas 1994	84	US$8
J.P. Vinhos Alentejo Tinto da Anfora 1991	84	US$10

Source: The Wine Spectator.

Forestry products

Portugal's forest industry has considerable potential. The country's natural suitability for forestry is so strong that it could occupy up to two-thirds of the national territory compared with the current 30 per cent. The 3.3 million hectares of land under afforestation produced export earnings of Esc274.4 billion in the first nine months of 1996 (see Exhibit 5.7).

Many experts believe that Portugal would be better off devoting more energy to developing the forestry industry than propping up agriculture whose economic importance has been steadily declining. Portugal is not a natural country for agriculture, and the constant breaking down of small plots into even tinier ones, particularly in the north, has made production very inefficient. There are an estimated 400,000 to 600,000 hectares available for afforestation. But it is not easy to convince farmers to grow trees instead of crops when food self-sufficiency is a pressing need for poor families.

Nevertheless, some progress has been made: investment by small private land owners was stimulated in the first years after Portugal joined the EC in 1986 by funds from the Afforestation Programme (PAF). In 1989 afforestation with eucalyptus became subject to restrictions after a surge in eucalyptus plantings. There were clashes between local populations and ecologists who protested that the tree dries up underground water resources; its shape encourages fast

Exhibit 5.7

Exports and imports of forestry products, January–September 1996 (Esc billion)

	Exports	*Imports*
Rosin products	4.86	0.84
Cork	81.61	6.12
Cellulose pulp	54.64	6.22
Paper	76.58	81.74
Furniture	12.54	8.70
Wood-based panels	17.82	4.06
Wood (round and sawn)	26.42	38.55
Total	**274.47**	**146.33**

rainfall erosion of topsoil and it sterilises the soil for a long period after it has been uprooted.

As in Spain, forest fires have taken a heavy toll. Between 1986 and 1993 416,740 hectares were destroyed and only 114,856 hectares were replanted with trees. In the 1994–99 period the goal is to cover 192,000 hectares with trees (32,000 a year compared with 14,000 in 1986–93).

Although export earnings are sizeable, Portugal only accounts for around 1 per cent of world pulp production and 0.3 per cent of paper output; demand for wood, however, accounts for 11 per cent of the world total and is growing at a rate of 1.5 per cent a year.[1] The industry has entered a period of raw material shortages, mainly brought on by increases in installed capacity since 1987 and higher capacity utilisation rates. Additionally, world-wide environmental restrictions, such as reduced felling in tropical forests, have affected production.

There are a small number of pulp producers and around 75 paper producers, most of them very small. The major ones are set out in Exhibit 5.8. The most integrated company is Soporcel. Portucel is the largest European producer of hardwood pulp (closely followed by Ence of Spain) and the second biggest producer of bleached eucalyptus market pulp in the world after Brazil's Aracruz. Portucel is expanding in the Iberian peninsula via acquisitions – primarily downstream in paper or upstream to increase its self-sufficiency in wood. The government is actively supporting consolidation within the domestic pulp and paper industry.

As well as importing more wood, Portugal has begun to manage forests more intensively – which requires closer involvement from pulp producers.

Portucel, 40 per cent privatised in 1995, plans to double output of its 70,000 hectares of eucalyptus forest by 2003 through more intensive management of its resources. The increase from 450,000 cubic metres of timber a year to more than one million will be achieved through the renewal of existing forests and the planting of genetically improved trees without any substantial increase in the area of forest it manages.

Expansion will enable the group to meet almost 50 per cent of its own timber requirements, up from 27 per cent in 1996.

Exhibit 5.8

Major pulp and paper companies

	Capacities ('000 tpa)
Portucel	615 Eucalyptus pulp
	60 Kraft sack-paper
Soporcel	420 Eucalyptus pulp
	260 Uncoated fine paper
Papeis Inapa	180 Uncoated fine paper
Cellulose do Caima	85 Eucalyptus pulp
	33,000 ha forestry

Source: HSBC James Capel.

[1] See the November 1995 report by Gesfinc, *Pulp and Paper – What is Changing in the Sectors*.

SONAE Indústria, part of Portugal's largest private group, became the fourth largest European woodpanels group after building up a significant stake in the Spanish company Tafisa and obtaining management control in 1993. SONAE has 5 per cent of the European market and 28 per cent of the Iberian market.

SONAE began by producing decorative laminates and bought a chipboard company in 1960. Between 1986 and 1990 it expanded rapidly through a series of acquisitions in Portugal and manufacturing facilities in Northern Ireland. The company now manufactures laminated, veneered and paper coated chipboard and fibreboard (principally MDF) as well as uncoated wood-based products. It also produces value-added products, mainly components for flatpack furniture, shelves and flooring.

Tafisa, the second largest wood-chip manufacturer in Spain, enlarged SONAE's chipboard capacity by 80 per cent and its MDF capacity by 70 per cent. Tafisa produces thin MDF, which complements the thicker product produced by SONAE. Tafisa also has manufacturing facilities in Canada.

The geographical diversity of operations is increasing with greater disparity between production plants. Exports account for some 80 per cent of SONAE Indústria's sales, the majority of these are into Spain. Production capacity of chipboard is being increased to 1.4 million cubic metres from just over 1 million through expansion in Spain and the start of operations in Brazil and Zimbabwe (to serve South Africa), and MDF capacity to 380,000 cubic metres from 260,000 through a unit in Brazil. SONAE reached agreement with the state government of Paraná in October 1996 to invest US$130 million in a plant producing chipboard and fibreboard. The joint venture with Brascan, a Canadian conglomerate, is due to begin production at the end of 1997; yearly output is forecast to reach 140,000 cubic metres of medium-density fibreboard and 100,000 cubic metres of chipboard.

The move to Zimbabwe and Brazil reflects SONAE's strategy of locating production units where wood is available at more competitive prices. The competitiveness of Portuguese products in the chipboard industry has been eroded by the high cost of wood and the escudo's strength; production capacity in Portugal is being reduced. The MDF product range is also being broadened and sales increased outside Portugal. After 1988, 70 per cent of production capacity will be located outside Portugal, up from 52 per cent in 1995 and none in 1992.

Cork

Portugal is the world's largest manufacturer of cork, accounting for around 55 per cent of total production and 70 per cent of world exports. Corticeira Amorim is the country's largest producer of cork products, accounting for one-third of output.

The cork industry in Portugal is predominantly a cottage industry with close to 900 enterprises employing 16,000 people. Most of the producers concentrate on cork stoppers for the wine and champagne industries. Amorim, in contrast, serves many different market segments, usually producing those products with the waste material from its stopper operations.

White agglomerates are used for a wide variety of household goods and decoration, and in footwear. Black agglomerates are used for acoustic purposes and insulation. Cork with rubber is used by the motor industry in engine parts as a shock absorber and sealant of engine joints. These areas, together with the flooring and wall covering product lines, use the waste material from the manufacture of wine and champagne corks. There is very little raw material wastage in the Amorim operation and as a producer of a global range of cork products the company can call upon the waste material from the small stopper producers.

Amorim has built up a strong distribution network; it has representatives in 30 countries and around 60 per cent of total sales are now distributed through group companies.

Exhibit 5.9

Structure of Corticeira Amorim's sales, 1999

	% of total
Corks	43
Flooring and wall coverings	33
Rubber cork	12
Compound agglomerates	10
Black agglomerates	2

Source: Amorim.

Raw material cork moved into a position of under-supply in 1996 where it is likely to remain for the rest of the decade. Cork trees must be 25 years old before the bark can be cut, and thereafter the process can only be repeated every nine years. As with other agricultural products, there are peak and trough years for the cork industry as the amount of trees that can be harvested varies.[2]

[2] This section draws on the July 1996 report by HSBC James Capel, *Portugal Coming of Age*.

6

THE COMMERCIAL BANKS

No sector of the Portuguese economy has undergone such intense change as banking, epitomised by the "multibank electronic purse" (known by its acronym as PMB), one of the most advanced systems in Europe. A shopper loads his PMB card into an automatic teller and uses it for purchases: the store owner inserts the card into the Portuguese-designed terminal and later deposits the day's earnings electronically.

The "electronic purse" was pioneered by Portugal's interbank system (SIBS), which has a giant computer housed in Lisbon and charges bank accounts weekly. SIBS also receives the information from Brisa's sensors which read car details at the entrance and exit of no-stop *Via Verde* lanes on toll roads. Brisa received the IBTTA Award in Washington in 1994 for electronic engineering and is preparing for the day when the EU picks a Europe-wide standard so that drivers can go from one end of the continent to the other without stopping at a toll gate. By being a late starter in information technology Portugal has been able to leapfrog from obsolete to cutting-edge technologies. The country also has one of the world's most advanced ATM networks – the Multibanco system – which enables holders of debit cards from any Portuguese bank to use any ATM for operations ranging from paying the electricity bill to booking a railway ticket.

Portugal's banking industry has changed beyond recognition since it was reopened to the private sector in 1984 and the country joined the EC in 1986. All banks were nationalised in 1975; today only Caixa Geral de Dépositos, the big savings bank, remains in the state's hands (with close to one-quarter of total assets), and it has been part of the public sector since it was established in 1876.

Six major steps were taken to transform the banking industry. First, the gradual liberalisation of deposit and lending rates from 1987 to 1992. Second, suppression of the legally determined specialisation of commercial banks and investment banks, which culminated in the creation of the present concept of a universal bank. Third, the setting-up of a wide range of non- monetary financial institutions, encouraged by tax incentives and the high net interest margins and credit ceilings. Fourth, the re-privatisation, since 1989, of several banks, coupled with the simplification of the rules on opening new branches. Fifth, the abolishing of credit limits, and the transition to an indirect method of monetary control, based on market mechanisms. Finally, the liberalisation of capital movements between 1986 and the end of 1992, just a few months after the decision to join the exchange rate mechanism (ERM) of the European monetary system.

Banks today are more solvent and more profitable; non-performing loans were down to around 7.4 per cent of total credit in 1996 from 9.5 per cent in 1993 and a peak of 19.3 per cent in 1986. Competition is intense; the net interest margin (the difference between the rates at which banks fund themselves and lend to customers) declined to an estimated 2.6 percentage points in 1996 from 5.6 in 1990, in line with what has been happening in most EU countries. The decline in Portugal, however, has been sharper (see Exhibit 6.1). The reduced margin is due not only to greater competition but also to the fall in nominal rates which implies a lower spread between sight deposits and the interest rates to which these balances are applied.

The margin appears to be stabilising after four years of rapid deterioration, but Portuguese banks will not see a return to margins in excess of 3 percentage points and the onus is on them to develop other income streams. The banks benefited in 1996 and 1995 from the strength in the bond market from which significant trading gains were earned, but the hallmarks of success in the future will be healthy fee and commission income and cost efficiency in operations. Banks are still heavily dependent on revenue from traditional financial activity; clients find it difficult to accept the idea of paying fees.

There are 46 banks in Portugal (26 in 1987), but the five largest groups (see Exhibit 6.2) – Caixa Geral; Banco Comercial Português and Banco Português do Atlântico; the Champalimaud group (Banco Pinto & Sotto Mayor, Banco Totto &

Exhibit 6.1

Net interest margin, 1991–96 (% points)

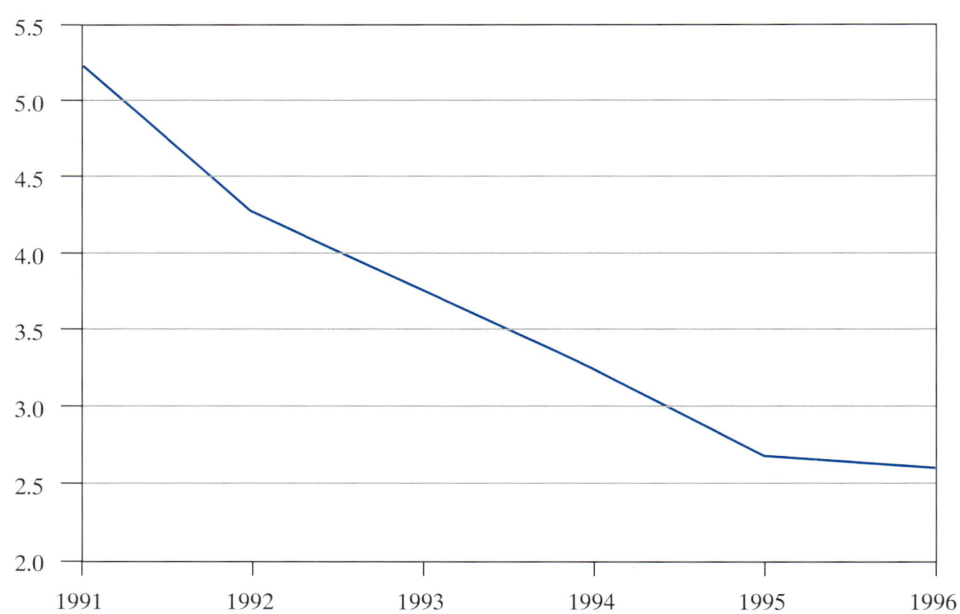

Source: Portuguese Banking Association.

Exhibit 6.2

Market shares of banking groups, 1995 (%)

	Assets	*Deposits*	*Loans*	*Branches*
Caixa Geral	24	30	27	18
Banco Comercial Português/ Banco Português do Atlântico	19	18	20	22
Banco Totta e Açores/ Banco Pinto e Sotto Mayor	16	20	18	17
Banco Português de Investimento/ Banco de Fomento e Exterior	11	10	10	11
Banco Espírito Santo	10	11	12	12
Mello	4	4	5	6
Other	16	7	8	14

Source: Portuguese Banking Association.

Açores, Crédito Predial Português and Banco Chemical); Espírito Santo; and Banco Português de Investimento/Banco de Fomento Exterior – control 80 per cent of total assets. The concentration is higher than in most EU countries. However, even if all the Portuguese banks were to merge into one, such a group would remain less than half the size of Deutsche Bank or Crédit Lyonnais.

Portugal had one bank branch for every 2,475 inhabitants in 1996, making it relatively over-banked (in Lisbon and Oporto but not elsewhere), compared with some EU countries with larger ratios, but nowhere near as much as Spain (see Exhibit 6.3).

Exhibit 6.3

Banking capacity in Europe

	No of banks	*No of branches*	*Staff employed*	*Population per branch*	*Catchment area per branch*	*% population employed in banking (%)*	*Market share of largest five (%)*
Germany	3,622	48,200	733,600	1,650	7.4	0.92	17
France	1,635	26,291	406,000	2,153	20.7	0.72	47
Italy	976	24,040	339,297	2,403	12.5	0.59	29
Spain	510	35,989	251,078	1,094	14.0	0.64	49
Switzerland	413	3,666	119,133	1,851	11.3	1.76	50
United Kingdom	324	17,722	430,800	3,230	13.8	0.75	57
Denmark	202	2,215	43,000	2,317	19.4	0.84	78
Belgium	133	7,800	60,300	1,272	3.9	0.61	59
Sweden	111	2,825	41,000	3,032	159.2	0.48	86
The Netherlands	110	7,440	147,733	2,019	5.5	0.98	81
Portugal	46	3,729	58,592	2,641	28.1	0.59	78
Total	**8,082**	**179,917**	**2.63 million**	**1,974**	**15.7**	**0.75**	–

Source: Central Bank reports; prepared by HSBC James Capel.

Exhibit 6.4

Basic indicators, 1991–95

	1991	*1992*	*1993*	*1994*	*1995*
Branches	2,802	2,991	3,336	3,377	3,729
Employees	61,055	60,772	59,74	58,610	58,592
Assets/employees (Esc)	263	309	372	426	481
Staff costs/assets (%)	1.4	1.4	1.3	1.1	1.0
Other admin costs/assets (%)	0.6	0.7	0.7	0.6	0.6
Net interest margin (% points)	4.5	4.3	3.6	3.2	2.6
ROA (%)	1.3	1.0	0.8	0.6	0.5
ROE (%)	19	13	12	9	7

Source: Portuguese Banking Association.

The average number of employees per branch was halved to 15 between 1990 and 1996 (Spain has seven), but it was largely achieved by building more branches and not shedding staff (see Exhibit 6.4). It is widely recognised that Portuguese banks are still overstaffed to a considerable degree; reducing the number of employees is probably the main challenge facing banks now that the map has been redrawn through privatisations and acquisitions (which are more of an accumulation of banks by groups than mergers in the strict sense of the word). An estimated 15,000 to 20,000 employees are estimated to be surplus to efficiency needs.

Tough competition and high overheads have dented profitability sharply: the average return on equity (ROE) dropped to an estimated 10 per cent in 1996 from 19 per cent in 1991 and return on assets (ROA) to an estimated 0.75 per cent from 1.3 per cent.

Background

The banks nationalised in 1975 were greatly weakened by the experience. Reasonably profitable and in some cases well regarded in international circles (particularly Banco Espírito Santo and Banco Português do Atlântico) before they were taken over, most became a pale shadow of their former selves. Several of them had been the financial arms of holding companies and by seizing the banks the revolutionaries gained control of 53 per cent of Portugal's fixed investment, and then depleted the banks to finance projects. Nationalisation and decolonisation, which brought back thousands of bank clerks from Angola and Mozambique, greatly increased the number of employees. During the chaotic first years after the revolution administered interest rates failed to keep pace with soaring inflation and real lending rates became negative. Deposit rates for domestic savers were also negative while remittances from emigrants were granted special high rates in the hope of attracting foreign currency reserves when capital was fleeing the country. The banks' capital shrank and their costs rose.

The impact on balance sheets of this post-revolutionary period took several years to come to light: accounts were either neglected or revamped to look more impressive.

Successive governments avoided revealing the true extent of the losses and only the advent of EC membership and the prospect of re-privatisation forced orthodox accounting and structural improvements onto the state banks. Only Banco Espírito Santo, from the outset, managed to reject attempts by the then Communist-influenced government to force the bank to provide loans; Banco Português do Atlântico, after two turbulent years, righted itself and opted for commercially-minded management. The other banks took far longer to recover from the state's flirtation with Stalinism.

The two banks that have emerged as the most aggressive and innovative, Banco Português de Investimento (BPI) and Banco Comercial Português (BCP) – and the ones that acquired the nationalised banks when they were reprivatised – were established after 1984 when the banking industry was reopened to the private sector. The Oporto-based BPI, the pioneer of post-1975 private Portuguese banking, which grew out of an investment company (SPI) established in 1981, acquired Banco Fonsecas & Burnay (BFB) in 1991 and Banco de Fomento Exterior (BFE) in 1996. BPI is now the investment banking arm of the group and BFB and BFE make up the retail banking arm. BCP, founded in 1985, acquired full control of Banco Português do Atlântico (BPA) in 1995. BCP's chairman, Jorge Jardim Gonçalves, left the chairmanship of BPA to establish BCP.

Encumbered with neither the high overheads of the banks that were nationalised in 1975 nor their bad debts, and styling themselves on sophisticated European or US models, the private Portuguese banks established after 1984 raced to the forefront of the market, although they still had to grapple with discrimination in the administration of credit ceilings, bureaucratic limitations on expansion, and a mass of constantly-changing regulations. For every four branches opened these banks were required to open a further branch in one of 40 more remote areas listed by the Bank of Portugal as locations otherwise unlikely to attract banks.

Interest rates, both for deposits (minimum) and loans (maximum), were set by the Bank of Portugal, which even standardised the cost of the financial services to be provided. In 1990, banks were still obliged to keep 17 per cent of their deposits, certificates of deposit, repurchase agreements and foreign currency deposits held by residents in the Bank of Portugal as a cash reserve requirement. They were liable to abrupt and arbitrary increases in their capital requirements or restrictions on their foreign currency swap facilities and above all, manipulation of credit ceilings to their detriment and in favour of the state banks.

The banking authorities tried to tie the opening of new branches by the private and foreign banks (such as Barclays and Lloyds), to buying a portion of bad debts from the state banks at premiums above their market value. The move, designed to make the banks "share the burden of the past" created a furore and led to a compromise solution: instead of having to take bad debts onto their own books, thereby tying up large sums of capital and requiring management time in the pursuit of loans which had never been their responsibility, the banks had to make a contribution to Finangest, the institution set up to deal with the problem of bad loans in the state banks. The "entry tickets" were criticised by Sir Leon Brittan, the then EC Commissioner for competition, who said they were "against the spirit of the single market".

The privately owned commercial banks – as well as BPI and BCP two others were established, Banco de Comércio e Indústria (now owned by Spain's Banco Santander) and Banco Internacional de Crédito (part of the Espírito Santo group) – were highly computerised and drew on the young MBA and economics graduates from Portugal's universities. The average age of employees today in BPI and BCP, in particular, is much younger than those in the former state banks and, inevitably, it is the older staff that are having to be shed. The average age of BCP's employees, for example, is 31 and BPA's 46.

Portuguese banks, until recently, have relied more heavily on interest income – 77 per cent of total income in 1994 – than most of their European counterparts, and have now begun to diversify their sources of income more strongly. Banks have been later than their EU colleagues in charging commission fees for services, while the less developed securities markets reduced the opportunities for realising gains on bond trading. This is changing rapidly, however.

Banks are also increasing the cross-selling of financial products and containing overheads more strongly. In addition, the level of general loan loss provision requirements is lower because of the improved economic climate.

Regulatory changes

The Deposit Guarantee Fund was established in 1994 with an upfront payment by participating financial institutions and annual contributions thereafter: the upfront payment is being depreciated over five years and was calculated on the basis of the average deposit balances held between May and December 1993. The rate for the annual contribution may vary between 0.1 per cent and 0.2 per cent of average yearly deposits, to which a multiplier (between 80 per cent and 120 per cent) is applied, inversely proportional to the average individual solvency ratio.

The limit on the full repayment guarantee of a depositor's balance is Esc3 million, while further guarantees are in place to reimburse 75 per cent of the additional amount up to Esc6 million and 50 per cent of amounts between Esc6 and Esc9 million.

The new cash reserve system came into effect towards the end of 1994 when the coefficient for calculating minimum reserves was cut to 2 per cent from 17 per cent (non-remunerated). Excess liquidity arising from the reduction was blocked in inter-bank negotiable Certificates of Deposit issued by the Bank of Portugal. There are non-interest bearing certificates (Series A) and those earning interest at rates defined by the Bank of Portugal (Series B).

The new system established a reduction in monetary assets (including the items "cash and other assets at the central bank" and "sight deposits at credit institutions"), in favour of investments in credit institutions, where the Certificates of Deposit, both interest and non-interest bearing, replaced cash reserves. The reserve base was also redefined (see Chapter 4). Only non- interest bearing reserves, which represent 2 per cent of deposits, are now found under monetary assets. The system's impact on bank results in the early stage was neutral but as the non-interest bearing Certificates of Deposit are unblocked they will represent potential future earnings.

The reduction in mid-1995 in the level of general loan loss reserves (from 2 per cent to 1 per cent of total loans plus guarantees) had little impact on banks other than freeing up reserves which could then be channelled into other areas. In most cases, banks were able to use the released general loan loss reserves to cover additional specific reserves for "doubtful debts" and sovereign risk, new areas of provisioning created by the authorities. Country risk had to be 25 per cent provisioned by the end of 1995 and fully covered in 1997.

While the general impact of the reduction in general loan loss provisions has been positive on bank earnings, the requirement to make provisions for the potential losses on public debt securities in the investment portfolio has been harder to absorb. A gradual system was established, requiring 25 per cent provisioning at the end of 1995, 50 per cent in 1996 and 100 per cent in 1997. The favourable trend in the bond markets, in the context of declining interest rates, helped to ease the pressure on most banks in 1995 and 1996.

Another change is in pension provisions. Pension liabilities for those employees who had already retired had to be fully reserved by the end of 1995; the cost of pension liabilities for employees who take early retirement may be deferred over a 10-year period; pension shortfalls for employees still in service may be deferred over a maximum period of 20 years, in line with international standards. Previously, legislation did not differentiate between the various categories of pensioners, with all obligations having to be reserved by the end of 1997. For those banks which had already met pension liabilities in full, like Banco Comercial Português, the new measures provided some relief, and the ability to defer costs relating to early retirement should facilitate further redundancies (this will particularly help BCP after its absorption of Banco Português do Atlântico). However, actuarial tables on which pension liabilities are calculated were also changed, in some cases giving rise to additional pension liabilities.

Exhibit 6.5 provides details of outstanding provisioning requirements faced by leading banks at the end of 1995.

Exhibit 6.5

Outstanding provisioning requirements

	Pension shortfall (Esc billion)	*% of equity*	*Treatment*
Caixa Geral	44.1	10.9	20-year amortisation
Banco Comercial Português	No outstandings	nil	–
Banco Português do Atlântico	17.6	13.2	20-year amortisation
Banco Pinto e Sotto Mayor	41.1	19.5	20-year amortisation
Banco Totta e Açores	9.6	6.8	Esc1.1 billion charged to income in 1995; the balance deducted from equity reserves in 1996.
Banco Espírito Santo	25.6	16	20-year amortisation
Banco de Fomento e Exterior	No outstandings	nil	–
Banco Português de Investimento	12.2	14.6	20-year amortisation

Source: IBCA.

Leading banking groups[1]

Caixa Geral de Depósitos

Caixa Geral de Depósitos, the government's depository and savings bank, is the largest banking group, with close to one quarter of total assets (see Exhibit 6.2). It controls the largest share of the lower income banking market, partly because all Portugal's civil servants, teachers and other public sector employees are paid through the bank.

The bank owns Fidelidade, the second biggest insurance group, with a market share of around 11–12 per cent, and Banco Nacional Ultramarino (BNU), the ex-colonial issuing bank, which it took under its wing after the 1974 revolution. Caixa Geral is unique in the EU because Portugal is the only country whose largest bank is state-owned; it is not expected to be privatised, however, unless the government is very hard pressed for funds, but BNU could be put up for sale.

Caixa Geral strengthened its international presence in 1995 when it acquired Banco Simeón, a small commercial bank with 59 branches, most of them in northern Spain. It also owns Banco Luso Español and Banco de Extremadura in Spain, Banco Financial Português in Brazil and Banque Franco Portugaise in France. With the purchase of Simeón, Caixa Geral increased its network in Spain to 146 branches, 126 of which are located in areas bordering Portugal.

The bank has registered a relatively high level of profitability (see Exhibit 6.6) in recent years, held up by improved income from securities trading and stronger contributions from group companies offering related financial services.

Banco Comercial Português

Banco Comercial Português (BCP), established in 1985, quickly sprang to national fame when it embarked on an aggressive expansion programme through its Nova Rede network of small highly automated branches. The network was revolutionary for customers: providing instant services and doing way with the legendary queuing. For the bank, Nova Rede was a way of getting round restrictions on opening branches and an innovative way of gaining market share. The great majority of the bank's clients use Nova Rede; the concept was an excellent way to achieve customer bonding. BCP also

Exhibit 6.6

ROA and ROE of banking groups, 30 June 1996

	ROA (%)	*ROE (%)*
Caixa Geral	0.8	10.1
Banco Comercial Português	0.8	9.1
Banco Pinto e Sotto Mayor[1]	0.4	8.7
Banco Espírito Santo	0.7	na
Banco de Fomento e Exterior[2]	1.9	23.9
Banco Português de Investimento	1.15	17.9

[1] Part of the Champalimaud group.
[2] Since acquired by Banco Português de Investimento.

Source: IBCA.

[1] This section draws on reports by HSBC James Capel.

embarked on a market segmentation strategy (today it has seven distribution networks targeting different segments), a concept barely developed in Portugal at that time.

Between 1987 and 1994 BCP's market share of total assets increased to 8.6 per cent from 1.9 per cent, and total loans grew to 9.2 per cent from 1.2 per cent. The bank was particularly successful in the cross-selling of mortgage, insurance, leasing and factoring products.

BCP decided in 1993 that it was approaching the end of its potential as a medium-sized specialist bank in the Portuguese market. Having fully exploited the niche area that it had created, internal expansion was becoming more expensive; this conclusion coincided with management's feeling that in order to compete effectively, a significant increase in critical mass would be required so that the bank could boost network efficiency and cross-selling potential, achieve a higher dilution of fixed costs and reduce vulnerability to competition threats. Its proposed purchase of Banco Pinto & Sotto Mayor was rejected in January 1994 and its initial bid for Banco Português do Atlântico (BPA) was declined in September 1994. In March 1995 BCP and Império, the insurance company, gained full control of BPA. BCP paid two times book value for BPA and that premium appears to have been spent on acquiring the customer base rather than on any particular operational strength or brand loyalty.

With this purchase BCP increased its share of total assets to 19 per cent from 9 per cent, becoming the second largest banking group after Caixa Geral. BCP and BPA between them constitute the largest financial group, with around 2.1 million customers (over 40 per cent of the total) and 780 branches (20 per cent of the total). BCP's capital adequacy ratio, based on the criteria of the Bank for International Settlements (BIS) dropped to 10 per cent after the BPA acquisition from 17 per cent before, but it was still above the 8 per cent yardstick.

BCP (with a 50 per cent stake) has first refusal on the 48 per cent stake that Império holds and can block the entrance of another banking institution into the share capital.

The rationale for acquiring BPA was solid and it triggered a scramble among the other banks for critical mass. BCP secured a dominant market share in banking and insurance (Ocidental, Bonança and BPA Vida became the largest insurance group); it acquired an untapped customer base (less than 7.5 per cent of BCP customers had a BPA account); the cross-selling contribution to net income was increased and rationalisation potential was achieved via reduced hiring at BCP and early retirement at BPA (whose employees are much older).

BPA was better placed than BCP in the north of Portugal; it had an above average non-performing loans' coverage ratio and the bank was well known to BCP management (Jorge Jardim Gonçalves of BCP having previously been the chairman of BPA). BPA was strong in the corporate banking area, but had neglected the retail sector during its privatisation drama. BCP launched hostile takeovers, one of which was blocked by the last government under pressure from BPA's industrial shareholders. Retail customers drifted away.

The strategy now is to concentrate on profitability and not on growth. This has meant getting to grips with the over-staffing problem, which BCP has done quickly and smoothly, and focusing on enhancing the cross-selling and fee income opportunities.

(BPA recorded fee income of Esc11 billion in 1994 from 1.2 million customers, while BCP earned Esc20 billion from 800,000 clients and 87 per cent of all insurance policies sold were through branches of the sister companies.)

The total number of employees released or relocated between the acquisition of BPA and the end of 1996 was 1,484, nearly one-fifth of the entire workforce at the time of the purchase. Of the 1,484 employees, 418 were relocated to other parts of the group and 1,066 employees were pre-retired or fired. Releasing employees was expensive; long-term workers received Esc20–25 million in indemnities.

The BPA brand was re-launched and a new sub-brand called Atlântico created which dovetails neatly with another new concept called *expresso! Atlântico* jointly developed by BCP and Jerónimo Martins, Portugal's second largest retailer. The Atlântico "shops", as the remodelled branches are called, are set out in an open plan design with a flexible format. There is no traditional counter. Customers are greeted by employees, sometimes standing at small moveable desks. If customers' needs cannot be met immediately, they are directed to glass-screened compartments for individual attention. Staff are trained to be able to deal with all products rather than concentrating on one area (a similar policy to that undertaken in Nova Rede) and thus the BCP management hopes that cross-selling at BPA will develop (the lack of it was one of BPA's weaknesses). The design of the Atlântico branch moves traditional banking methods towards the retail model; the stores are high-tech and employ videoconferencing facilities with a centralised specialist office. This small office is off-site and can be contacted by any of the new stores. It contains a small team of product specialists who can answer customer queries if they cannot be fielded by the generalist in the store.

BCP is opening "in-store" branches in the Pingo Doce supermarkets owned by Jerónimo Martins. This is in line with BCP's segmentation strategy and is part of a general move in Portugal among retailers; SONAE has also launched a banking service within its Modelo and Continente stores, although the SONAE concept of financial stores – Universo Bank – is quite removed from the traditional bank branch. The products offered include cheque accounts, deposit accounts, ATM cards, credit cards, investment funds, time deposits, long-term savings plans, mortgages, consumer loans and insurance. Market research showed that the great majority of Pingo Doce customers valued convenience and proximity as being the key variables behind selecting a bank. BCP also planned to establish branches in the Feira Nova hypermarkets and Recheio cash and carry chains of Jerónimo Martins.

BCP would like to broaden its market by selling financial products across post office counters. The move, involving competition with other banks for an exclusive post office contract, would hurt Caixa Geral which dominates the lower income segment of the banking market.

Integration of BCP and BPA has proceeded according to plan. There was a unified branch platform in July 1996 and a single software platform as of April 1997.

With 10 Portuguese investment banks, including Banco Cisf, owned by BCP, and intense competition from the main international merchant banks, BCP decided it made no sense to set up an investment banking unit for BPA. Instead, BPA concentrates on universal banking for large corporate customers.

In the international field, BCP has a cross-participation agreement with Spain's Banco Central Hispano (BCH). BCP has 3 per cent of BCH and 50 per cent of Banco Banif, a private bank for high net worth customers, and BCH has 20 per cent of BCP. BCP also controls 10 per cent of Mexico's Bital, which was planning to establish a presence in the US to serve Hispanic clients, and is associated with the Mozambican state in Banco Internacional de Moçambique.

Banco Português de Investimento

Banco Português de Investimento (BPI) began life in 1981as a financial service company , specialising in medium- and long-term corporate lending. It was the first private financial institution to be created after the 1974 revolution and in 1985 was converted into an investment bank. BPI forged a reputation in the 1980s for innovation. It pioneered, for example, the creation of such products as Navigator bonds (escudo-denominated Eurobonds), was the first Portuguese bank to go public and has been the most active bank in Portugal's privatisations. BPI and Banco Espírito Santo, the other leading bank in privatisations, placed around three-quarters of shares with one-fifth of the total number of branches between them. Like BCP, BPI's staff is young and very loyal, and solvency and profitability ratios have also been high. Non-performing loans represented only 2.6 per cent of total lending at 30 June 1996, compared with a banking industry average of above 6 per cent, and NPL coverage was 120 per cent.

BPI acquired 70 per cent of Banco Fonsecas & Burnay (BFB) in 1991 and full control in 1994. In August 1996 it bought 65 per cent of Banco de Fomento e Exterior (BFE), thereby establishing the fourth largest banking group. The purchase of BFE was crucial to the long-term evolution of BPI. If BFE had been acquired by one of the other interested parties (Banco Finantia or the Amorim group), BPI would have been left as a medium-sized bank in a sector dominated by four much larger groups. BPI had expanded by increasing its branch network but it was late in pursuing this strategy (Espírito Santo carried out the majority of its branch expansion in 1994 and 1995) and would not have attained the necessary critical mass until the end of 1997, during which time it would have been competing head-to-head with the four established banking groups. To ensure the success of its bid, BPI had to bid higher than it had originally anticipated.

The retail network of BPI in the north complements that of BFB in the south while the concentration of BPI in large corporate lending balances out BFE's concentration in small/medium corporate and retail lending.

After it acquired BFE, BPI used its branch network to move aggressively into the mortgage loan business. The mortgage portfolio stood at Esc119 billion on 30 June 1996, up from Esc8 billion in 1991. Launching a credit card with the largest retailer in Portugal in 1995 enabled BFB to become the third largest credit card issuer with a market share of around 18 per cent. The introduction in 1994 of a life capitalisation product with a guaranteed rate of return pushed BPI's life insurance business to second place in the industry from a starting position the previous year of below 20.

BFE was in much better shape than BFB was when it was acquired in 1991 (it was virtually bankrupt with a NPL ratio of 12.1 per cent when the equivalent ratio for BPI was 0.1 per cent) and it is enhancing BPI's position in retail banking.

The Champalimaud group

The Champalimaud group – named after António Champalimaud, Portugal's richest individual, now in his 70s, and one of the leading entrepreneurs before the 1974 revolution – consists of Banco Pinto & Sotto Mayor (BPSM), Banco Totta & Açores (BTA), Crédito Predial Português (CPP) and Banco Chemical. After his business interests were nationalised Champalimaud went on to make a new fortune based on cement and farming in Brazil before returning to Portugal in the late 1980s.

The jewel in the crown is BTA which is in far better financial shape than its parent, BPSM. There has been a certain amount of friction between the two management bodies, with the overall strategic evolution of the group the losing party. The structure of the group (see Exhibit 6.7) is rather misleading and suggests it is the third largest. In practice, this is not the case. BTA and BPSM were still operating in 1996 as two completely separate banks, both as distinct franchises and separate back offices.

All but Banco Chemical (a member of the US Chemical Bank group) were nationalised banks that were re-privatised; in BPSM's case 80 per cent was acquired in 1994 by Mundial Confiança, one of the largest insurance companies which Champalimaud re-acquired, and the bank's control reverted back to him. Mundial Confiança stands to benefit considerably from the cross-selling of its insurance business with the 630-strong retail branch network of BTA, BPSM and CPP. BTA bought Crédito Predial in 1992 (its stake stood at 48 per cent in 1996) and BPSM acquired 45 per cent of BTA in 1995.

BTA is Portugal's second largest retail bank in consolidated asset terms and has more than 400 branches, including 145 belonging to CPP, which has the second largest market share of mortgages after the state savings bank Caixa Geral. The share of mortgage business has increased steadily in CPP's loan portfolio since privatisation (over 70 per cent compared with 56 per cent in 1992). BTA's mortgage business has been concentrated in CPP.

Exhibit 6.7

Champalimaud financial holdings

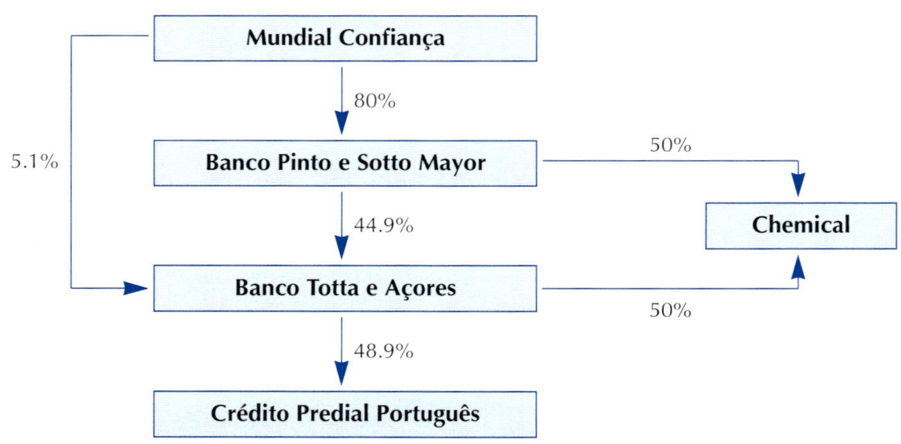

Source: HSBC James Capel.

Banco Chemical, which was the front runner amongst its peer group of 17 majority foreign-owned banks in Portugal in terms of profitability and innovation, is the corporate/investment banking arm of the group. (As Manufacturers Hanover, before its merger with Chemical, it earned in one particular year in the 1980s with one branch and 28 employees more than Banco Português do Atlântico with its 450 branches and 5,000 employees.) Chemical is a top-tier bank to most of the 250 largest companies in Portugal, has significant relationships with every major institutional investor in the country, and has been a major provider of funds and advisory services to major government companies and the Portuguese Treasury.

Under a restructuring programme known as Project Harmony, several group companies were to be merged and cross-selling potential strengthened. The potential for cross-selling at BTA is enormous; its parent Mundial Confiança is one of Portugal's insurance giants. Project Harmony will ensure that the banks operate more as an integrated group.

The Espírito Santo group

The Espírito Santo group is growing organically rather than through acquisitions. It has transformed itself into a major player in a relatively short space of time. The number of Banco Espírito Santo branches was around 450 at the end of 1996, up from 240 in 1992, with a further 50 branches of Banco Internacional de Crédito (BIC), a mortgage specialist.

Espírito Santo group, which incorporates both the commercial bank and the investment bank Banco Essi, saw net profits after tax increase by 27.7 per cent (US38.7 million) at the end of December 1996. The trend was continued with the commercial bank posting first-quarter results of Esc6.9 billion, an increase of Esc2.2 billion. The result reflected sustained increases in net interest income, commissions, trading and insurance revenues, against a background of good economic conditions in Portugal.

Espírito Santo – probably the family to suffer most from the 1975 nationalisations – is strong in capital markets (through Banco Essi). Together with BIC it has developed a new business strategy in the area of mortgage loans, resulting in an increase in their joint market share from 11 per cent at the end of 1995 to 13 per cent at the end of June 1996. It also has a majority stake in Tranquilidade, the country's largest insurance company (which it had previously owned).

Increased activities in securities markets and its prominent role in corporate finance work led to an increase in Banco Essi's revenues by 30 per cent during 1996. The bank's involvement in the secondary offering for Portugal Telecom, and IPOs of Telecel and CIMPOR, established the bank as the leading domestic corporate finance house. Further success in fixed income with domestic placements of bonds for the Kingdom of Sweden, Banco Sul America, Lehman Brothers, Banco Bozano Simonsen, SNCF, and Portugal Telecom have established Essi as one of the leading domestic investment houses.

Espírito Santo is now moving into China. It formed a partnership with Everbright, China's second-largest financial group, in 1997 under which Everbright was to acquire 48 per cent of Banco Espírito Santo do Oriente, the wholly-owned bank based in the Portuguese enclave of Macao, which will be handed over to China in 1999.

Exhibit 6.8

Espírito Santo financial holdings

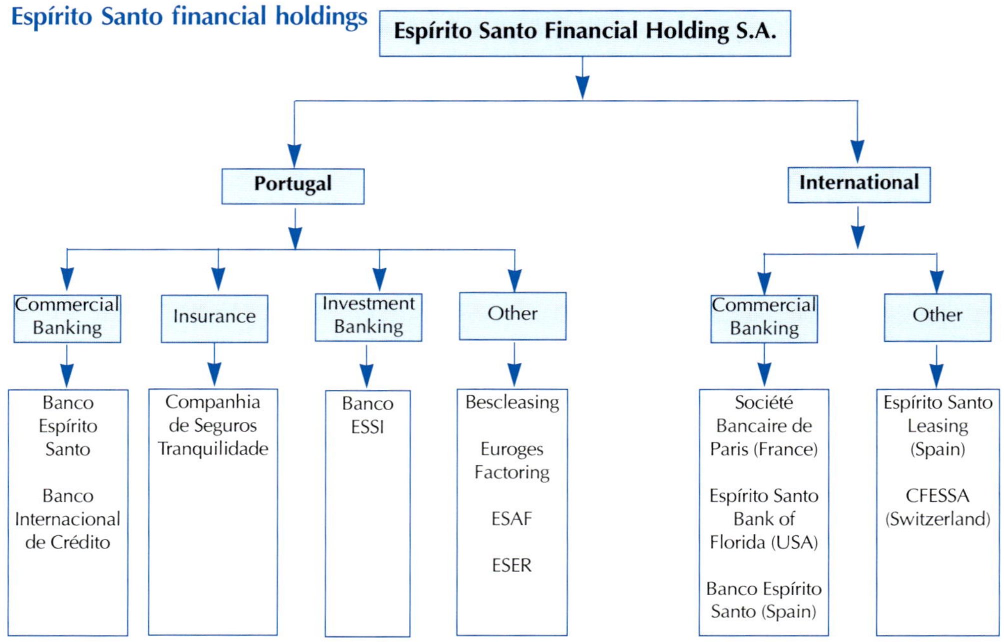

Source: Espírito Santo.

The new bank will develop a retail network in southern China and provide Everbright's corporate clients, who are mainly based in northern China, with a "gateway" for raising finance abroad.

Foreign banks

Foreign banks were a major innovative force in Portugal between 1984 and the early 1990s, exercising an influence out of all proportion to their tiny share of the market. Portuguese banks caught on, particularly after privatisation began, and today the eight foreign banks with local subsidiaries – which accounted for 8 per cent of assets in 1995 and 3 per cent of total profits – are finding the going very tough.

Manufacturers Hanover (now Banco Chemical, see above), the first-established foreign wholesale bank, led the way. Lloyds Bank, which came to Portugal in 1862 at the height of Anglo–Portuguese trade, was the largest force in retail banking. Sensing opportunities in a market which is a logical extension of its domestic market and frustrated by the limited prospects of its financial service company in Lisbon and the long queue for licences, Spain's Banco Bilbao Vizcaya (BBV) acquired Lloyds in 1991. The assets of BBV parent bank represent some 60 per cent of the total assets of the Portuguese financial system.

BBV has moved from a merchant to a universal bank, increasing the number of branches to 60 in 1996 from 12 (it planned to open 30 more in 1997) and radically changing the structure (94 per cent of employees are account managers compared with 40 per cent in 1991). Its branches have a smaller number of staff than the Portuguese banks (10 people compared to 15) and on average handle twice the volume of business of its Spanish branches. Of the 840 companies with a turnover of more than Esc4 billion a year, BBV does business with 720.

The Spanish banks are strong in Portugal; Banco Santander had 78 per cent of Banco de Comércio e Indústria (BCI), whose shares were suspended from trading in February 1977, after several years of weak performance by the bank, and now own close to 100 per cent. Santander's investment banking arm, Banco Santander de Negocios, is much more successful than BCI. Banco Central Hispano has 20 per cent of Banco Comercial Português.

Barclays, which first came to Portugal in 1981 with a representative office, had 67 branches in 1996. In 1995 it added private banking activities to corporate banking, fund management and insurance.

Madeira offshore centre

More than 30 financial institutions operate out of the Portuguese island of Madeira including Chemical Bank, Citibank, Deutsche Bank, ABN-Amro Bank and Crédit Lyonnais, as well as every Portuguese bank. In 1995 Banco Itaú, a large Brazilian bank, became the first Latin American institution to set up in the international business centre (IBC), which also comprises a free-trade zone, an international services hub and an international shipping register.

Companies setting up in Madeira (see the chapter on foreign investment) are governed by the same corporate law and central bank regulations as their counterparts on the mainland. They enjoy total exemption from taxes on profits and capital gains until the end of 2011 provided operations are exclusively carried out with non-residents or with other entities established within the IBC.

As an integral part of Portugal and hence of the EU, investors also benefit from total exchange freedom. Until 1996 only branches of well-known banks were allowed to operate within the IBC. Since then a new provision makes it possible for new banks to be created within the IBC, providing them with a passport to operate anywhere within the EU.

Madeira is one of the few jurisdictions outside Britain and the United States to recognise the establishment of offshore trusts; the settler of the trust is free to determine the country whose law it wishes to govern the trust.

Santa Maria in the Azores is also an offshore centre, but only five institutions were operating there in 1996.

7

INVESTMENT BANKS

Most of Portugal's investment banks are linked to the main commercial banks, with the notable exception of Banco Português de Investimento (BPI) which began life as an investment bank and then moved, through acquisitions, into the full range of banking activities.

The investment banking market is even more overcrowded and competitive than the retail market; there are six Portuguese banks, and all the big international names such as Rothschild and JP Morgan either have a representative in Portugal or send people from London. Portuguese bankers joke that it is difficult to get a seat on the regular flights between Lisbon and London because there are so many investment bankers travelling between the two cities. The investment banks are playing a prominent role in Portugal's ongoing privatisation process. Project finance is a relatively new activity that is attracting interest; the government is keen to encourage greater private sector participation in building roads, bridges, schools and hospitals for budgetary reasons.

BPI is at the forefront of investment banking in Portugal (see Chapter 6). Apart from BPI, the other main Portuguese investment banks are Banco Cisf (part of the Banco Comercial Português/Banco Português do Atlântico group), Banco Essi (part of the Espírito Santo group), Banco Mello, Banco Finantia and Banco Efisa. Efisa and Finantia are independent in the sense that they do not belong to one of the banking groups. Amongst the foreigners with a strong presence in Portugal is Spain's Banco Santander de Negocios.

Banco Cisf began as a financial service company in 1984 and in 1992 Banco Comercial Português (BCP) acquired full control. After BCP acquired Banco Português do Atlântico (BPA) in 1995 the two banks concentrated their specialist capital markets, financial services and financing units in Banco Cisf (in which BPA now has a 50 per cent stake). BPA focuses on short-term commercial banking relations with companies. Cisf is responsible for integrated management of the group's treasury activity and for brokerage business through its subsidiary Cisf Dealer. Another subsidiary, Cisf Risco, operates in the field of risk capital. The enlarged network of retail branches resulting from the BCP/BPA group has given Cisf greater capacity for originating investment banking business and stronger placement power. Among its "firsts" was the launch in 1996 of a 20-year escudo bond issue for the European Investment Bank. The bank is particularly active in the domestic and Navigator bond markets and in financing large investment projects.

Banco Essi is the investment banking arm of the Espírito Santo group, and is particularly strong in research.

Banco Finantia lost to BPI in its bid for Banco de Fomento Exterior (BFE) when it was privatised in 1996. BFE would have given Finantia, established in 1986, a deposit-taking base and greater placement power. Some analysts believe that the smaller investment banks not linked to one of the banking groups are vulnerable when there is a shake-out among investment banks. Business will drop off after the privatisation process is completed, though there will still be plenty to do in Portugal's fragmented corporate sector among the plethora of small and medium-sized companies needing financial services or embarking on mergers and acquisitions.

Banco Efisa was established in 1994 from the merger of a financial service company (Efisa) and a leasing company (Geoleasing). It has earned a reputation for innovation: it co-arranged the first credit-enhanced structure in the escudo market. The Esc45 billion deal, for special purpose vehicle Polo Securities, was arranged so that a loan could be advanced to a state company. The transaction was secured on a credit insurance policy.

Project finance

Portugal is ideally suited for project finance – the country still has a lot of catching-up to do in infrastructure and it has to exercise budgetary restraint to meet the convergence criteria for European monetary union.

Two big projects are currently underway. The Esc180 billion Vasco da Gama bridge, the longest continuous river crossing in Europe, is being constructed across the Tagus in Lisbon under a build, operate and transfer (BOT) contract by Lusponte, a consortium led by Trafalgar House of the UK (since acquired by Norway's Kvaerner). Turbogás, Portugal's first natural gas-fired power plant, is being built at Tapada do Outeiro, near Oporto. This Esc100 billion project is largely financed by a syndicate of Portuguese and international banks, including the European Investment Bank.

Lusponte also took over the operation and maintenance of the nearby April 25 bridge. The 12 km Vasco da Gama bridge will be completed in time for Expo '98. One problem that had to be ironed out was the toll to be charged on the bridge. Lusponte believes a toll of less than Esc300 would mean a commercial loss. But the toll on the April 25 bridge, a few miles up river, has been frozen by the government at Esc150 until April 1998. When the last government raised the toll from Esc100 to Esc150 in June 1994, motorists blockaded the April 25 bridge and clashed with riot police. The same toll will have to be charged for the two bridges if the Vasco de Gama crossing is to fulfil its prime purpose of easing traffic congestion on the existing bridge.

The government was also planning to create two new motorway concessionaires – the Northern Concessionaire and the Western Concessionaire. – to replace the single pre-1997 operator Brisa. Brisa would deliver existing stretches to the new companies and in return would take a stake in them.

The Northern Concessionaire would be responsible for the A7 (Póvoa de Varzim–Chaves) and A11 (Esposende–Casteloes). Of the 189 km, 21 km were in operation in 1996 and the rest (166 km) was still to be built. Banco Efisa estimated the construction cost at Esc140 billion, on top of which there would be maintenance costs of Esc2 billion a year and large repair costs, every 12 years, of Esc10 billion. This concession is expected to generate revenue of Esc10.4 billion a year in tolls (ie, excluding income from service stations, resting areas and advertising).

The Western Concessionaire would take over the A8 (Lisbon–Leiria) and A13 (Caldas da Rainha–Santarém). Of the 168 km, 66 km are already in operation and 18 km under construction in 1996. The concessionaire would have to build the rest.

The government also planned to award 315 km of roads in areas where traffic is much lower in the form of DBFOs (design, build, finance and operate) and using the shadow toll system. Operators would count cars as normal but bill the state for the respective tolls rather than charge the motorist directly. The six projects under these conditions are: IP2 (Castelo Branco–Guarda); IP3 (Régua–Chaves); IP4 (Leixoes–Agua Santas); IP6 (Abrantes–Gardete); IC1 (Ilhavo–Coimbroes) and IC4 (Guia–Lagos).

The Portuguese financing market has developed considerably over the past few years and can accommodate structured finance operations of up to 17 years' maturity, as demonstrated by the deals for Lusoponte and the Turbogás power plant.

8

INSURANCE COMPANIES AND OTHER INSTITUTIONAL INVESTORS

When fire swept through the Chiado district in the heart of old Lisbon in 1988 only 10 per cent of the losses were covered by insurance. The level of insurance coverage has improved considerably since then but Portugal is still under-insured compared with other EU countries. Total 1996 premiums amounted to Esc925.9. billion (5.6 per cent of GDP) compared with an EU average of 7–8 per cent.

The Portuguese insurance sector still has high growth potential. Total premium income increased 18.3 per cent in 1996 after rising 24.6 per cent in 1995 and 19.3 per cent in 1994 (see Exhibit 8.1). The driving force behind the surge in premiums is the rapid growth in life business, largely due to the spectacular rise in bancassurance (see Exhibit 8.2). More than 80 per cent of new life income is earned from policies sold through bank branches, up from 30 per cent in 1992. Bancassurance in life business is stronger than in any other EU country.

Exhibit 8.1

Growth in total insurance premiums, 1992–96

	Esc billion
1992	431.8
1993	526.8
1994	628.5
1995	782.9
1996	925.9

Source: Portuguese Insurance Association.

Bancassurance

The sector is very fragmented; there are close to 100 companies including the branches of EU firms, the largest of which belong to Portuguese banks (see Exhibit 8.3). The strongest banking group in the insurance sector is Banco Comercial Português/Banco Português do Atlântico which owns Ocidental, Bonança and BPA Vida (with a market share of around 20 per cent in life business and 28 per cent in non-life). Caixa Geral owns Fidelidade, Mundial Confiança is part of the Champalimaud group (Mundial acquired Banco Pinto & Sotto Mayor in 1994), Tranquildade belongs to Espírito Santo, Banco Português de Investimento has BPI Vida and Banco Mello Império. The 10 largest companies accounted for 65 per cent of business in 1995.

A large number of foreign companies have flocked to Portugal, attracted by the growth potential and the country's high savings rate, but their penetration is not very

Exhibit 8.2

Relative share of bank assurance, 1991–95 (%)

	Life	*Non-life*	*Total*
1991	13	0	4
1992	31	1	10
1993	36	1	15
1994	49	1	23
1995	76	3	44

Source: Portuguese Insurance Association.

Exhibit 8.3

Ranking of insurance companies, 1995

	Life	*Non-life*
Tranquilidade	1	4
Ocidental	2	9
BPI Vida	3	na
Fidelidade	4	2
Mundial Confiança	5	3
Império	6	1
Group Aliança UAP	7	6

Source: Portuguese Insurance Association.

high (27 per cent in 1995 between majority-owned firms and branches of EU and non-EU companies).

Years of inefficient control when they belonged to the state (the insurance companies passed into the public sector when the banks that owned them were nationalised in 1975) and low investment in information technology have left Portuguese insurance companies with higher general expenses than most of their EU counterparts, though this is improving. Mundial Confiança's general expenses, for example, represented 16.8 per cent of 1995's total premiums, down from 20 per cent in 1994.

Growth has been sustained for several years by high demand for lump sum investment products known as *prémio único,* typically of eight years maturity and offering attractive returns as they are linked to fixed-rate bonds, and, to a lesser extent, by pension savings schemes, though their development potential is much higher. The *prémio único* accounted for 38 per cent of total premiums in 1995, up from 2.7 per cent in 1992, and if it tailed off suddenly companies would suffer a sharp drop in premium income. Growth of motor premiums has slowed significantly after a disastrous year in 1992 when companies wrote policies indiscriminately in a bid for market share. The motor business, however, continues to have a high claims ratio, reflecting Portugal's appalling road accident record, said to be the worst in the EU.

The ISP, the insurance sector's regulator, lays down strict provisioning requirements for areas such as life, where the company's potential liability is a long-term one, in order to allow for the risk of early redemption and ensure that policyholders' claims can be met. The aim is to determine actuarially the net present value of the company's future liabilities, with the level of provisioning required varying according to the risk insured.

Investment

Portugal's insurance companies play a fundamental role as institutional investors; they have become much more professional about financial asset investment. The idea that a company's portfolio of financial assets, as well as its real estate, can be subject to

Exhibit 8.4

Investment policy limits

An insurance company may invest no more than:
- 5 per cent of its assets in transferable securities issued by the same body.

Exception:
- the 5 per cent limit may be raised to a maximum of 10 per cent; however, the total value of the securities held by a company in issuing entities in each of which it invests more than 5 per cent of its assets must not exceed 25 per cent of the value of its assets. This restriction does not apply to government debt.
- 20 per cent of its assets in deposit accounts and certificates of deposit.
- 60 per cent of its assets in bonds and commercial paper.
- 20 per cent of its assets in units of mutual funds.
- 25 per cent of its assets in listed shares.
- 3 per cent of its assets in cash and current accounts.
- 20 per cent of its assets in securities issued by or loans to companies that belong to the same group as the insurance company.
- 10 per cent of its assets in a single property.
- 10 per cent of its assets in unlisted bonds.
- 50 per cent of its assets in real estate shares and units of real estate funds.

Prepared by Barclays Bank in Portugal.

permanent rotation without putting at risk the integrity and quality of the technical reserves and on the basis of the opportunities offered by the market, is a relatively new concept in Portugal. The Portuguese financial markets offer day-to-day investment opportunities that cannot be ignored without a considerable opportunity cost.

Companies' investment is guided by certain limits (see Exhibit 8.4).

Mutual funds

Assets under the management of investment funds (mutual funds and real estate funds) stood at Esc3.1 trillion at the end of 1996 (18.7 per cent of GDP compared with 26 per cent in Spain). Again, the banks are very strong in this sector, particularly Caixa Geral through Caixagest and Banco Comercial Português, and Barclays among the foreign banks. Investment limits for mutual funds are set out in Exhibit 8.5.

Pension funds

The potential for growth in private pension schemes, launched in 1987, is high as Portugal, like all EU countries, will face a social security crisis unless reforms are implemented. The Portuguese are also great savers. Assets under pension fund management stood at Esc1.6 trillion at the end of 1996 (9.9 per cent of GDP), up from Esc106 billion in 1989.

The elderly dependency ratio (the number of people aged 65 and over per 100 people aged 15–64) has been fairly stable over the past 15 years (at around 27), but the World Bank expects slowing population growth and healthier pensioners to push it up

Exhibit 8.5

Mutual fund investment limits

Restriction and legal limit

1. Issuing company

A mutual fund may acquire no more than:

- 10 per cent of the non-voting shares of a single issuing body.
- 10 per cent of the debt securities of a single issuing body.
- 10 per cent of the units of a single mutual fund.

Exception:

- Transferable securities issued by or guaranteed by a EU member state or its local authorities.
- Transferable securities issued by an international organisation of which one or more EU state is a member.

2. Total fund assets

A mutual fund may invest no more than:

- 5 per cent of its assets in transferable securities issued by the same body.

Exception:

- The 5 per cent limit may be raised to a maximum of 10 per cent; however, the total value of the transferable securities held by a mutual fund in issuing bodies in each of which it invests more than 5 per cent of its assets must not exceed 40 per cent of the value of its assets.
- the 5 per cent limit may be raised to a maximum of 35 per cent if the transferable securities are issued or guaranteed by an EU member state, local authorities or by international bodies of which one or more EU states is a member.
- The 35 per cent limit may be raised to 100 per cent if there are at least six different issuers, but securities from any one issue may not account for more than 30 per cent of total assets.
- 10 per cent of its assets in transferable securities other than those referred to above, including debt instruments.

3. Assets of mutual funds

A mutual fund may invest no more than:

- 20 per cent of its assets in the units of a single mutual fund.

4. Cash funds

A mutual fund has to invest at least:

- 35 per cent of its assets in transferable securities with residual maturity of 12 months.

Prohibition:

- Cash funds cannot invest in shares, convertible bonds and subordinated debt instruments.

Prepared by Barclays Bank in Portugal.

to 38 by 2020. With public finances under pressure to meet the fiscal conditions for European monetary union, the state will find it increasingly difficult to meet future social security obligations (see Chapter 2), and the likelihood is of real reductions in basic state pensions in the future.

The minimum and maximum limits for pension fund portfolios are set out in Exhibit 8.6.

Exhibit 8.6

The maximum limits which condition the composition of pension fund portfolios (%)

	Maximum limit
Time deposits and certificates of deposit	20
Bonds and commercial paper, except public debt	60
Participations in mutual funds	20
Shares listed in OECD stock exchanges	35
Land and buildings	45
Mortgage loans and loans granted to participants of closed pension funds	25
Unlisted and other securities not previously referred to with the exception of public debt	5
Other deposits in credit institutions and interbank deposits	5
Cash and sight deposits	3

Prepared by Barclays Bank in Portugal.

9

RETAILING

Market profile

Portugal's plethora of small shops, the largest number in relative terms in the EU, are increasingly under threat from the big new supermarket and hypermarket chains. Almost 5,000 local grocers closed between 1989 and 1994. The squeeze has coincided with sluggish consumer spending growth. Private consumption growth fell from an average of 5.3 per cent between 1986 and 1992 to less than 1 per cent between 1993 and 1996. However, last year the growth in consumption increased again to above 2 per cent.

The country, however, still has almost three times as many small grocers as the EU average – 3.8 per 1,000 inhabitants in 1993 compared with an average of 1.4 (see Exhibit 9.1). Based on the turnover of the largest modern retailers and on Nielsen's estimations, in 1995 the 35,097 small Portuguese grocers and small independent stores accounted for 75 per cent of the retail food market (fresh and non-fresh goods) compared with 23 per cent for modern supermarket and hypermarket networks. Including non-food goods, the share of the traditional, usually family-owned shops is larger (see Exhibit 9.2).

On the whole, small retailers in Portugal are of a poor standard.[1] They dominated the market until the early 1990s and generated healthy income from their shops, helped by the outdated commercial leases on which most of the retail space is held. Many retailers are still in property owned by their family from the 1940–60s and pay low rents. The new rental law allows the revision of past rents for up to 90 per cent of accumulated inflation, but rents had already lost touch with the market as they were frozen when passed from one family member to another. Indeed, one could even sell the contract on without the

Exhibit 9.1

Number of food stores per 1,000 inhabitants, 1993

Portugal	3.8
Italy	2.5
Greece	2.4
Spain	2.3
Ireland	1.7
Norway	1.3
Belgium	1.3
Austria	1.2
Finland	1.0
Germany	1.0
Switzerland	1.0
Denmark	0.8
Sweden	0.8
France	0.8
United Kingdom	0.7
Netherlands	0.5

Source: Distribução Hoje.

[1] This chapter draws extensively on the October 1996 Retail Sector report by Espírito Santo Research and on the November 1996 report on Modelo Continente by HSBC James Capel.

Exhibit 9.2

Retail market share (food and non-food)

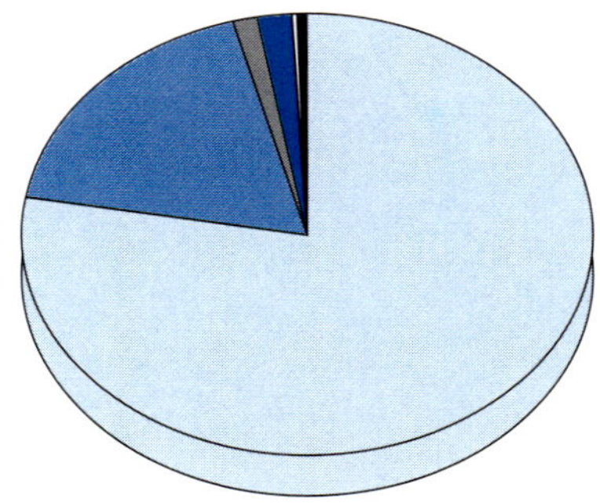

- Traditional stores (79%)
- Hypers & supers (18.2%)
- Hard discount (1.4%)
- Satellite stores (2%)
- Mail order (0.4%)
- Category killers (0.3%)

Excluding Madeira and the Azores.
Source: A.C. Nielsen.

Exhibit 9.3

Market share of the five largest retailers, 1995 (%)

Norway	84
Denmark	71
France	61
United Kingdom	51
Ireland	44
Portugal	34

Note: Market shares relate to the five largest operators in each country.

Source: A.C. Nielsen.

supervision of the landlord. Many contracts remain in place which bear no resemblance to the market price of the property. The rents are so low that even with declining market share small retailers are able to generate sufficient income to survive. However, with low rental income, landlords are unable to maintain properties adequately, which contributes to the decay of city centres.

Large-scale retailing has been growing quickly; the five largest hypermarket and supermarket groups – Continente and Modelo (part of SONAE), Pao de Acúcar (acquired by France's Auchan in 1996), Pingo Doce (part of the Jerónimo Martins group) and Carrefour – accounted for 34 per cent of the total market in 1995 (see Exhibit 9.3), though the level of concentration is still lower than in other European countries.

Portugal had 44 hypermarkets in 1996 with an area of 2,000 sq metres or more (see Exhibit 9.4). This is the equivalent of one for every 220,000 inhabitants, more than double the number of potential customers per hypermarket in Spain and seven times higher than the ratio in France. One quarter of them are in the Lisbon area.

As elsewhere in Europe, the growing strength of large-format stores and the lobby of small retailers has resulted in restrictions being placed on hypermarkets and supermarkets, limiting both the amount of business they can do and their ability to increase it. The granting of new permits for large-format stores has slowed down to a trickle, particularly for the major retailing groups: Modelo Continente, the core of SONAE; Jerónimo Martins; Pao de Acúcar; and Carrefour. Although the freezing of permits for new projects was never formally approved, in practice very few new permits were granted between 1994 and 1996.

These difficulties forced retailers to follow the international trend by developing new formats. Permits for smaller sales areas were granted at the discretion of municipal authorities. This situation led to a redefinition in 1995 of what constitutes a large

Exhibit 9.4

Hypermarkets

	Portugal	*France*	*Spain*
Number of hypermarkets	44	1,030	240
Total sales area ('000 sq m)	235	5,706	1,832
Shop floor area (sq m)	5,340	5,551	7,635
Population (millions)	9.3	57.6	39
Inhabitants per shop	212,200	32,339	94,251
Inhabitants per sq m	40	5.8	12.3

Note: Portuguese figures do not include Madeira and the Azores. Portuguese hypermarkets have a minimum of 2,000 sq m, while the minimum in France and Spain is 2,500 sq m.

Source: Espiríto Santo Research.

retail area. Decree Law 83/95 reduced the lowest sales area to be classified as a large retail area from 2,500 sq metres to 2,000 sq metres in municipalities of more than 30,000 people, and to 1,000 sq metres in those below 30,000. This led the major groups to confine their strategies to the development of supermarkets, discount and hard-discount stores, while foreign hard-discount chains, such as Lidl and Día, expanded their operations more quickly.

Opening hours

The conflict between traditional commerce and large-scale retailing generated a heated national debate over Sunday opening hours. The previous centre-right government cut almost unrestricted Sunday opening hours to six hours for hypermarkets and other large stores in January 1995 in response to strong lobbying from small shopkeepers. After the Socialists came to power in October 1995, the law on permitted hours of business was re-examined and Sunday opening for big stores was reduced from six to five

Exhibit 9.5

Opening hours for large retailers

	Previous	*Present*
Definition of large stores for legislative purposes	> 2,500m^2	> 2,000m^2 in towns > 30,000 people > 1,000m^2 in towns < 30,000 people
Monday to Saturday	10am–10pm	10am–midnight
Sundays/holidays (Jan–Oct)	6 hours	8am–1pm
Sundays/holidays (Nov–Dec)	10am–10pm	10am–10pm

Source: HSBC James Capel.

hours, and restricted to the morning, against 10 hours for other outlets (see Exhibit 9.5) as of July 1996, but not without claiming a victim. Daniel Bessa, the then economy minister, resigned in disagreement over the reduction. The regulation on Sunday opening hours having been in force for a year, DECO, the national consumers' association, and APEO, the modern retailers' association, now claim the legislation needs to be reviewed, and unrestricted Sunday trading should be permitted to better serve the consumers because the current restrictions have not resulted in any improvement in the traditional retailing sector, as recognised even by small shop-keepers.

For some operators Sunday has gone from being the second best selling day of the week to one of the worst.

A decree-law regulating permits for the opening of large retail areas was due to be approved during 1997. The government defines such areas (known as UCDRs) as:

- large retail areas (according to the definition in Exhibit 9.5) and also aggregations of retail establishments;
- retail establishments with a sales area of more than 300 sq metres if they belong to a group or banner whose total selling area is equal to or more than 10,000 sq metres; and
- wholesale traders belonging to a group or banner whose total selling area is equal to or greater than 50,000 sq metres.

The legislation would make the government responsible for practically all new openings (the powers of local authorities were removed) and thus it controls the potential growth of the major retail groups. The factors taken into account when studying authorisations include the UCDR's ratio of sales areas per thousand population and the market share in the area of influence (all municipalities within a circle, of a defined radius, with the intended hypermarket at its centre) or at the national level, of the company, group or banner to which the unit belongs.

The main players

Expansion of the major groups is expected to slow down because of the opening restrictions, the already substantial selling space achieved in some areas and the good regional coverage attained.

SONAE

Modelo Continente, part of SONAE, Portugal's largest priveate sector group, is Portugal's largest retailer by sales. The company runs three retail franchises: Continente, hypermarkets; Modelo, mini-hypermarkets; and Champion, supermarkets. Modelo Continente also has a minority stake in Día, a hard discounter controlled by France's Promodès.

Continente purchased Modelo in October 1995. The advent of legislation limiting large store openings, restrictions on Sunday openings and a stagnant retail environment led SONAE to merge the two activities in order to generate an integrated planning structure and to realise significant cost efficiencies, particularly in logistics.

At the end of 1996 Continente had four licences, all of which are to be anchor stores in group shopping centres. This gives it a competitive advantage as its growth is assured. The Colombo and Vasco de Gama stores (expected to be opened in October 1997 and the first quarter of 1999, respectively) will be the two largest Continente hypermarkets in operation. The Colombo shopping centre, designed and developed by SONAE, on the outskirts of Lisbon will be the Iberian peninsula's biggest at 122,000 sq metres. The other two Continente stores (at Maishopping and at Loureshopping) will be opened in the last quarter of 1997 and the second quarter of 1988, respectively.

SONAE had 37 Modelo supermarkets in 1996 and eight Continente hypermarkets. In May 1996, SONAE opened its first Champion store in Oporto and had three by the end of January 1997. These are smaller stores (1,000–1,500 sq metres) for Oporto and Lisbon, which could eventually be extended to Portugal's other large cities. They are sited close to office buildings and large residential areas, and great emphasis is placed on fresh produce. SONAE plans to set up around 20 Champion stores, while the number of Continente hypermarkets could increase above 12 by one or two more stores by the year 2000 and the number of Modelo markets is expected to grow by 12 units per year.

Another growth area for SONAE is the new Specialised Retailing format, which will comprise MaxMat stores, the SONAE Quelle catalogue, and between three and five new store formats ranging from computers to sports goods to perfumery. The company aimed to have eight MaxMat building material stores by the end of 1997 and 40 in the Iberian peninsula by 2000.

Having built up a strong customer base and successfully launched a Visa Universo credit card in 1995 (the first co-branded credit card launched by a European retailer), SONAE moved into banking in 1997 with Universo Banco. This bank – the largest of its kind in Portugal and one of the first *supermarket banks* in Europe – with its 43 innovative financial branches located in the SONAE hypermarkets and supermarkets focuses on consumer credit, mortgage insurance and savings products. It does not handle deposits because this would be an unprofitable business for such a specialised bank. The credit card entitles Sonae's customers to vouchers worth 1 per cent of their sales, and in addition it can be used in certain other businesses, such as Petrogal, the state's oil concern, which gives customers a 3 per cent discount on petrol purchases. The card's main purpose was to forge customer loyalty rather than generate another source of profits, but it broke even in 1996.

Portugal's small market and the limitations on supermarkets and hypermarkets have made SONAE look abroad in order to keep on growing. SONAE expects to expand in Brazil, particularly after 1998 when most of its investment in its own country will have been completed. SONAE acquired, through Modelo Investimentos Brasil, control of Companhia Real de Distribução (CRD), ranked eighth among Brazilian retailers, in July 1995. CRD has hypermarkets (known as Big Shop), and a network of supermarkets (REAL); the chain's expansion plans envisage seven new hypermarket openings by 1998, which will double the sales area of 55,000 sq metres. SONAE's aim is to be one of the three largest retailers in Brazil, an ambition which will probably demand mergers or acquisitions within the sector.

SONAE's objective is to give CRD the critical mass to impose its presence in the market, thereby enabling it to become better known and competitive with Brazilian retailers such as Carrefour and Wal-Mart. The latter's sales volume is roughly eight times that of CRD. With a per capita income in Brazil less than half that of Portugal's and a population 16 times larger, it is calculated there is room for 175 hypermarkets in this giant country. There were 67 in 1996.

Jerónimo Martins

The other big Portuguese player is Jerónimo Martins (JM) which owns the Feira Nova hypermarkets (eight in 1996), the Pingo Doce supermarkets (106) and the Recheio cash and carry stores (22). In order to be able to maintain its growth, JM, like SONAE, began to look abroad and it bought Lillywhites of Piccadilly Circus, the sporting goods and sportswear shop in London and Eurocash, Poland's largest chain of cash-and-carry stores. JM's turnover has grown from US$200 million in 1989 to more than US$3 billion today.

Lillywhites has provided Martins with a springboard from which to expand its retailing businesses and strengthen its non-food sector. The group plans to open Lillywhites outlets in Europe, Asia, Latin America and Africa. In the UK, Martins plans to increase its stores from four to 15 by 1999, placing itself in the upper end of the market. In Poland the aim is to operate 103 Eurocash stores by 1998 and also to expand in retailing through a network of 300 supermarkets under the Biedronka banner by the same year. Biedronka is Eurocash's largest customer and JM has an option to buy it in 1998.

10

DIRECT FOREIGN INVESTMENT

General

Decree-Law No. 321/95 of 28 November has amended and substantially simplified the legal and procedural regime applicable to foreign investment operations in Portugal.

The aforesaid legislative innovation is part of a gradual process of lifting of barriers to the free economic initiative of foreign entities in Portugal and the progressive flexibility and liberalisation of the corresponding exchange operations which commenced several years ago.

The Decree-Law stipulates, among other innovations, the express revocation of Decree-Law No. 197-D/86 of 18 July, which approved the "Foreign Investment Code", and of Ruling Decree No. 12/87 of 19 January, which until now established the regime of fees payable to obtain the authorisation and registration of foreign investment operations in Portugal.

For all intents purposes, the Foreign Investment Code has disappeared from the Portuguese legal order, the regime having undergone profound modifications tending to expedite foreign investment operations and which also permit the suppression of disputable formalities and of significant costs to the economic agents and to the state itself.

The legal concept of foreign investment

The law describes foreign investment operations in Portugal as being "all acts and contracts entered into by non-resident individuals or companies which have as an objective or effect the creation, maintenance or strengthening of stable and lasting economic links relative to a company incorporated or to be incorporated in Portugal, the following acts or contracts being considered as such:

(a) the creation or increase of capital of branches or other forms of representation of non-resident companies or of new companies exclusively owned by the investor;
(b) the participation, acquisition and subscription of holdings, free or onerous, total or partial, in new or already existing Portuguese companies;
(c) the execution and amendment of consortium or joint venture agreements when the respective activity is totally or partially undertaken in Portuguese territory, as well as operation and management agreements relative to resident companies or real estate located in the national territory;

(d) The creation of or participation in groups of companies, under any form whatsoever;
(e) the paying up of supplementary payments of capital or partners' loans;
(f) the execution and amendment of contracts for the transfer of technology and technical assistance, whenever there is a direct or indirect participation of the assignor in the capital stock or in the results of the profitable activity of the assignee; and
(g) long-term loans with a participation nature, being understood as being those which have a term exceeding five years and are destined to maintain lasting economic links with a company incorporated or to be incorporated in Portugal."

However, the legal definition of foreign investment operations is slightly broader and also considers as foreign investment (in this case "indirect") the acts previously referred to made by Portuguese companies the capital stock of which is participated in the first degree by non-resident foreign individuals or companies.

The qualification of an entity as non-resident results from the legal definition set forth in the exchange Portuguese regulations applicable at the time of the operation.

As far as the participations in companies by shares are concerned (S.A. companies and "in commandité" by shares), there is an express legal presumption as to the existence of stable and lasting economic links with the foreign investors when the joint participation of non-resident entities exceeds 20 per cent of the respective capital stock or when the participation individually held by one sole non-resident entity exceeds 10 per cent.

The previous regime

Until the enactment of the new legal regulations, the regime of the so-called "Prior Declaration of Foreign Investment" was in force and required the (direct or indirect) foreign investors to submit their projects for prior approval to ICEP – Investimentos, Comércio e Turismo de Portugal (hereinafter called ICEP), for the purpose of the generality of investments in Portugal.

The subsequent implementation of the investment projects concerned, generally made through notarial acts and the import of funds to Portugal, could only be made after the issue of the Prior Declaration of Foreign Investment, failing which such investment would not produce effects, particularly of an exchange nature.

The new regime

With the new regime, the requirement to obtain the Prior Declaration has been abolished, with the exception of the foreign investment projects specified in Article 12 of the new law: any project which "due to its nature, form or implementation conditions may affect the public order, safety or health, as well as those which refer to the production and trade of arms, ammunitions and war material or which involve the exercising of powers entrusted to public authorities".

It is well understood that special care is required with these specific types of investment projects, which are still subject to the prior authorisation from ICEP, which is only granted after the competent entities have been consulted, the investigations deemed necessary have been made, and when all supplementary clarification that may have been requested from the potential foreign investors has been obtained.

The basic rule applicable to foreign investments in general, whether originating from member countries of the European Union or not, is their complete equality to investments made by national entities, having the "same rights and guarantees conferred to national investments and access to all incentives" foreseen for national entities, such projects however being subject to the principles in force of an economic nature, to the law in general and to the national legal order.

Acquisition of real estate

With respect to the acquisition by non-resident entities of real estate located in the Portuguese territory, these operations adopt the same procedures as the legal regime applicable to foreign investment operations when such acquisition is destined for the creation, maintenance or strengthening of stable and lasting economic links relative to a company incorporated or to be incorporated in Portugal.

Investment contracts

In turn, and as far as foreign investment projects which are considered as having special interest for the national economy are concerned, these can be submitted to the contractual regime governing Foreign Investment Contracts by means of Investment Contracts to be executed between the foreign investors and the competent national public entities.

For these contracts, it is possible to agree on the settlement of any disputes or litigation between the parties by arbitration, with the exception of those relating to tax matters.

Registration of operations

The obligation to obtain the Prior Declaration of Foreign Investment was replaced by a system of registration "a posteriori" of the operations concerned, as well as of the operations of liquidation of foreign investments (operations of foreign disinvestment).

Under the legal terms now in force, both the entity receiving the investment and the foreign investors concerned have the joint and several obligation to communicate to ICEP the implementation of the referred operations within 30 days after conclusion, failing which a fine between Esc20,000 and Esc500,000 in the case of individuals, or between Esc200.000 and Esc6 million in the case of companies is due, ICEP being responsible for the instituting of the respective misdemeanour proceeding and the Board of Directors of ICEP for the application of the fines.

The legislation currently in force expressly safeguards the enforcement of the provisions regarding the safeguarding of competition, in particular as to operations of companies having a monopoly, as well as the legislation regarding the restriction of the participation of non-resident entities in the capital of certain companies or types of companies.

Finally, it is also stipulated that, when exceptional circumstances occur which impose restrictions to capital operations with states that are not members of the European Union, similar restrictions may also be imposed to foreign investment operations.

The legal regime presently in force replaced prior formalities which did not take into account the merit of the project and which in practice proved to be bureaucratic and useless, as much to the investors as to the state.

11

THE EQUITY MARKET

The Lisbon Stock Exchange has changed beyond recognition since Portugal's "big bang" in 1991. Although still small and underdeveloped by European standards, the stock market is playing an increasingly important role in the country's financial system, spurred on by privatisations, – most of which have been carried out through the exchange – the sharp fall in interest rates and the improved profit outlook of companies.

The BVL-30 index was one of the fastest-growing in the EU in 1996, rising 34.8 per cent in escudo terms and 28.8 per cent in dollar terms (see Exhibit 11.1). The index rose 19 per cent in the first three months of 1997. The rally reflected the sharp narrowing of the risk premium of Portuguese bonds: the 10-year government

Exhibit 11.1

BVL30 Index, January 1993 to April 1997

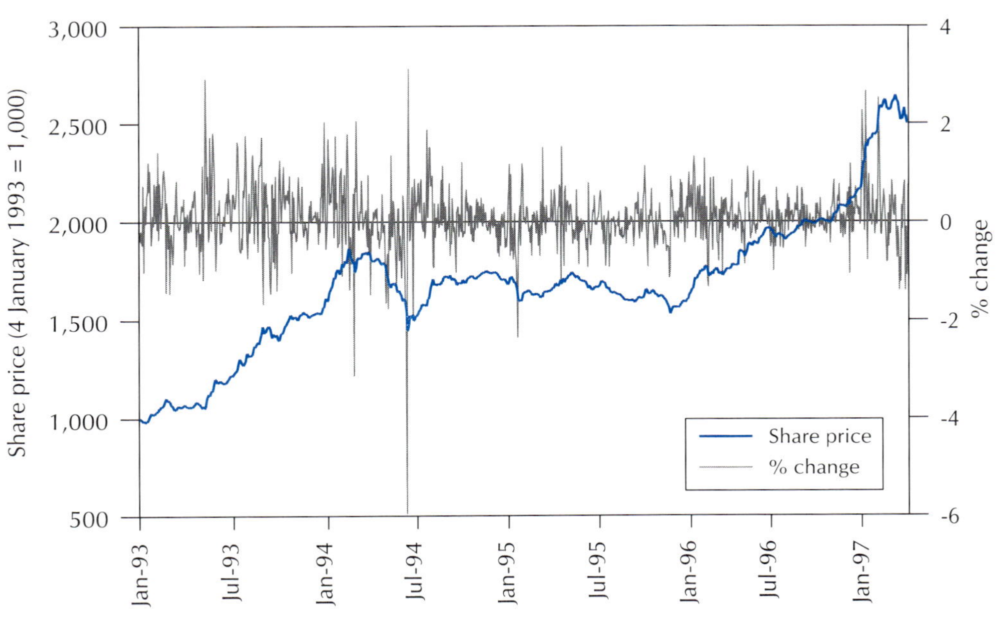

Source: Lisbon Stock Exchange.

Exhibit 11.2

Yields, August 1994–December 1996 (% points)

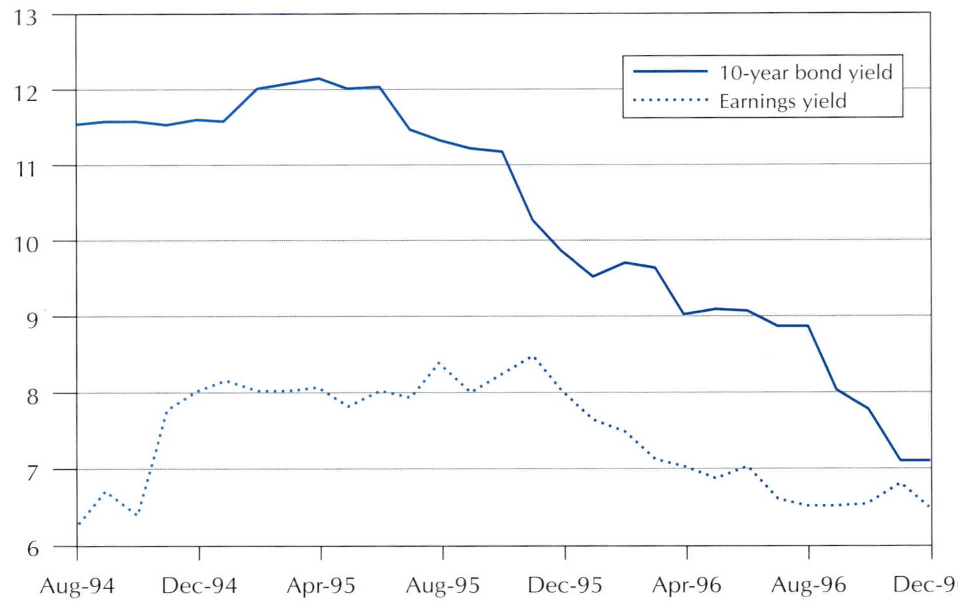

Source: Lisbon Stock Exchange, Santander Investment.

Exhibit 11.3

Market multiples, 1996

	P/E	*P/BV*
France	48.7	1.88
Germany	27.6	2.69
Greece	11.0	2.11
Ireland	12.8	2.36
Netherlands	17.8	2.69
Portugal	16.0	1.77
Spain	16.8	2.09
Switzerland	20.5	2.87
United Kingdom	14.9	2.87

Source: Morgan Stanley Capital International.

bond yield dropped by 2.95 points in 1996 to 6.85 per cent and the yield gap with Germany narrowed from 380 to 106 basis points.

The gap between 10-year yields and earnings yields of Portuguese shares has fallen considerably over the past few years and was 0.6 points at the end of 1996 (see Exhibit 11.2). The spread was smaller than most other European markets. Given that the gap was at an historic low and the positive bond market prospects (see Chapter 12), the stock market's upward potential in 1997 was substantial. Earnings per share growth was expected to remain robust, reflecting the scenario of non-inflationary economic growth and lower interest rates.

Market valuations compare favourably with other European markets, leaving the Portuguese market looking relatively inexpensive both in terms of P/E and P/BV (see Exhibit 11.3).

Market profile

After the 1974 revolution, the Lisbon and Oporto stock markets were closed down for three years. The April 25 *coup* brought a period of wild speculation to an abrupt halt; in the two years before the revolution the vaulted marble hall of the Lisbon exchange was so full of investors that they were crowded out into the street where frantic trading of shares was carried out from vans loaded with share certificates. At the height of the speculative madness, when companies refused to offer more share certificates, brokers offered clients slips of paper which read "worth 100 shares of company X". Investors would gather at the Café Central to strike up deals. It was like a lottery. Middle class investors took out loans to buy shares and enlisted gardeners, chauffeurs and maids to act as "fronts" to acquire more shares. When the Lisbon market re-opened for share transactions the number of listed companies had shrunk from 150 to 23.

The market almost withered away after losing its main stars to nationalisation. Up to 1984, both the state and private sectors were financed by the banking system, which collected almost all household savings in the form of term deposits. Between 1985–90, under the stimulus of EC membership, tax incentives, high economic growth and the first privatisations, the number of listed companies on the Lisbon Stock Exchange increased eight-fold to 184, and to 155 on the Oporto Stock Exchange (145 were listed on both).

During this period, however, there was another bout of heavy speculation. The upturn in the economy combined with the lack of experience of domestic investors and a defective regulatory framework fuelled a meteoric rise in share prices. Many Portuguese investors got their fingers burnt in the October 1987 crash. The BVL general index fell 37 per cent in 1998. By the end of 1990 the market was still at a level considerably lower than in 1988, and 1991 and 1992 were also negative years, partly due to the high opportunity cost linked to investment in shares (high real interest rates). The market boomed in 1993 and was flat in 1994 and 1995. The exchange's new premises were opened in 1994.

The Oporto market ceased to operate when Portugal's derivatives market was launched in the northern city in June 1996, and Lisbon became the only cash market. At the end of 1996, 267 companies were listed (including those listed only in Oporto which were transferred to Lisbon) and market capitalisation of shares was Esc3.8 trillion (23.3 per cent of GDP), up from Esc1.28 trillion in 1991 and Esc33.9 billion in 1986. Total capitalisation (ie, of all securities) was Esc10.6 trillion (64.7 per cent of GDP) compared with Esc8.7 trillion at the end of 1995.

The driving force behind the increase in capitalisation (see Exhibit 11.4) has been the listing of large new companies, chiefly as a result of privatisations, beginning with banks such as Banco Totta e Açores in 1989 and insurance firms (Império in 1992) and then industrial companies like Petrogal (oil), Cimpor (the second biggest cement producer in the Iberian peninsular) and Portugal Telecom.

Liquidity has also grown strongly as a result of an increase in turnover at more than twice the rate of growth of market capitalisation. The average daily trading volume was Esc3.6 billion in 1996 (US$23.3 million), up from Esc2.4 billion (US$15.5 million) in 1995 and Esc695 million (US$4.5 million) in 1992, though this is still low in international terms. The basic problem for investors has been the lack of market liquidity which for any except the largest stocks can be painfully thin.

Exhibit 11.4
Market capitalisation of shares, 1991–96

	Esc billions
1991	1,284
1992	1,430
1993	2,193
1994	2,586
1995	2,743
1996	3,828

Source: Lisbon Stock Exchange.

Several steps have been taken to try to increase turnover and encourage what the government calls "democratic ownership" (a policy started by the previous centre-right administration under the title of "popular capitalism"). Commissions charged on small retail trading have been lowered and the government has offered significant discounts to retail investors in privatisation offerings.

A record 86,000 individuals applied for shares when 45 per cent of Cimpor, Portugal's biggest cement producer, was privatised in October 1996, while the flotation of Telecel at the end of 1996 was the largest private operation of its kind in the country, and it became the fourth biggest listed company in terms of market capitalisation. The share price of Telecel, Portugal's largest mobile phone operator, gained 19.5 per cent on its first day of trading. Share capital increases, flotations and privatisations generated around Esc600 billion in 1996, 24 per cent of the market capitalisation at the end of 1995. The most significant privatisation in 1997, and the largest to date, was 20–25 per cent of Electricidade de Portugal (EDP), the national power company, which was expected to raise Esc200–300 billion. Privatisation issues will continue to improve market structure and depth, and also the degree of transparency, as these companies are more sensitive to minority shareholders' needs regarding information flows.

Portugal's big banks are building up their mutual fund base as a way to increase fee income and offset the sharp fall in net interest margins; pension funds and the life insurance sector are also growing. Greater investment in shares by these funds can be expected. Investment in equities by mutual funds grew 141.3 per cent in 1996 to US$700 million, and by pension funds 23.5 per cent to US$900 million.

Portugal is thus well on the road to changing from an emerging to a developed market, offering the high growth of the former with the low risk of the latter. The Lisbon market still features in emerging market indices (such as that of the International Finance Corporation), to the chagrin of stock market officials, although Portugal's per capita GDP is well above the emerging market definition. The transition to the main European or world market listings could take place in 1977 or 1998, when Portugal will probably qualify for entry into the first round of European monetary union. Lisbon would be officially re-rated as a developed market when the BVL index is given a mainstream weighting by indices such as Morgan Stanley Capital International and FT/S&P Actuaries. The reclassification would be determined by Lisbon's size, in terms of market capitalisation and trading volume, as well as by the balance of listed companies and the regulatory environment. Market capitalisation of shares was US$24.6 billion at the end of 1996, about one-seventh of Spain's. The transition would substantially increase trading volumes. International funds that have not previously invested in Portuguese shares would be attracted to allot part of their portfolio in accordance with the weightings Lisbon is given by mainstream indices.

There are three markets in Lisbon, each one with specific requirements for listing/trading:

- Shares and several other securities are continuously traded by a computer-link system (Tradis) on the market with official quotations;
- The second-tier market is for securities that do not fulfil the requirements of the market with official quotations; and
- The market without quotations is for securities that do not fulfil the requirements of the other two markets.

The only securities that can be negotiated on the market for block trading (known by its Portuguese acronym as MEOG) are bonds or similar securities listed on the market with official quotations and registered as book-entry securities with the central securities depository; they must have a minimum nominal value of Esc10 billion. The deals effected on MEOG must have a minimum value of Esc175 million if the securities are issued by the Portuguese or foreign governments and Esc100 billion if they are bonds issued by companies. The MEOG is a registration market, which means that it is only intended for registration of previously agreed deals. In this market there are no unmatched bid and ask positions.

Trading practices

Using an order-driven automated trading system (Tradis), brokers enter buy and sell orders via terminals in their office. Trade matching takes place on a continuous basis throughout the day. Tradis is fully integrated with the central securities depository (Central). Interbolsa, established by the Lisbon and Oporto exchanges, is responsible for managing the integrated trading and settlement systems. On T (trade date), brokers specify which accounts at the Central are to be debited/credited on settlement date. Indirect market participants, which include custodian banks, have until T+1 to specify the relevant accounts.

For depository-eligible securities, trades are matched on T+1 and locked in once any discrepancies are resolved, with the transfer (but not delivery) of securities taking place on T+3. An overnight batch processing takes place at the Central and details of the adjusted balances delivered to the Bank of Portugal for the exchange of cash across accounts the following day (T+4).

Technically, fails are not allowed in the Portuguese market. Cash or securities must theoretically be in the relevant account on trade date. In practice, however, an informal matching process is carried out among market participants alongside the official timetable to ensure that settlement can occur on the night of T+3/4. The settlement structure (see below) makes turnaround trades technically impossible since securities delivered into the system on T+3 for overnight settlement are not credited to the buyer until T+4, and therefore not available for onward delivery until that evening.

Short selling, the selling of shares not owned in the hope of buying them later at a lower price, and stock lending were due to be allowed in 1997. This and opening of a "repo" market will be an important stimulus fot the Oporto derivative market, whose

Exhibit 11.5

Trading systems and hours

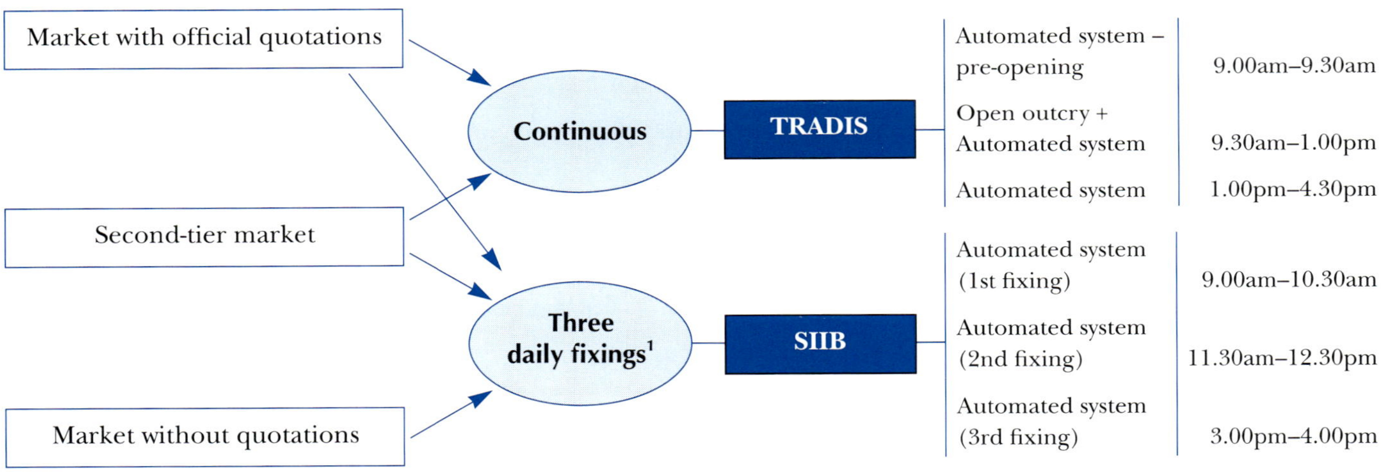

[1] Rights are traded through the system applied to the securities from which they are detached.
Monday–Friday. Exceptions: public holidays.

Source: Lisbon Stock Exchange.

main contract, the PSI-20 stock index, has helped attract new investors to the Lisbon cash market (see Chapter 13). The suspension of stocks for as long as four days for dividend payment was abolished in early 1997. Dividends are now paid before trading begins and no suspension in the trading of the stock is required. Trading hours (see Exhibit 11.5) depend on the market segment.

Exhibit 11.6

Market capitalisation by sectors, 1996 (Esc million)

Sector	*Capitalisation*	*% of total*
Banks	1,783,871	32.9
Telecommunications	1,482,175	27.3
Retail	467,305	8.6
Building materials	389,597	7.2
Forest products	341,702	6.3
Multi-industry	255,850	4.7
Insurance	224,477	4.1
Beverages & tobacco	110,138	2.0
Capital goods	92,802	1.7
Construction	92,659	1.7

Source: Lisbon Stock Exchange.

Banks dominated the market until 1995 when the partial privatisation of large companies such as Portucel Industrial and Portugal Telecom reduced the banks' share of total capitalisation and helped make the market more representative of the whole economy. At the end of March 1997 banks accounted for 33 per cent of total market capitalisation (see Exhibit 11.6), down from 55 per cent in 1993, and after the initial share offering of Elecricidade de Portugal (EDP) during 1997 they were expected to fall to around 25 per cent. The main listed companies include

Exhibit 11.7

Ten largest companies by market capitalisation, March 1997 (Esc million)

Company	*Capitalisation*	*% of total*
Portugal Telecom	1,186,550	21.9
Banco Comercial Português	341,715	6.3
Telecel	295,625	5.4
Cimpor	294,000	5.4
Banco Espírito Santo	282,978	5.2
Banco Português do Atlântico	277,200	4.6
Jerónimo Martins	245,637	4.6
SONAE	226,600	4.5
Continente	212,806	4.2
Banco de Fomento Exterior	209,200	4.2

Source: Lisbon Stock Exchange.

Barbosa & Almedia, the biggest glass container manufacturer in Portugal; Corticeira Amorim, the world's leading cork producer operating in diversified segments; Efacec, the largest electrical equipment manufacturer; Engil, a large construction company; Jerónimo Martins, one of the major players in retailing; SONAE, the country's largest private conglomerate; and Vista Alegre, the leading Portuguese china and porcelain pro-ducer with a world-wide brand name.

Of the 10 largest companies by capitalisation, five are banks (see Exhibit 11.7). Banco Português do Atlântico had the largest capitalisation until Portugal Telecom's second privatisation tranche in 1996 (see Exhibit 11.7). The most actively traded shares are set out in Exhibit 11.8.

Foreign investors play a leading role in the market. At the end of 1996 shares

Exhibit 11.8

Ten most actively traded shares, January–March 1997 (Esc million)

Company	*Value*	*% of total*
Portugal Telecom	122,200	25.0
Telecel	45,819	9.4
Cimpor	45,200	9.2
SONAE	33,585	6.9
Banco Comercial Português	31,958	6.5
Banco Totta e Açores	26,692	5.7
Banco Português de Investimento	17,565	3.6
Espírito Santo	16,816	3.4
Jerónimo Martins	10,306	2.1
Portucel	10,079	2.1

Source: Lisbon Stock Exchange.

Exhibit 11.9

Transaction fees (%)

Securities	*Stock market fee*[1]
Stock exchange market	
Bonds: national public debt and similar funds	0.02
Bonds: medium-/long-term fixed coupon Treasury bonds (OTs)	0.004
Bonds: public foreign funds and other	0.02
Participation bonds and investment trust units	0.02
Shares	0.04
Rights	0.05
Special market for block trading	–
Over-the-counter market	
Listed securities	0.4
Unlisted securities	0.05

[1] Due by the seller and by the buyer on the transaction value. Other charges: brokerage and banking fees deal negotiable.

Source: Lisbon Stock Exchange.

held by non-residents amounted to Esc6.3 billion (26 per cent of the market capitalisation). Net foreign investment in equities in 1996 amounted to US$2.9 billion. However, in terms of free float (ie, not controlled by long-term shareholders) it is estimated that these investors hold more than 50 per cent of the market. Their role in terms of liquidity and price formation has been preponderant.

Costs for investors

Transactions are subject to different charges, depending on whether they are effected on or outside the stock exchange. The fees are paid by both the seller and the buyer and are charged on the traded amount (see Exhibit 11.9)

Clearing and settlement systems

The central securities depository manages and operates the registration and control of book-entry securities; the deposit, custody and control of fungible securities and the clearing and settlement of transactions.

The basic features of the system (see Exhibit 11.10) are:

- Any transfer of ownership is immediately registered on the trading system, with the identification of the intervening brokers;
- Brokers must report on the trade date the origin of the executed trades; if the order has not been received directly from the final orderer, they must enter into the system the name of the ordering financial intermediary;
- In the event of a sale, financial intermediaries, whether brokers or not, must hold in their accounts with the Central a suitable position in those securities;

- On the third working day after the trade date, the accounts of the selling brokers or financial intermediaries are debited and the accounts of the purchasing brokers or financial intermediaries are credited;
- The securities credited in the accounts of the purchasing financial intermediaries become available for trading only after financial settlement takes place; and
- Financial settlement of deals is centralised by the Bank of Portugal and takes place on the fourth working day after the trade date.

The Lisbon Stock Exchange has its own clearing and settlement system for securities not registered with the Central, known as SICOB.

Portugal is close to the top in the GSCS benchmarks drawn up yearly for emerging markets on the basis of settlement, safekeeping and operational risk.

Exhibit 11.10

Clearing and settlement system

Securities		*Securities settlement (T: trade day)*	*Financial settlement*
Registered with the Central (CSD)[1]	Fungible	Clearing of the accounts held by financial institutions and brokers/dealers with the Central for the net positions resulting from all the trades on T: night of T+3[3].	Debit and credit of the accounts held by the clearing parties with Banco de Portugal: T+4
Non-registered with the Central (CSD)[2]	Fungible	Fortnightly physical clearing between financial institutions and brokers/dealers of the deal of the fortnight: 5th working day after the 14th and after the last day in the month[4].	
	Non-fungible	Physical delivery of the securities by the selling financial institution to the selling broker/dealer: T+1.	
		Physical delivery of the securities by the selling broker/dealer to the buying broker/dealer: T+2.	
		Physical delivery of the securities by the buying broker/dealer to the buying financial institution: T+3.	

[1] The Central Securities Depository (CSD) and National Clearing and Settlement System are managed by Interbolsa.

[2] The clearing and settlement system is called SICOB and is managed by the Lisbon Stock Exchange.

[3] The credit entries effected on T+3 in the securities accounts of financial intermediaries and stockbrokers become effective only after financial settlement on T+4.

[4] When the seller is a private investor brokers/dealers must deliver the relative securities to the Lisbon Stock Exchange for custody.

Source: Lisbon Stock Exchange.

The leading indices

The principal indices are the BVL Geral (1,000 on 5 January 1988) and the BVL 30 (1,000 on 4 January 1993). The latter is based on the most representative companies in terms of liquidity and capitalisation. The BTA index published by Banco Totta e Açores continues to be used by some foreign investors for historic reasons, though it is not a weighted index. The BVL indices only take into account the shares listed and not all the shares representing the whole of the share capital of each company.

Data disclosure services

The Stock Exchange Interactive Information System (SIIB) provides access via computer-link to the market's database. The system provides on-line information on the ongoing session and stored information on securities and issuers.

Telebolsa provides on-line access to information on the prices of the securities traded in each session. Information is passed via television channel in teletext.

Exhibit 11.11

Taxation system (%)

	IRS		*IRC*			*ISD*
	Residents	*Non-residents*	*Residents*		*Non-residents*	
	Rates	*Rates*	*Withheld rates*	*Final rates*	*Rates*	*Rates*
Income						
Interest from public debt						
general rule	20	20	20	36	20	at source 5%
issued between 91–95	20	20	20	36	20	exempt
issued between 4/5/89–90	20	20	20	28.8	20	exempt
issued up to 3/5/89[a]	exempt	exempt	exempt	exempt	exempt	exempt
Interest from bonds						
general rule	20	20	25	36	20	at source 5%[b]
issued between 1990 and 15/10/94	25	25	25	36	25	exempt
issued in 1989[c]	16	16	16	28.8	16	exempt
issued in 1988[a]	6	6	6	6	6	exempt
Dividends						
general rule	25	25	25	36	25	at source 5%
listed companies[d]	12.5	12.5	12.5	18	12.5	at source 5%
privatised companies (during 5 years)[d]	12.5	12.5	12.5	18	12.5	at source 5%
listed privatised companies	6.25	6.25	6.25	9	6.25	at source 5%
Income from participation bonds						
general rule	20	20	20	36	20	exempt
issued between 1990 and 15/10/94	25	25	25	36	25	exempt
issued in1989[c]	16	16	16	28.8	16	exempt
issued in 1988[a]	6	6	6	6	6	exempt
issued in 1987	exempt	exempt	exempt	exempt	exempt	exempt

Exhibit 11.11 *continued*

Taxation system (%) *continued*

	IRS		*IRC*			*ISD*
	Residents	*Non-residents*	*Residents*		*Non-residents*	
	Rates	*Rates*	*Withheld rates*	*Final rates*	*Rates*	*Rates*
Income from investment fund units						
securities investment funds	exempt/20[e]	exempt	20	36/20[f]	exempt	exempt
real estate investment funds	exempt/20[e]	exempt	20	36/20[f]	exempt	exempt <Esc250,000
Capital gains[g]						
Shares						
general rule	10	10	–	36	exempt	
held for over 12 months (since 1992)	exempt	exempt	–	36	exempt	
held for over 24 months (up to 1992)	exempt	exempt	–	36	exempt	
acquired before 31/12/88	exempt	exempt	–	36	exempt	
Public debt bonds	exempt	exempt	–	36	exempt	
Bonds, participation bonds and other debt securities	exempt	exempt	–	36	exempt	
Investment fund units						
up to 1994	exempt	exempt	–	36	exempt	
from 1994 onwards	10	exempt	–	36	exempt	

[a] Taxation of capital tax on issue date.
[b] Bonds issued before 1996 are exempt from Gift and Inheritance Tax.
[c] The income from bonds and participation bonds issued in1989 benefits from a 20 per cent reduction for the purpose of IRS and IRC taxation.
[d] Dividends are considered only for 50 per cent of their total amount net of other fiscal incentives for the purpose of IRS and IRC taxation.
[e] Respectively not included or included in a commercial, industrial or agricultural activity.
[f] For entities, whose main line of business is not a commercial, industrial or agricultural activity.
[g] Capital gains less capital losses.

Source: Lisbon Stock Exchange.

Taxation

Transactions are subject to personal income tax (IRS) or corporate income tax (IRC), charged on income and capital gains, and gift and inheritance tax, either withheld on the income or on the transfer amount (see Exhibit 11.11).

IRS is applicable to the whole income of resident individuals and the income produced in Portugal by non-resident individuals. In the case of non-residents, IRS is withheld at source; rates may be reduced by double taxation agreements.

12

THE DEBT MARKETS

Increased government borrowing requirements and greater corporate finance needs have spurred the development and sophistication of the Portuguese debt markets.

After the 1991 "big bang" which modernised the Lisbon stock market, the need to comply with EU convergence criteria and the prospect of falling interest rates in Portugal led the Treasury to begin issuing fixed-rate coupon bonds known as *obrigaçoes do Tesouro* (OT) or Treasury bonds.[1] They also reduced recourse to floating-rate instruments. The full liberalisation of capital flows at the end of 1992 eliminated the differentiation between resident and non-resident borrowers and eased Portuguese interest rates.

OTs are the chief public debt instrument and dominate the government bond market, representing around 70 per cent of the total outstanding par value of the

Exhibit 12.1

Bond market capitalisation, 1986–96 (Esc billion)

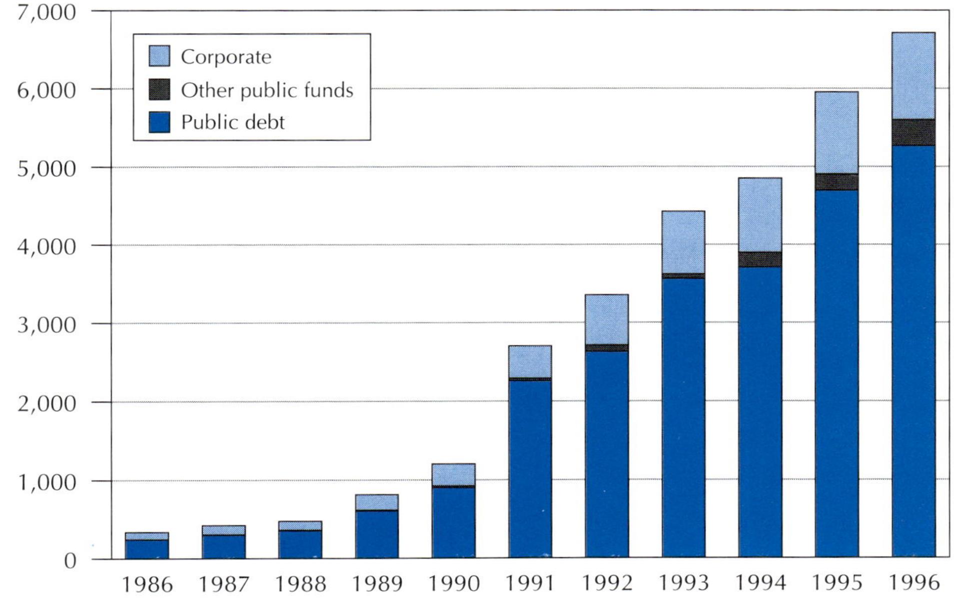

Source: Banco Essi.

[1] This chapter draws on reports by Banco Essi and Banco Santander de Negocios Portugal.

Exhibit 12.2

Bond market turnover, 1986–96 (Esc billion)

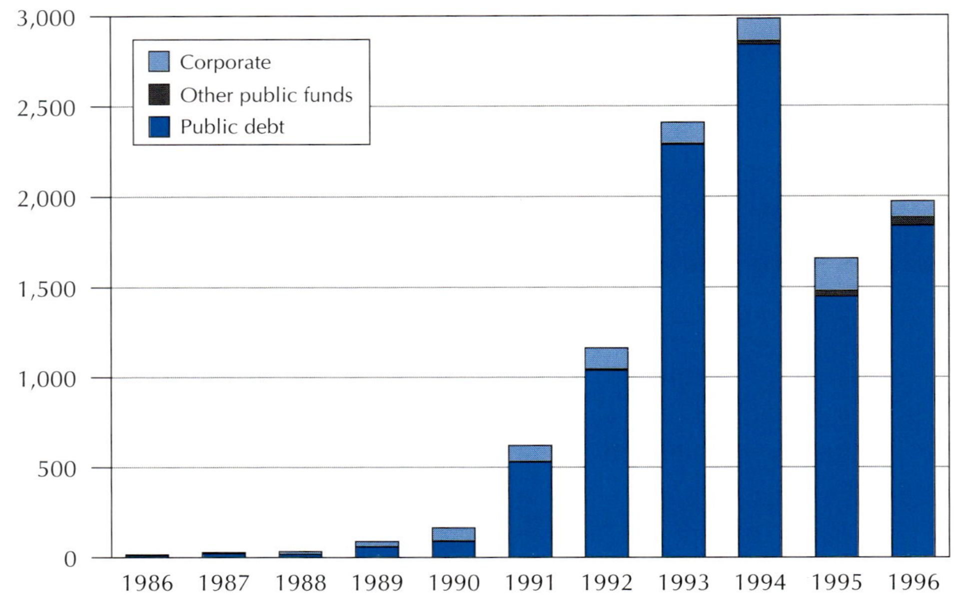

Source: Banco Essi.

domestic debt listed on the Lisbon market, with the fixed rate coupon segment accounting for over two-thirds of the value. Until 1993 the longest maturity was five years. Since then the Treasury has lengthened the maturity of its debt, issuing OTs with maturities of up to 10 years. This has have given Portugal a long-term benchmark and allowed the construction of a yield curve which can be used as an instrument of comparison with the international markets.

The OTs are listed on the Lisbon stock market. The coupon has a fixed rate throughout its life and interest is paid annually (on the older issues – prior to 1994 – interest is payable semi-annually). Total bond market capitalisation grew to Esc6,711 billion in 1996 from Esc5,953 billion in 1995 and turnover reached Esc1,971 billion, up from Esc1,658 billion in 1995 (see Exhibits 12.1 and 12.2).

Primary Treasury bond market

OTs are issued by the *Junta de Crédito Público* (JCP) through competitive auctions. Announcements of new issues – whose main features are set out in Exhibit 12.3 – are made by fax by the JCP at least two working days before the auction day. There is an indicative calendar published by the Treasury for government bond issues. Auctions are typically held on Tuesday or Thursday mornings, with the first week of the month set for 3-year issues, the second week for 5-year issues, the third week for 10-year issues and the last week for floaters. Each issue is fungible with the previous one at the same maturity. The bonds are normally traded on the exchange five days later.

Bids have to be submitted (to one-sixteenth of a percentage point) by 1600 hours

Exhibit 12.3

Main features of Treasury bonds

Issuer	Republic of Portugal
Rating	Moody's Aaa – Standard & Poor's AAA
Denomination	Esc10,000
Maturities	From two to 10 years
Day count	Annual rates (Act/365)
Call or put features	None
Redemption	Bullet
Form	Book entries
Clearing	Central de Valores Mobiliários
Primary dealers	Financial institutions subject to cash reserves
Size in primary	Esc1 million with multiples of Esc100,000
Size in secondary	No limitations
Financial settlement	T + 4
Tax	Withholding tax 20 per cent; none for foreign investors and financial institutions
Brokerage fees	According to the market where they are traded; none on the special market for block trading
Issuance method	Competitive auctions
Primary results	Announced by fax by the Junta de Créditor Público
Secondary results	Reuters page 0#PTTSY=IN

Source: Banco Essi.

to the Bank of Portugal on the last day before the auction. A maximum of five bids per institution are authorised. The minimum bid is Esc1 million, with increments of Esc100,000. Auctions are the American-style tender: the Treasury sets the highest interest at which the bonds are awarded. Bids submitted at rates below the maximum rate are ordered lowest rate first and are satisfied until the amount is allocated. Bids at the cut-off rate are sorted according to a pro rata system, and the Treasury decides whether to limit the allocation at this rate or fully satisfy it.

The chief players are institutional investors. Market makers selected by the JCP (known as *Operadores Especializados de Valores do Tesouro* or OEVTs) ensure liquidity in both the primary and secondary markets. They are obliged to participate in the primary market, and have a special tranche of the issue put at their disposal at non-competitive prices (ie, the lowest price at the auction). This extra amount is calculated from a coefficient of 33 per cent of the total issue, and each market maker's amount depends on their share in the last three tenders. The OEVTs also have to ensure all government bond transactions in the secondary market, with minimum amounts and bid-ask spreads previously determined for each type of bond. For OTs the amount is set at Esc500 million and the maximum price spread is 0.5 per cent.

Large-volume bond trading is carried out on the market for block trading – known as MEOG – which was created in 1994 in order to reduce transaction costs by putting an end to both stock exchange and broker/dealer fees. This market is responsible for a considerable share of turnover (see Exhibit 12.4).

Exhibit 12.4

Capital market turnover structure, 1996

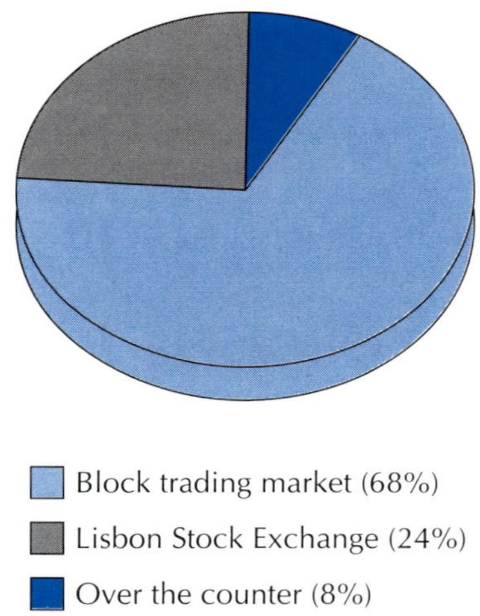

Source: Banco Essi.

The performance of the Portuguese bond market in 1996 was very positive, with a sharp fall in yields resulting from better political and economic conditions than the other southern European countries. The 10-year yield dropped by 2.95 points to 6.85 per cent – far steeper than the most optimistic expectations – and the differential with Germany narrowed to 106 basis points from 380. The Portuguese market is closely linked to the Spanish market and generally moves in line with it.

The importance of other listed government bonds is negligible. FIPs (*Fundo de Investimento Público*) are long-term floating rate negotiable bonds listed on the Lisbon stock market. They have a bi-annual coupon and their maturities range from seven to 12 years. They stopped being issued in 1993. OCAs (*Obrigaçoes de Capitalização Automática*) are bi-annual coupon floating rate notes, with a six-year maturity. The last issue outstanding matures in 1997.

Treasury bill market

Treasury bills have maturities of 91, 182 and 364 days and are issued at a discount (see Exhibit 12.5). They have become less of a monetary and more a short-term fund raising instrument for the government as the Bank of Portugal has its own money market instruments (see Chapter 4). Auctions are announced several days in advance, normally at the beginning of new cash reserve periods. Bids can only be placed by financial institutions subject to cash reserve requirements. The minimum bid is Esc50 million with increments of Esc10 million. Like Treasury bonds (see above) auctions are by American-style tender.

Corporate bonds

This market has been growing steadily, both in terms of capitalisation and turnover (see Exhibit 12.6). Corporate borrowers have a strong preference for 10-year bonds which account for around half of total issues in terms of the outstanding par value amount. Most of the issues are floating rate notes which pay interest on a bi-annual basis and are indexed to the main reference rates (see Exhibit 12.7).

The Navigator bond market

Navigator bonds (*Caravelas*) are escudo-denominated bonds issued by non-resident borrowers (usually supranational entities and sovereign borrowers). The first issue by a supranational entity was made in 1988 by the European Investment Bank and the

Exhibit 12.5

Main features of Treasury bills

Issuer	Republic of Portugal
Rating	Moody's Aaa – Standard & Poor's AAA
Form	Certificates
Clearing	Bank of Portugal
Primary dealers	Financial institutions subject to cash reserves
Maturity	Primary: three, six and 12 months
Quoting type	Annual rates (Act/365)
Size in primary	Esc50 million with increments of Esc10 million
Size in secondary	No limitations
Payment date	T + 2
Tax	Both parties withholding tax: 20%
Brokerage fees	None
Payments	In accordance to discounted yield formula (redemption at par)
Primary results	Reuters page BPDH
Secondary timing	Normal working day

Source: Banco Essi.

Exhibit 12.6

Corporate bond capitalisation and turnover, 1986–96 (Esc billion)

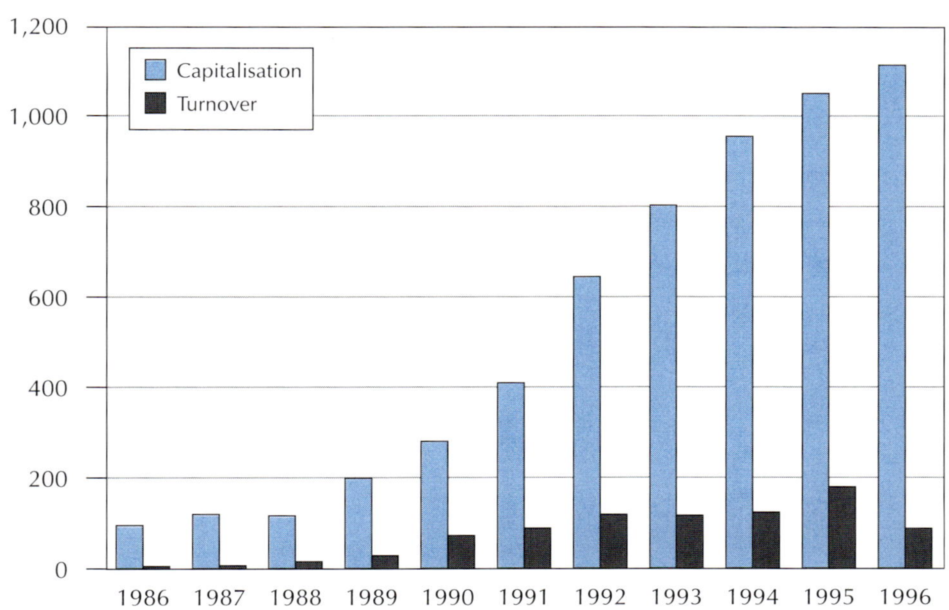

Source: Banco Essi.

Exhibit 12.7

Main reference rates

Main reference rates of interest rates	*Description*
TRO (*Taxa de Referência para Obrigações*)	Rate determined by administrative procedures, which was substituted by TD3 multiplied by a factor of 1.1.
TD3	Average of the nominal gross annual rate for deposits between 180 days and one year, weighted by the amounts of the three financial institutions with the greater share of these deposits.
TBD (*Taxa Base de Desconto*)	Discount rate of the Bank of Portugal.
TBA (*Taxa Base Anual*)	Nominal semi-annual rate, announced by the Bank of Portugal, corresponding to the average annual effective rate weighted by the amounts of the last 12 T-bill auctions of all maturities.
APB (90/180 days) (*Associação Portuguesa de Bancos*)	Rate announced by the Portuguese Banking Association equivalent to the simple arithmetic average of prime rates given by the eight financial institutions for each maturity (the highest and lowest rates are excluded).
Lisbor – Lisbon Interbank Offered Rate (One, three, six months and one year)	Average interbank offer rate of the eight major banks (excludes the two highest and lowest rates) for each tenor, and announced on a daily basis on Reuters page LBOA at 11am.

Source: Banco Essi.

first by a sovereign was the Republic of Ireland in 1993. The market has grown strongly since July 1994 when the need for prior authorisation from the Treasury was abolished (see Exhibit 12.8).

Maturities for this type of debt range from three to 10 years, and most issues are fixed rate notes. The first floating rate note indexed to Lisbor was issued in 1995.

Commercial paper

Portuguese and foreign companies can issue commercial paper (promissory notes with a fixed maturity of less than one year) provided they fulfil the following conditions or the issuer presents a bank guarantee:

- minimum capitalisation of Esc1 billion or the foreign currency equivalent;
- profits made in the last three years; and
- rated by an agency registered with the stock market regulatory body.

The minimum volume for each issue is Esc10 million. Most issues are made on a discount basis.

Exhibit 12.8

Navigator bond issues, 1988–96 (Esc billion)

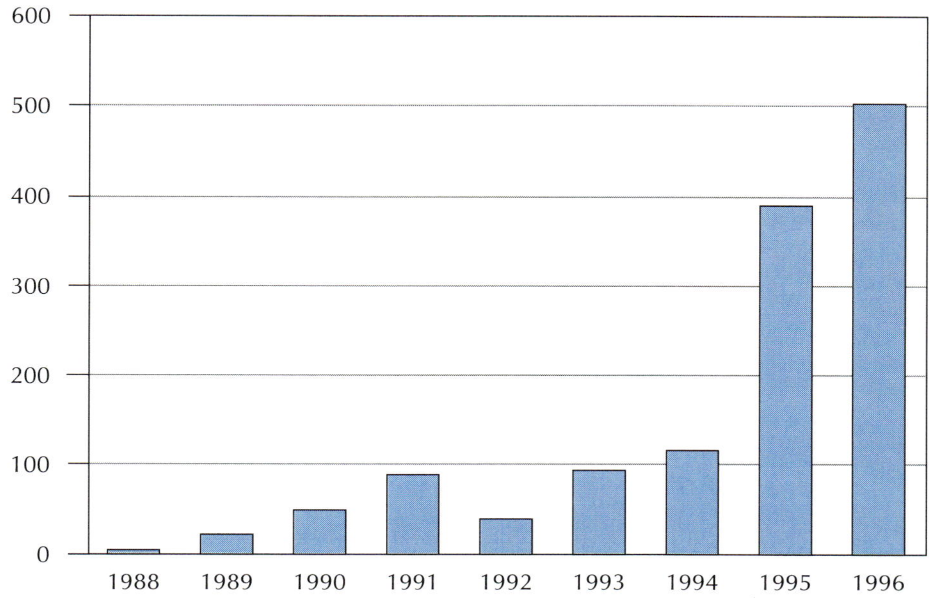

Source: Banco Cisf.

13

THE DERIVATIVES MARKET

Portugal launched a futures and options market in 1996 when the more than 100 years old Oporto Stock Exchange, housed in an impressive neo-classical building in the old city, ceased to operate and derivatives began to be traded in a new tower block in another part of the city. The tiny market trades futures contracts on a purpose-designed 20-share index, the PSI-20, on a 10-year notional Treasury bond (OT10) and on Lisbor 3-months (see Exhibit 13.1). The previous lack of a derivatives market had sidelined a large number of investors because they were unable to hedge their positions. The timing was fortunate: the Portuguese equity market was one of the best performers in Europe in 1996.

The market is modelled on Spain's very successful Meff, which since 1990 has been one of the fastest-growing European derivatives markets. Barcelona, where futures and options on Spanish bond and money-market contracts are traded, assisted Oporto with the technology for fully-automated trading (which allows trading to be done anywhere in the country) and an integrated clearing system. Lisbon is the only cash market (the equities that had been listed only in Oporto were transferred to Lisbon).

The Oporto market intends to gradually expand the range of contracts traded. A repo market and short-selling are expected to be introduced. Foreign investors, in particular, will be more tempted into the Portuguese financial markets as they can now hedge escudo investments.

Trading has been thin. In its 82 trading days in 1996, 11,222 contracts on the 3-month Lisbor rate were traded with a value of Esc1.1 trillion. The daily trading volumes, however, have been irregular, fluctuating between zero and a maximum of 405 contracts. Open interest has been gradually increasing, to stand at 1,600 at the end of 1996. The more liquid contracts were the longer-dated ones, particularly the June and September 1997 contracts.

The average number of contracts traded on the PSI-20 index was 622 in 1996, with the great majority of operations being speculative, although open interest showed an upward trend (possibly reflecting the increasing number of hedging operations). Liquidity averaged Esc320 million a day in 1996. The low level of liquidity can be explained by the lack of liquidity in the underlying market, and particularly of some of the shares in the PSI-20 index. As a result, arbitrage movements that generate most of the futures market liquidity in more developed markets were difficult to implement, a

Exhibit 13.1

Contract summary

	OT10	*PS120*	*Three-month Lisbor*
Contract size	Esc10,000,000	Esc100 × Index	Esc100 × Index
Underlying asset	Domestic 10-year government bond with an 8 per cent coupon rate	PS120 Portuguese Stock Index	Three-month Lisfra
Tick size	One basis point	1 index point	1 basis point
Maximum daily price fluctuation	+/- 140 ticks	+/- 120 ticks	+/- 40 ticks
Initial margin/contract	Esc400,000	Esc35,000	Esc300,000
Daily settlement price	Weighted average of the prices of the last 12 deals of the trading session	Weighted average of the prices of the last 12 deals of the trading session	Weighted average of the prices of the last 12 deals of the trading session
Contract months	March, June, September, December	Current month, following month and next month of the March, June, Sep-tember, December cycle.	March, June, September, December
Last trading day (T)	Two working days before third Wednesday of the contract month	Third Friday of contract month	Two working days before third Wednesday of the contract month
Settlement method	Physical delivery	Cash settlement	Cash settlement
Settlement price at maturity	NA	Average of 30 index values calculated with 1 minute intervals on the first 30 minutes of the last 45 minutes of the cash market session	NA
Deliverables	Fixed-rate government bonds with maturities of not less than 6.5 years*		

* OT 10.625% Jun-03; OT 8.875% Jan-04; OT 11.875% Feb-05; OT 9.500% Feb-06.

Source: Banco Essi.

poor correlation between the PSI- 20 index and the corresponding futures contracts. The contracts with the highest liquidity were those closest to maturity.

Banks, as well as brokers and dealers, can be both trading and clearing members of the exchange.[1]

Bids are introduced into computer terminals located on the premises of market participants and are then fed into a central computer on the premises of the managers, where they are matched with bids pending on the market. The IT system known as SEND immediately broadcasts the operation resulting from the matching of

[1] This chapter draws extensively on reports by Banco Santander de Negocios Portugal and Banco Essi for technical details and operational procedures.

two bids of opposite signs or, provided that the type of bid used so permits, the balance awaiting fulfilment. In addition to ensuring the deal and its disclosure, SEND also automatically calculates the financial movements connected with the user- member, allowing real-time monitoring and providing, in relation to prices prevailing on the market at any given moment, full information: margins to be deposited on open positions, either the member's own or those of his customers; daily adjustments to be made; gains or losses realised on closing positions; charges owed on the operations; or premiums payable to option sellers.

SEND provides front-end users with real-time information and dealing capabilities on: market transactions, including best bids and offers by price and volume; positions by account holders; status of pending orders and modifying and cancelling of orders.

Market members can introduce a wide range of buy or sell orders using SEND (see Exhibit 13.2).

There are also market maker orders (equal to two limited orders – one buy and one sell – for the same contract maturity) and straddle orders (equal to immediate limited orders – one buy and one sell – for two different contracts or two different maturities of the same contract).

The trading limits applied to clearing members are:

Daily operational limit Margin requirements due at the end of the trading session may not exceed the permanent guarantee.

Exhibit 13.2
Types of offers

Name	*Price limit*	*Amount*	*Date*
Limited	Specified	Partial amounts accepted	Non-executed balance remains pending
Limited immediate	Specified	Partial amounts accepted	Non-executed balance cancelled
Attack	Not specified initially. After acceptance, specified by best price	Partial amounts accepted	Non-executed balance cancelled
Best	Not specified. All prices accepted	Partial amounts accepted	Non-executed balance cancelled
Stop (loss/gain)	Triggered when last trade price reaches trigger price and then becomes a best offer	Partial amounts accepted	Non-executed balance cancelled
Limited stop (loss/gain)	Same as stop but a limited offer is generated instead.	Partial amounts accepted	Non-executed balance remains pending
All or nothing	Specified	All or nothing	Cancelled if not executed immediately

Source: Banco Essi.

Global risk exposure	Overall margin requirements may not exceed 30 per cent of the institutions' net worth.
Position concentration	Overall position in a contract including customer positions and trading member positions cannot exceed one-third of open interest.

The concentration limits applied to individual customers by themselves or in association with other parties are:

- no investor may hold more than 5 per cent of the open interest in each contract maturity;
- no investor may hold positions representing more than 4 per cent of the capitalisation value of the underlying deliverables; and
- in the case of contracts on indexes, no investor may hold positions representing more than 1 per cent of annual turnover of the underlying assets of the index.

The clearing house intervenes as a counterpart in deals made, playing the role of buyer *vis-à-vis* the seller and of seller *vis-à-vis* the buyer and, once the deal is closed, it manages the resulting positions, conducting the operation settlement, position-clearing and credit-risk control.

The system of guarantees (see Exhibit 13.3) rests on daily adjustment of gains and losses; initial and extraordinary margins; maximum price fluctuation limits; permanent guarantee and operating limits and additional clearing guarantee. All guarantees have to be in the form of cash deposited at the account held by the Oporto Derivatives Exchange Association (ABDP) at the Bank of Portugal, or by a number of selected Portuguese government bonds deposited in the ABDP account at the clearing house.

Exhibit 13.3
Types of guarantee

Type	*When due*	*Purpose*	*Amount*
Initial margin	Upon registering contracts and delivered before opening of next trading session	Cover own default risk	Depending on contracts
Extraordinary margin	Upon request of ABDP to all holders of open positions	Cover own default risk	Depending on contracts
Permanent guarantee	Upon becoming member of next trading session	Cover own default risk	At least Esc20 million*
Additional guarantee	Upon becoming member and revised quarterly of next trading session	Cover default risk of other clearing members	Esc5–240 million depending upon volumes

* Depends upon margins due by clearing member in one session – has to cover overnight risk.

Source: Banco Essi.

Operational procedures

A customer may request the opening of more than one account or sub-account with the same or with different clearing or trading members. At each bank a futures account is represented by a five-digit code as defined by the Oporto Derivatives Exchange. The first three digits represent the account holder, and the last two its different sub-accounts. Sub-accounts of the same account will always offset initial margin requirements on a consolidated basis. Revaluation adjustments, however, will always be made at the individual sub-account level. If a customer has two different accounts – eg, proprietary and customer – then initial margin requirements will not offset between them.

A client who works through various members may request the opening of an account specifically for the purposes of consolidating and clearing positions to which all the trade executed by other members will be automatically transferred. In order to implement this automatic procedure of transfer of executed trades, transitory or give-up accounts need to be created with other members. At the same time, a global account has to be created to consolidate all executed transactions, becoming the automatic recipient of all transactions executed in related give-up accounts.

The market has quickly proved its usefulness. Whether it has a life after European monetary union and the launch of a single currency will depend on the market's ability to be innovative. Alliances with the Spanish and Brazilian derivatives markets are one possibility to guarantee survival.

14

SECURITIES AND STOCK EXCHANGE REGULATIONS

Introduction

After several decades of stagnation, which reflected the lack of dynamism of the economic policies then prevailing in Portugal, the Portuguese stock market experienced significant growth in the years following 1972. At that time the market's regulatory system could be found mostly in two statutes, the old Commercial Code of 1898 and the Decree of 10 October 1901. However, the system was obviously inadequate for an active modern market, having been designed for a relatively inaccessible market dominated by the wealthy Portuguese bourgeoisie of the late 19th century.

Legislative Decree No. 8/74, which came into force in January 1974, thoroughly reformed the operations of the market and the activities of brokers. It was a comprehensive and general statute, intended as a response to increasing demand and as an instrument for creating a modern market, but before it could be fully implemented the revolution of 25 April 1974 led to the closing of the two Portuguese stock exchanges.

Their reopening two years later had no real meaning, since the conditions which would have encouraged the growth of the capital market did not exist. Portugal was entering one of the worst economic crises in its history; the political atmosphere in which the Constitution of 1976 was drawn up was hostile to the development of private enterprise or capitalist markets; foreign disinvestment was increasing; and the traumatic experiences of those who had invested between 1972 and 1974 still exerted a decisive influence over their thinking. It was only after 1985, when an upturn of the economic cycle began, that real development of the capital market occurred, creating (by Portuguese standards) boom conditions which attracted foreign institutional investors alongside very strong participation by domestic investors. Against this background the regulations provided in Decree No. 8/74 already appeared old-fashioned, both in comparison with other European markets and in view of the actual needs of the Portuguese stock market.

It was clear that a thorough reform of the regulatory system was required. The work of a specialised committee under the National Securities Market Council led to the formulation and enactment of the Securities Market Code as Legislative Decree No. 142/A of 10 April 1991. The Code (also known as the Sapateiro Law, after the jurist who chaired the committee) is now one of the principal statutes to be reckoned with in the field of Portuguese securities law, on a par with the Commercial Companies Code enacted in 1986.

Regulatory agencies

The key regulatory agencies in Portugal – those individuals or entities, public or private, which are responsible for the organisation and functioning of the securities markets, controls over the activities performed on such markets, and the fulfilment of applicable legal and regulatory applicable provisions – are the Securities Market Commission (*Comissão do Mercado de Valores Mobiliários*, or CMVM), the National Securities Market Council (*Conselho Nacional do Mercado de Valores Mobiliários*, or CNMVM), the Clearing House (*Central de Valores Mobiliários*) and the two stock exchanges.

The Securities Market Commission

The Securities Market Commission (referred to as "the Commission" throughout this chapter) is a public regulatory authority with administrative and financial autonomy and with its own assets, subject to the supervision of the Ministry for Finance. It is responsible for the development and supervision of the Portuguese securities market and is therefore in charge of the general functions of regulation, supervision, control and promotion of the securities market and the activities performed, directly or indirectly, on it by all agents. To enable the Commission to exercise its duties it has been entrusted with extensive powers, some of which are quasi-judicial.

The Commission has a board of directors, charged with exercising those powers; a consultancy board, which gives opinions on matters presented by the board of directors and brings forward any proposals it may find appropriate to the proper functioning of the markets; and a control and supervisory commission, which is responsible for supervising the financial and accounting operations of the Commission itself.

The Commission's regulatory powers enable it to propose new legislation to the Ministry for Finance and to issue its own regulations and technical rules. Its supervisory powers in relation to market orientation and coordination give it a position of outstanding importance, corresponding to the traditional functions of any capital markets commission, and making it an arbitrator among the participants in the market; it also has an important role in relation to insider trading and market manipulation, ensuring application of the appropriate penalties. Its powers in relation to promoting the development of the securities market include giving operational support, providing incentives and developing research, publications, training and similar activities.

The Commission has a leading role in the functioning of the market through its control over the whole range of market participants. It oversees the work of the stock exchange associations, the stock exchanges and their management and control bodies; the institutions that organise, manage, operate or control other secondary markets; and those that operate special systems of stock exchange transactions or transactions in other secondary markets, settlement and clearing of the correspondent transactions, securities deposit or assembly registration and control, and other similar systems and services; financial intermediaries. It also has control powers in relation to issuers (with the exception of the Republic of Portugal itself) and investors. In connection with the exercise of its control powers over these entities the Commission operates a special service which receives any reports and complaints that may be presented by any investor, or any other interested party, regarding illegal or irregular acts or related incidents in the securities market.

In addition, the Commission cooperates with the corresponding authorities of other member states of the European Union and of any other states and also assists the government and the Ministry for Finance in all matters relating to the securities market.

The National Securities Market Council

The National Securities Market Council is a consultative body of the Ministry for Finance, created by the Securities Market Code. It is chaired by the minister and includes representatives of several organisations participating in the market. It has power to give opinions on the general policies of the government that either directly concern the securities market or have a significant impact on it; on any law relating to the securities market; on the regulations through which the Ministry for Finance exercises powers under the Code (in cases where the law requires prior consultation with the Council); on the creation and closing of stock exchanges; and on the creation of new types of markets, entities, intermediaries or financial instruments within the securities market. In addition the Council gives its opinion, on a regular basis, on the condition and evolution of the securities market and presents appropriate recommendations and suggestions for improving its structure and operation.

The Clearing House

The Clearing House was created by the stock exchange associations with the compulsory affiliation of financial intermediaries. It supervises the administration and functioning both of the registration and control system for uncertificated securities and of the deposit and control system for registered securities. It also creates the necessary conditions for completing the physical clearing of purchase and sale operations regarding uncertificated and registered securities executed on the stock exchanges and in other secondary markets. The Clearing House is thus the appropriate entity for the financial settlement of transactions. It may also undertake the safekeeping, on behalf of affiliated financial intermediaries, of all or part of the registered securities deposited with them at any given time.

The stock exchanges and the stock exchange associations

The two stock exchanges, in Lisbon and Oporto, are financial establishments providing facilities and systems endowed with the necessary means for the creation and operation of a free open market for the purchase and sale of securities in appropriate conditions of efficiency, continuity and liquidity. By themselves or through third parties they ensure that appropriate registration, compensation and clearing services are provided and they must disclose detailed and up-to-date information concerning securities transactions.

It should be noted that both exchanges were created and are administered and maintained by the stock exchange associations, which are non-profitmaking bodies under private law. They too are subject to authorisation from the Ministry for Finance, after consultation with the National Securities Market Council and the Commission, and to subsequent registration with the Commission. Apart from creating, administering and maintaining the exchanges, the associations are also in charge of promoting the liberalisation and integration of the securities market in general, and, in particular, the appropriate development, improvement and modernisation of the structures and operational systems of the stock markets; promoting and controlling the intermediary securities services within the exchanges; and promoting the application of savings to securities.

Each association has a general meeting, a board of directors, a delegate director and a statutory audit committee. The regulatory powers vested in these associations allow them to control the activities of those associated in them (whether members of the exchange or not) as well as the directors, managers, representatives and their assistants, and other workers or representatives of exchange members, in relation to their obligations within the exchange, and any other individuals directly connected with them. They may also control the activities of any individual on the exchange, to ensure compliance with the rules governing their activities and the general order and discipline of the market.

Issuing securities

Registration procedures

It is important to distinguish between certificated and uncertificated securities, and, within the certificated category, between registered and bearer securities.

Uncertificated securities

The introduction of uncertificated securities was one of the main innovations of the Securities Market Code and was aimed at bringing Portuguese legislation closer to other systems and providing an incentive to further growth of the securities market. Uncertificated securities do not have order numbers and are realised by inscription in accounts opened in the names of the respective holders, through which their nature, characteristics and legal situation are proved. All operations and rights regarding such securities are processed and registered by means of entries and appropriate notes in such accounts. On the date that an account is opened the account is considered to be a common subscription account. It is only converted into an uncertificated securities registration account once the acts and formalities required by special legislation for the incorporation of the securities have been completed (provided that no such acts or formalities have already been completed before the opening date).

The registration and control system for uncertificated securities is jointly operated by the issuers, the Clearing House and the financial intermediaries (such as credit institutions and finance companies) authorised and registered by the Commission for the rendering of such services. Stock exchange transactions in uncertificated securities require intermediation by a financial institution authorised to operate transfers in an electronic environment by credit to the buyer's account and by debit to the seller's account. The uncertificated securities must either be blocked in the respective accounts by the financial intermediary, or reported in specific sub-accounts of the general accounts of the respective holders. These rules also apply, with the necessary adaptations, to transactions on the over-the-counter market and on the special secondary markets, provided that the uncertificated securities meet the conditions legally necessary for transactions in those markets.

The Clearing House and the financial intermediaries are subject to the rules of client's privilege (professional secrecy) regarding the registrations themselves, the corresponding facts and all the documents on which the registrations are based.

In addition, and without prejudice to the supervision and control duties and specific responsibilities of the Clearing House, the Commission is responsible for the general supervision of the functioning of the registration and control system for uncertificated securities, as well as the activities of the institutions operating within it.

Unless resulting from the victim's fault, and without prejudice to any disciplinary or criminal sanctions, the financial intermediaries in charge of the uncertificated registration services are liable for all damages suffered by the securities owners, by holders or beneficiaries of other rights, burdens, restrictions or bindings existing on such securities, or by third parties, as a result of irregularities, deficiencies, mistakes or delays in the execution of such registrations.

The Ministry for Finance is responsible, on the initiative of the Commission and in consultation with it, for issuing regulations governing the organisation and functioning of the registration and control system for uncertificated securities.

Authorisation of securities issues

Securities may only be issued by corporate entities or other public or private entities for which authorisation has been given by general or special legislation or by their own articles of association. Issues of securities do not otherwise depend on administrative authorisation, apart from two categories of issue which must be authorised by the General Directorate of the Treasury (*Direcção Geral do Tesouro*, or DGT), notwithstanding that such authorisation is within the competence of the Ministry for Finance. The two categories are: issues which, because of the nature of the securities or the activities of the issuers, are expressly dependent on authorisation under special legislation; and issues submitted for authorisation by the Ministry for Finance in the national interest or in the general interests of the market.

Further, for the purposes of administrative or statistical information, and without prejudice to the legal powers of the Bank of Portugal in relation to foreign exchange matters, the following issues may depend on the submission of a prior declaration to the Ministry for Finance: issues to be executed in Portugal and expressed in a foreign currency; issues to be executed in Portugal by public or private entities not resident in the country; and issues to be executed in foreign markets by public or private entities which are resident in Portugal.

Subscriptions for securities

Subscriptions for securities may be public or private, direct or indirect. Under the terms of the Securities Market Code a public subscription is one which is offered to an indeterminate number of people, or to a determinate number of people not identified in advance, by any means of public trading, or in which securities are issued by public subscription companies or offered simultaneously for public and private subscription. All other subscriptions are considered private, including subscriptions of shares corresponding to capital increases by conversion of shareholders' loans into stock capital or by entries in assets different from money – provided that, in the latter case, there is no public securities transaction offer – as well as subscriptions of shares resulting from the transformation, merger or demerger of the issuer.

A subscription is considered to be direct when the offer to investors is directly made by the issuer, with or without the support, or the partial or total guarantee of placement, of authorised intermediaries. It is considered to be indirect when the issue is subscribed by one or more financial intermediaries obliged to offer it to investors on the terms and conditions set forth in a contract entered into with the issuer for that purpose. The form of a subscription is defined either in the statute or regulation under which the issue is authorised, or at the time of placement, according to the market circumstances and the best interests of the issuer, by the appropriate administrative body.

Documentation, marketing and distribution

The placement of an issue with investors can be carried out by the issuer itself or through authorised financial intermediaries.

Duties of intermediaries

Marketing by financial intermediaries is compulsory for any issue with a public subscription. A market-making contract must be agreed between the issuer and the intermediaries, to define the intermediaries' duties and obligations in compliance with the administrative rules of the Commission. In this contract the intermediaries undertake to underwrite the issue; to guarantee its placing in whole or in part; to buy any securities subject to guarantee which are not subscribed for by investors; and to place the issue, without commitment to subscribe any part not subscribed for by the public.

Financial intermediaries also have important duties in relation to the registration procedure. They must examine and assess, jointly with the issuer, the feasibility and appropriateness of the issue and its conditions, in particular regarding issue price. They must prepare, or revise and reformulate where necessary, the drafts of the prospectus and the advertisement launching the public offer. They may demand from the issuer all documents, studies or other essential data and must make every effort to check that the information contained in the prospectus and other relevant information given to the market, with their intermediation, during the period of registration and placing of the issue, is sufficient, true, objective and up to date. They must also organise and submit the issue registration application to the Commission, assist the issuer in all subsequent procedures and agree the issue timetable with the issuer.

Financial intermediaries may group together in order to place any securities issue. Under the Securities Market Code the contract in such cases must be a group or consortium contract, under which the intermediaries act as a placing syndicate.

Registration documentation

Any public offer for subscription in the Portuguese market requires prior registration with the Commission. An application to register must be accompanied by the following documents:

- a copy of the minutes or resolutions of the board of directors of the issuer;
- documents proving that all necessary administrative authorisations, registrations or prior declarations on which the issue depends have been granted;

- an up-to-date copy of the issuer's by-laws;
- a certificate from the Commercial Registry or, when the entity is not subject to commercial registration, an equivalent document, proving the existence and the date of incorporation of the issuer, the amount of its registered capital, and the identities of all the members of its administrative and supervisory bodies;
- reports of the issuer's board of directors, the accounts, the opinions of the supervisory body, and legal certification regarding the accounts for the last three accounting periods, whenever the entity is legally obliged to supply these documents;
- a copy of the market-making contract entered into with the financial intermediary or intermediaries in charge of the issue distribution;
- a copy of the liquidity contract, if any, provided that it is not part of the market-making contract;
- a draft of the issue prospectus; and
- a draft of the advertisement regarding the public offer for subscription.

If the issue is intended for the incorporation of a company, the application to register must also be accompanied by:

- a declaration identifying all those responsible for the company's incorporation;
- a document showing the number and value of the subscribed and fully paid shares held by each of those responsible;
- a certified copy of the complete project for the company's incorporation;
- a certificate proving that the project has received provisional registration; and
- a study of the technical, economic and financial feasibility of the issuer or the specific undertaking in question.

The issue prospectus

The issue prospectus must contain all information that, according to the nature of the issuer and of the securities, may be reasonably regarded as necessary for investors to form a grounded judgement on the issuer's activities, registered capital, financial situation, results, perspectives and other relevant characteristics, as well as on the rights inherent in the securities. The prospectus should thus include, for example, information about the entities responsible for publishing it, details of the terms and conditions of the issue, legal identification of the issuer, a description of the issuer's activities and financial statements, including balance sheets and accounts for the last three years.

The legal entities responsible for the validity, adequacy and accuracy of the information contained in the prospectus are the issuer, the members of its board of directors, the members of its audit board or equivalent, the chartered accountants certifying the accounts in the prospectus, any persons mentioned in the prospectus as having participated in its preparation, the managers and the underwriters.

Both the issue prospectus and advertisement concerning the public offer for subscription must be jointly published in a national newspaper, in stock exchange quotation reports and in brochures that may be freely obtained by the interested parties from the registered offices of the issuer and intermediaries, the open establishments of the intermediaries and the Portuguese stock exchanges. Publication must take place, at the latest, on the working day before the date fixed for the beginning of the subscription.

Advertising

The Commission must notify the fact of registration to the issuer and to the financial intermediary or syndicate in charge of market-making. From the notification date the interested party must make every effort to complete all necessary procedures for market-making. Publicity for any public offer must be approved by the Commission before it can be published, provided that approval is assumed if the Commission has not made a decision within five days after receiving the material to be published. Advertising relating to the issue placement may only begin following the publication of the advertisement concerning the public offer for subscription and the issue prospectus, unless the Commission authorises prior publicity on certain conditions and within limits established for the purpose. Any publicity issued in disregard of these requirements may attract criminal penalties. In any case the entities responsible for such illicit publicity must indemnify the investors for any damage caused by their activities.

Withdrawal or cancellation of public offers

Following the beginning of the subscription period a public offer for securities subscription may only be withdrawn with authorisation from the Commission and must be justified by abnormal and unforeseeable changes in the circumstances on which the issuer based its decision to carry out the operation. At any time the Commission may cancel the operation, order the withdrawal of the offer or forbid it whenever the offer breaches any applicable regulations or involves fraud.

Non-domestic issuers

The issue and placement on the Portuguese market of any securities of non-resident issuers require prior authorisation from the Ministry for Finance and the Bank of Portugal.

In order to be acceptable to the Portuguese authorities any prospectus published by an issuer from another member state of the European Union (EU) must have been approved by the relevant authorities of the issuer's home state and may only be published in relation to:

- a public offer for subscription or sale occurring at the same time, or within a short period, both in Portugal and in another EU country;
- admission to official quotation in another EU country occurring at the same time as, or within a short period before or after, the public offer for subscription or sale in Portugal or the admission to listing on a Portuguese market; or
- a public offer for subscription or sale in another EU country less than three months before the admission to listing on the Portuguese official market.

The prospectus must be translated into Portuguese and must include references to the managers in charge of rendering financial services to the issuer, the tax treatment of securities in Portugal and the publication of advertisements to investors.

Market intermediaries

Under the Securities Market Code financial intermediaries are private or public, individual or corporate entities authorised to operate in the securities market by carrying out activities of financial securities intermediation. However, although the Fifth Title of the Code is headed "Financial Intermediaries", it applies only to private entities, since the Bank of Portugal and other public bodies are governed by separate and specific regulations.

Definition of intermediation activities

The following activities, when carried out on a professional basis, are considered as activities of financial securities intermediation:

- receiving and executing investors' orders concerning securities subscriptions or transactions;
- dealing in securities on one's own account;
- canvassing and advising investors in subscriptions, purchases, sales, exchange or other securities operations, as well as clients of any other securities intermediation services;
- placing securities issued by any entities on the primary market;
- rendering services in relation to the organisation, registration, launching and execution of public offers for securities transactions;
- opening and operating certificated securities deposit accounts and registration of uncertificated securities, as well as rendering services concerning the rights inherent in them;
- managing securities portfolios owned by third parties and executing portfolio operations as and when authorised by their holders;
- creating and administering real estate and securities investment funds and performing trustee duties relating to securities belonging to such funds;
- providing consultancy on securities investments; and
- rendering any other securities-related services to issuers, offerors or investors, provided that such services are permitted under the applicable regulations.

Authorisation of intermediaries

The incorporation of financial intermediaries and the conducting of any of the activities listed above require prior authorisation by the Ministry for Finance or, in cases where its powers have been delegated, by the Bank of Portugal or the Commission. Authorisation depends on certain conditions: the intermediary must possess its own financial resources in sufficient amounts for, and the organisational, human and material resources technically appropriate to, the type and volume of activities to be performed. The individuals in charge of the direction and supervision of the internal activities of the company must be competent, must possess appropriate experience in performing such activities and must not be incapable of, or prohibited from, performing their duties under the terms of the Securities Market Code. Anyone applying for authorisation must provide the necessary documents to confirm these conditions, any documents specified in the regulations regarding each category of financial intermediaries and any other documents that may be laid down as necessary in an administrative ruling by the Ministry for Finance. In addition the applicant must provide a statement of the intended activities, the main operations to be executed, the services to be rendered within the scope of those activities and the internal structure of the company.

An authorisation to incorporate a financial intermediary automatically includes authorisation to perform the intermediation activities allowed by the applicable regulations, provided that each activity is specified in the articles of association of the intermediary. Any alteration in these articles of association is itself subject to prior authorisation by the Bank of Portugal unless it is the result of a merger, a split or a modification of the objects of the intermediary. In these cases the alteration, like the event which leads to it, depends on authorisation by the Ministry for Finance.

Deeds of incorporation or alteration of the articles of association cannot be executed unless it is proved before a notary that the required authorisations have been obtained beforehand. It should be noted that authorisations are nullified in cases of express waiver by applicants; failure to begin the activity within 12 months after the date of the authorisation notice; or failure to incorporate the financial intermediary within six months after that date.

Registration of intermediaries

A financial intermediary can begin carrying out intermediation activities once it has been duly registered with the Bank of Portugal and the Commission. An application for registration must be submitted to the Bank within 30 days after the date of the authorisation notice, or, in cases of incorporation, after the definite incorporation date, and must provide the following information about the intermediary:

- its trading name;
- the date of its incorporation, in the case of corporate entities;
- its professional headquarters or main registered offices;
- the intermediation activities it is authorised to carry out;
- its registered capital;
- the identities of (for corporate entities) the members of its administrative and supervisory bodies, or (for individual entities) those responsible for the administration and supervision of the authorised activities;
- the identities of its agents with administrative powers; and
- the location and date of creation of any branches, subsidiaries, agencies or delegations, and their respective registered capital.

In the case of a financial intermediary with main registered offices in a foreign country, the application for registration must also provide the date on which it was authorised to establish or to begin operating in Portugal, the capital with which it operates, the identities of those responsible for the representation, administration and supervision of its activities in Portugal, and the location of the main premises, branches, agencies, subsidiaries and other representations in Portugal.

Once an intermediary authorised to conduct activities in Portugal has been registered, the Bank of Portugal sends a copy of the registration to the Commission in order to effect simultaneous registration with both institutions.

Regulation of intermediaries

The regulatory powers vested in the Commission allow it to issue regulations and technical rules on intermediation activities, setting out, for example, the prudential limits to the execution of operations by authorised intermediaries in order to guarantee their solvency. Intermediaries are subject to the principles of lawfulness, truth, objectivity, opportunity and clarity whenever they give any information (including any kind of publicity) to the public, to clients or to regulatory authorities. They must carry out their activities bearing in mind their duty to reinforce investors' trust in the securities market by operating with commercial probity, in order to ensure the regular functioning, the transparency and the credibility of the market. They must also ensure high levels of competence and diligence in performing services to clients and must ensure equality of treatment for all clients.

Client's privilege

Financial intermediaries, those responsible for their administration and supervision, other employees, their agents and any other person that renders services for intermediaries, whether on a permanent or an occasional basis, are all subject to the rule of client's privilege regarding operations executed and services rendered to clients, as well as regarding information about them, or about third parties, acquired while carrying out intermediation activities.

Without prejudice to other sanctions foreseen in the Securities Market Code, any breach of the rules set out in the Code itself, in applicable regulations or in Commission rules obliges an intermediary to indemnify all damage suffered by third parties as a result of the violation. According to the general requirements of civil liability established in the Civil Code, damage can include violation of rights or protected interests, actual material damage, acts causally linked to damage, unlawful conduct and negligence (except where the law expressly provides for no-fault liability).

Exchange listing

In order to be traded on a stock exchange, securities must be admitted to listing and registered by the competent authority, and they must be fully paid up, free of any charges, and not subject to any restriction or limitation on rights or conveyance. Under the Securities Market Code the securities admitted to trading are the following:

- domestic and foreign government stocks, and securities comparable to them;
- shares and bonds, including cash bonds, issued by companies and other domestic or foreign entities;

- equity securities;
- close-ended investment trust units;
- other securities tradeable on the exchange under rulings issued by the Ministry for Finance after consultation with the Commission; and
- any economic rights detachable from any of the securities listed, or created in relation to them, and capable of being traded independently (such as warranties).

The admission of government stocks to trading on an exchange depends on an order from the Ministry for Finance, but the admission of any other securities requires a prior decision from the competent authorities, confirming that all the applicable legal and regulatory conditions have been met.

Securities issued by international financial entities or international organisations may also be listed on a stock exchange, provided that a schedule has been established by the Ministry for Finance after consultation with the Bank of Portugal and the Commission.

The stock market in Portugal has three sectors: the main board, known as the market with official quotations (MOC); the second market (SM); and the unlisted securities market (UM).

The market with official quotations (MOC)

The MOC is a nationwide market resulting from the linking of the two Portuguese stock exchanges by a single computer trading system. The admission of securities to this market is subject to the decision of the Ministry for Finance, unless compulsorily required by law, but the MOC also imposes its own strict rules for admission, which also govern the performance of all subsequent duties related to the market and to mandatory publication of information.

Conditions for admission to listing

The admission of shares to listing on the MOC depends on the following conditions (among others). The issuer must have been incorporated and operating, under the terms of applicable legislation, for at least two full years, and must provide proof that it is in a healthy and appropriate economic and financial condition. The expected market capitalisation of the shares must not be less than the limit imposed by the Commission and by the time of admission to listing there must be a sufficient spread of shares among investors, of not less than 25 per cent of the registered paid-up capital.

Similar conditions apply to the admission of bonds to listing, with two important variations. The amount of the bond loan cannot be less than the limit established by the Commission; and proof must be provided that the payment of capital and bond interest is reasonably guaranteed.

Convertible bonds and bonds or other securities which give rights to shares subscription or acquisition may only be admitted to quotation provided that the shares into which the bonds and securities are converted are either already listed on the MOC or will be admitted to listing simultaneously.

Any entity which already has securities listed on the MOC and wishes to issue new securities of the same nature and category must apply to have them listed within 90 days after the date of their issue. This period may be extended by the Commission if requested by the issuer.

The admission and readmission of any securities to listing on the MOC, when such admission does not result from a legal provision or does not depend on a decision from the Ministry for Finance, depends on a decision to be taken by the stock exchange associations following a request from interested parties represented on the exchange where admission is sought.

An application for admission to listing must mandatorily contain all the information and explanations necessary for the association to assess the application and any additional information may be asked for by the appropriate exchange if considered necessary for the purposes of assessment. The decision on the application must be notified to the applicants within six months after the date of the application, or after the date of the receipt of the last documents called for during the application process.

Admission to listing may be refused on the grounds that the applicant is ineligible; that any document, information or explanation has not been provided; that the documents or resolutions, acts or facts aimed to be certified, registered or marketed do not accord with applicable legal and regulatory provisions; that the issue has not been properly approved by the competent officials or bodies of the issuer; or that the project has not been approved by the competent authority. In addition, the admission to listing of securities already listed in another EU member state may be refused whenever the issuer has not respected the duties arising from admission in that state. Any of these faults or defects may be rectified by the applicants within a reasonable period laid down by the competent stock exchange association.

The prospectus for admission to listing

Domestic and foreign government stocks; bonds or other securities issued by companies benefiting from a state monopoly; and shares resulting from a capital increase by reserves incorporation issued by a company which already owns shares of the same category may all be admitted to listing without prospectus. For any other securities for which listing on the MOC is sought the issuer must publish a prospectus duly approved by the Ministry for Finance after consultation with the Commission, or by the Commission alone according to the case, before transactions can begin.

The prospectus must include, for example, information about the entities responsible for its contents, details of the terms and conditions of the issue, the legal identification of the issuer, a description of the issuer's activities and a statement of the nature, amount and characteristics of the securities to be admitted to listing. In addition, the prospectus must include the conclusions of the auditor's report, as well as those of a study on the technical, economic and financial viability of the issuer, and it cannot be published before being approved by the competent authority.

After the approval, and without prejudice to other forms of publication used by the issuer (in particular by means of publicity in one or more newspapers with a large circulation in Portugal), the prospectus must be published by means of a brochure that may be freely obtained by any interested party among the general public from the registered offices of the issuer, the intermediary in charge of managing the securities in question and the stock exchanges. The complete text of the prospectus should also be simultaneously reproduced in the exchange's official list. Publication must take place at least eight working days before the beginning of trading in the securities.

Seeking admission to listing on a foreign exchange

If admission to listing on a foreign exchange is being sought and the securities are already listed on Portuguese exchanges, the issuer must provide the Portuguese exchanges and the Commission with the following information:

- a copy of the admission application and any documentation accompanying it;
- documents proving compliance with all legal and regulatory provisions regarding capital movements involved in the admission to listing on a foreign exchange and the consequent clearing and settlement;
- a copy of any relevant correspondence exchanged with the foreign authority competent to decide on the application and with the foreign authority in charge of the market; and
- information on the outcome of the application.

The second market (SM)

The SM is intended for securities issued by small and medium-sized companies and therefore its entry requirements are easier to meet than those imposed on the MOC as far as minimum capital, reserves and dispersion of capital are concerned. It also involves lower admission and maintenance costs for issuers, since admission to quotation in this market is the stock exchange's responsibility.

On the SM the requirements regarding listing conditions, permanence in the market and information to be given to competent authorities and to the public are also significantly fewer and less onerous than on the MOC. However, the quality of information provided to the authorities and to investors must not be lessened and conditions to ensure an acceptable minimum of regularity in market operation and appropriate prices must be created and maintained.

Securities eligible for listing on the SM may only be admitted and traded on one of the two Portuguese stock exchanges. The requirements for admission to listing on the SM are broadly the same as on the MOC.

Three years after the date of the definite admission of securities to listing on the SM, and with a view to transferring the securities from the SM to the MOC, the board of directors of each exchange analyses:

- the development of the market, the degree of liquidity and the regularity and transparency of securities transactions;
- the spread of securities among the public;
- the quality, regularity and punctuality of information disclosure by the issuer;
- the accuracy of all accounting systems and procedures for accounts control adopted by the issuer;
- the volume of the issuer's market capitalisation and its own capital; and
- its economic and financial situation.

The unlisted securities market (UM)

The UM was conceived to include securities that do not fulfil the listing requirements on either of the other two sectors of the stock market. Admission and information requirements for this market are generally less rigorous than those imposed in the other two markets, but a minimum level of information is required from issuers, in order to keep the market reasonably informed about the issuers and the securities.

Securities suspended or excluded from the MOC or the SM may be traded on the UM for a short period, under conditions laid down by the board of directors of the relevant exchange. The issuer must comply throughout the suspension period with all the provisions regarding information to which it was subject (on the MOC or the SM) before the suspension.

The prices on the UM are not considered as quotations for any legal purposes. The following securities may be traded on the UM:

- rights of subscription and incorporation rights regarding securities admitted to quotation in the MOC, the SM or the UM itself;
- securities excluded or suspended from the MOC or from the SM and which can be traded on the UM under the Securities Market Code;
- securities admitted to quotation on the SM on a conditional basis, during the period of the execution of capital operations or subsequently, provided that, in the latter case, the admission has expired and the trading of the securities in the UM is permitted by the competent authorities; and
- any other securities issued by domestic entities and admitted to listing on the UM by the board of directors of the appropriate stock exchange association.

Securities issued by foreign entities, whether EU or non-EU, may only be admitted to listing on the UM if all the conditions for admission of domestic securities of a similar nature have been verified. In respect of non-EU issuers (but not of issuers from other EU member states), the Portuguese authority competent to decide on admission may require that the securities to be listed are already quoted on a stock exchange in the country where the issuer has its registered offices, or on a stock exchange in the country where the securities were issued.

The over-the-counter market

The over-the-counter market comprises all securities purchases and sales executed outside the stock exchanges and the special secondary markets. The securities tradeable on the over-the-counter market include both securities not admitted to quotation on the exchanges or the special markets, and securities admitted to quotation on an exchange or a special market, whenever operations on such securities may be executed on other markets.

Futures and options

The Oporto Derivatives Exchange, which came into operation early in 1996, is administered by a managing authority which has power to license entities to operate in the derivatives market. The authority includes a compensation section which ensures registration, compensation and payment of all operations, as well as risk assessment of the operations in order to allow participants to adopt defensive measures.

During the first stage of its development the exchange will operate only with financial derivatives. Derivatives contracts must be prepared in writing and have the minimum content established by law.

Insider trading and disclosure of interest

Article 666 of the Securities Market Code governs insider trading and applies to members of the board of directors of a listed company, shareholders, other employees, consultants and any other person that, because of his or her occupation or public position, has knowledge of price- or risk-sensitive information, these individuals being considered "primary insiders" since they have direct access to information. The Code also establishes penalties for persons who have obtained unpublished sensitive information, directly or indirectly, from a primary insider.

The following actions connected with the use of price-sensitive information are strictly forbidden: acquiring shares in the company with which the information is connected; passing on information outside the circle in which the insider obtained the information; and asking another person – the so-called "tipee" – to buy the company's shares on the basis of information received.

Any breach of confidentiality by a primary insider is punishable by a term of imprisonment, not exceeding two years, and a fine. Any breach by a tipee is punishable by a term of imprisonment, not exceeding 18 months, and a fine.

It should be noted that, in relation to the placement of securities with Portuguese investors, both foreign and domestic issuers are equally subject to the provisions of Article 666 and must comply with the regulations in force and applicable to them.

Other related matters

Collective investment institutions and mutual funds

Under Legislative Decree No. 276/94, issued on 2 November 1994, collective investment institutions are institutions, with or without legal capacity, established to invest capital received from the public in securities portfolios. Mutual funds are collective investment institutions representing gatherings of assets owned by several individuals or corporate entities that are not responsible for the debts of the funds or of the fund management companies. The funds are divided into shares with similar characteristics – the trust units – and may be open-ended or close-ended funds, depending on whether there is a fixed or a variable amount of trust units.

The establishment of mutual funds in Portugal is subject to prior authorisation from the Commission after consultation with and approval by the Bank of Portugal. The management of a mutual fund must be undertaken by a fund management company, or by a credit institution if its own funds exceed Esc1.5 billion. The fund management company must be incorporated under the Portuguese Companies Code; it must take the form of a limited liability joint stock company; and its registered capital must be represented by registered shares or bearer registered shares.

Take-overs

The rules governing take-overs differ as between privately owned companies and companies under state control. The privatisation of state-owned companies takes place by means of a sale of shares representing its capital, or an increase of its registered capital through a public tender, an offer on a stock exchange or a public underwriting appeal.

As for private companies, there are two different types in Portugal: limited liability quota companies (*sociedades por quotas* or Lda) and limited liability joint stock companies (*sociedades anónimas* or SA). Transfers of participation in a quota company must be recorded in a deed of transfer of quotas, executed before a notary, and then registered at the competent commercial registry. Purchase and sale contracts for the transfer of shares in SAs are not subject to any specific contractual form and the transferee of bearer shares becomes a partner of the company without any prior registration. Nevertheless, the transmission of registered shares does require a written statement about the title and registration in the company's book. It should be noted that the company's articles of association may impose restrictions on transmission of registered shares by subjecting any transmission to the consent of the company. They can also give other existing shareholders a first option right to the transmission of registered shares and impose other restrictions in the interests of the company.

Take-over rules apply only to public SA companies, defined by law as companies with all or part of their registered capital distributed among the general public following incorporation by means of a public subscription, an increase in capital through a public subscription, listing on a stock exchange or being the target of a public offer or sale on a stock exchange. Public take-overs are governed by the Securities Market Code and by regulations issued by the Commission. A take-over offer may include shares in the company or convertible bonds or other securities conferring a right to underwrite or acquire shares of the company.

Take-over procedures

Public offers must be conducted by a financial adviser (a bank or a brokerage company) chosen by the offeror, which will act as its representative during the whole take-over procedure and will be responsible for preparing, announcing and implementing the offer. The offer may be in cash, securities or partly in cash and partly in securities. The offeror is allowed to present, as an alternative, a proposal in cash and one or more proposals in securities, or even mixed proposals, provided that they are not less than the highest price paid, directly or indirectly, by the offeror in the three months before the date of publication of the preliminary announcement of the bid. The execution of any public offer is subject to prior registration with the Commission and the offer period may range between 30 and 40 days, subject to the Commission's approval.

Take-over procedures are also subject to such general principles as freedom to make an offer without any prior administrative authorisation; equal treatment of shareholders in equal positions; timely disclosure of adequate, accurate and updated information; and simultaneous disclosure of the bid to the bearers of the securities covered by it.

All information and publicity related to the bid must be submitted to the Commission for prior approval and any person or entity involved with the bid who supplies any information is responsible for its contents. Any advertisements or similar publicity must comply with the rules of care required for the bid documentation and can only be issued to the public after the definitive announcement has been published.

Compulsory take-overs

The Securities Market Code requires that any individual or entity intending to acquire securities issued by a public company must make a take-over bid whenever:

- the purchaser already holds securities granting more than 50 per cent but less than two thirds of the voting rights of the company and intends to acquire in each calendar year securities granting more than 3 per cent of those voting rights, or to acquire securities which, added to those already held, would grant the purchaser two thirds or more of the voting rights; or
- the securities to be acquired, alone or added to those already held by the purchaser, will grant the latter more than 50 per cent of the voting rights corresponding to the capital of the company; or
- where neither of these situations applies, the securities to be acquired, alone or added to those held by the purchaser itself or by any third parties and which should be considered as held by the purchaser as of 1 January of the previous year, grant to the purchaser more than 20 per cent of the votes corresponding to the capital of the company.

In the first and third cases the bid may cover the amount of securities the bidder intends to acquire, as long as the minimum amount of 5 per cent is guaranteed, and in the second case the bid must cover all the securities of the company (including convertible bonds and other securities conferring a right to underwrite or acquire shares of the company at any title).

A compulsory full take-over offer must also be made where a person or other legal entity becomes the owner of shares conferring more than 50 per cent of the voting rights of the company, except where the participation was acquired pursuant to a full take-over offer previously made, or to a clearance granted by the Commission, or under a legal exemption provided for in the Securities Market Code, due to such events as acquisition of securities by inheritance or legacy; acquisition of shares, directly and indirectly, within a privatisation process; or a merger between two companies, provided that the merger project clearly states that, as a result of the merger, some shareholders will acquire a participation which would otherwise require them to issue a mandatory take-over bid.

In all these situations the purchaser is allowed to proceed without a take-over bid provided that, after completion of purchase, the Commission is informed.

Criminal or other sanctions apply to cases where the rules on compulsory take-over bids have been breached. The purchaser may be subject to a fine, imposed by the Commission, ranging between Esc500,000 and Esc300 million and to being banned for five years from exercising the rights attached to the acquired securities, while retaining the corresponding liabilities and being responsible for damages caused to the seller of the acquired securities and to the holders of securities which would have been covered by such an offer.

Mergers

Mergers between two or more companies are regulated by the Companies Code. The most important document to be prepared in a merger process is the merger project, which must be jointly prepared by the boards of directors of the companies involved. The merger project includes the references determined by law, sets out the features of the merger – in particular the measures to ensure protection of shareholders' and creditors' interests – and explains the economic and financial advantages arising from the proposed merger.

Mergers are subject to approval by the shareholders' meetings of the companies involved; execution of the required deeds before a notary; and registration with the commercial registries. It should be noted that 30 days must be allowed to pass before registration can be filed, to allow any opponents of the merger to express their views.

Legislative Decree No. 371/93, the Portuguese Competition Law, governs concerted practices, abuse of dominant position and merger control. Under its provisions all companies involved in a merger process, apart from credit or financial institutions or insurance companies, may be subject to merger control. This means that merger projects must be submitted for approval by the Portuguese Anti-trust Authority (DGCP), before completion of the transaction and/or before a take-over bid, in two types of situation: whenever the merger would create or strengthen a national market share of more than 30 per cent for a specific good or service; and whenever the enterprises which are to be merged had an aggregate turnover during the preceding corporate year exceeding Esc30 billion (net of taxes directly related to this aggregate turnover).

Tax considerations

The tax benefits provided in Portugal in relation to securities may be either dividends benefits or stamp duty benefits.

Dividends benefits

Under Article 31 of the Portuguese Fiscal Benefits Regime (EBF), dividends from securities admitted to stock exchange trading are subject to a more favourable fiscal regime, since only 50 per cent of their value is taken into consideration when applying income tax, whether for individuals or for companies. The expression "securities admitted to stock exchange trading" means that the relevant fiscal benefits cover not only securities admitted to listing on the Market with Official Quotations but also securities admitted to the Second Market and the Unlisted Market.

Circular No. 19/90, dated 6 April 1990, issued by the General Directorate of Contributions and Taxes (DGCI), establishes the benefit computation on the basis of income net of inheritance and gift tax (at 5 per cent). Following an amendment introduced by Legislative Decree No. 252/89 (August), the inheritance and gift tax by adjustment applies to all registered or bearer shares of companies with registered offices in Portuguese territory.

The tax regime for dividends from securities admitted to stock exchange trading operates as shown in Exhibit 14.1, taking gross dividends of 100 as an example.

Further, if the holder of the dividend is resident in a country with which Portugal

Exhibit 14.1

Tax regime for dividends from securities admitted to stock exchange trading

(Taking gross dividends of 100 as an example)	
As regards individual income tax	
Inheritance and gift tax by adjustment (100 × 5%)	5
Deduction foreseen in Article 31 of EBF (100 × 50%)	50
Income subject to taxation	50
As regards corporate income tax	
Inheritance and gift tax by adjustment (100 × 5%)	5
Deduction foreseen in Article 31 of EBF (100 × 50%)	50
Deduction foreseen in Article 45 of the Corporate Income Tax Code (CIRC) aiming to avoid double taxation of distributed dividends ((100 − 5 − 50) × 95%)	42.75
Profit subject to tax	2.25

(Article 45 of the CIRC applies only to the amount of dividends subject to taxation.)

has entered into an agreement to avoid double taxation (ADT), the tax due is the amount calculated according to the national provisions when, and only if, they are inferior or equal to the limit of the ADT.

On the other hand, if the profits are allocated by a company resident in Portuguese territory to a company resident in another EU member state – provided that the conditions set out in Article 2 of EU Directive 90/543 of 7 July 1990 (the Parent-subsidiary Directive) apply to both companies, and that the direct participation of the company abroad in the registered capital of the company in Portugal exceeds 25 per cent over two successive years – then the corporate income tax rate is 15 per cent until 31 December 1996 (without prejudice to any lower rate under the terms of the ADT in force); 10 per cent from 1 January 1997 to 31 December 1999; and 0 per cent from 1 January 2000 onwards.

Stamp duty exemptions

Under Article 1 of Legislative Decree No. 273/88, dated 3 August, stamp duty is not applied either to operations on securities executed in stock exchange sessions; or to the same operations executed out of stock exchanges regarding bonds or similar securities, provided that any of the participants is a credit or para-credit institution operating on its own account.

Conclusions

The Portuguese stock market is now recovering from the losses and investors' mistrust of past years, caused by such events as the 1989 exchange crash, and is showing a high rate of growth due to both external and internal factors. Non-residents' demand for shares is increasing, driven by rising confidence in the country and in its capital market; the portfolios managed by institutional investors in different parts of the world are becoming increasingly internationalised; the Portuguese external account is in a healthy condition; and the authorities are maintaining a stable foreign exchange policy. At the same time some Portuguese companies are growing within the increasingly integrated European Union, which encourages demand for their shares; and the government's privatisation programme is bringing more and more companies onto the market.

Against this background there have been several innovations in the Portuguese stock market, most notably, perhaps, the agreement between the two stock exchanges to cease dealing largely in the same securities. Instead, the Lisbon Stock Exchange is now the main location of the securities market while the Oporto exchange became the Oporto Derivatives Exchange (see above) at the beginning of 1996. In addition, liquidity contracts have been introduced and the Second Market has been enlarged, incorporating new companies and stock.

15

THE REGULATORY ENVIRONMENT

The legal system

The Portuguese legal system is based on the Roman-Germanic system and therefore may be characterised as being conceptualist, systematic and abstract. Law is intended as a model of social organisation.

Most common forms of business entities

General

Portuguese companies are mainly governed by the Portuguese Companies Code (Código das Sociedades Comerciais) and by the Securities Market Code (Código do Mercado de Valores Mobiliários).

There are two main forms to conduct corporate business operations in Portugal: (1) limited liability joint stock companies (sociedades anónimas – SA), hereinafter referred to as SA; and (2) limited liability quota companies (sociedades por quotas – LDA), hereinafter referred to as LDA.

As to SA companies whose shares are listed on the Portuguese Stock Exchange, there are special legal obligations that must be complied with.

Formalities

In order to incorporate a company (SA and LDA) in Portugal it is necessary to obtain a certificate from the Companies Registration Office (Registo Nacional de Pessoas Colectivas – RNPC) authorizing the use of the intended corporate name.

Following the deposit in a bank of the paid-up capital (in cash), a public deed of incorporation, including the by-laws, must be signed before a Notary Public by all shareholders or their duly empowered representatives.

However, after incorporation, the management of the newly incorporated company is entitled to withdraw the registered capital from the bank.

Contributions in kind are also accepted as payment of capital, but require a certificate of evaluation issued by an independent chartered accountant.

Subsequently, the company must file a statement at the local Tax Department, declaring the commencement of its activity, and register its incorporation (i) at the local Commercial Registry, (ii) at the RNPC and (iii) at the local Social Security Department.

The by-laws are published in the Official Gazette and in a local newspaper.

If any of the shareholders is a non-resident, the incorporation must be communicated, within 30 days, to ICEP – Investimentos, Comércio e Turismo de Portugal, a government agency which keeps records of foreign investments.

In some special cases and depending on the activities to be carried out, a prior authorization from ICEP may be required before incorporation.

Branch

An overseas company may conduct its business operations in Portugal by setting up a branch. For that purpose, as well as to determine the relevant scope of activities of the branch, the capital to be allocated and the appointment of a general representative of the company in Portugal for the branch, a resolution of the relevant corporate body of the parent company pursuant to its by-laws or the applicable legal provisions must be adopted. Subsequently, a request for the corporate name and permitted scope of activities of the branch must be filed with the RNPC. The company must also submit the registration of the branch to the local tax department and the Commercial Registry, including the by-laws and the resolution of the parent company published in the Official Gazette and in a local newspaper.

Corporate boards

In case of SA companies, two different management and control structures are alternatively stipulated: (i) a Board of Directors (Conselho de Administração) and a Fiscal Board (Conselho Fiscal); or (ii) a Board of Directors (Direcção), a General Board (Conselho Geral) and a public chartered accountant (Revisor Oficial de Contas).

As from early 1997, and should the shareholders so decide, the law allows the Fiscal Board to be replaced by a single supervisor (Fiscal Único), which must be a public chartered accountant.

The Board of Directors is composed by an odd number of members, as specified in the by-laws. Directors are either appointed on incorporation or elected by the shareholders' meeting, for a term set out in the by-laws that may not exceed four years; directors may be re-elected.

The Board is empowered to carry out the company's business and daily management powers may be delegated either to any director (Administrador-Delegado) or to a committee of directors (Comissão Executiva).

In principle, the Board meets monthly and the meetings require the presence (or representation) of the majority of the appointed Board members, the resolutions being adopted by the majority of the votes of those present or duly represented. However, for special cases, the law establishes and the by-laws may create special majorities.

In case of LDA companies, the management is entrusted to one or more managers who are not necessarily organized in a Board. The company may have any number of managers, as specified in the by-laws.

Managers are either appointed on incorporation or elected by the General Meeting. If no term is stipulated in the by-laws or in the respective election's resolution, the managers will remain in office until they resign or are replaced.

In certain cases, should LDA companies meet certain minimum requirements, the law demands such companies to have a Fiscal Board or a single supervisor to control the activities carried out by the management.

Shareholders and capital

In case of SA companies, a minimum of five shareholders is usually required. Shareholders may be national or foreign individuals or legal entities. The minimum share capital is Esc5,000,000 and at least 30 per cent of the contributions in cash must be paid up on incorporation.

All shares must have the same face value, which can not be less than Esc1,000. Shares may be nominative or to the bearer and are represented by certificates which may include one or more shares.

In case of LDA companies, a minimum of two partners was traditionaly required for the incorporation of this type of company; however, as from early 1997, LDAs are allowded to have one single "partner" as from its incorporation or at any time thereafter.

Partners may be national or foreign individuals or legal entities. The minimum registered capital for LDA companies is Esc400,000 and at least 50 per cent of the contributions must be paid up on incorporation (in any case, the amount corresponding to the minimum capital must be always paid up).

At the moment of incorporation, each partner has only one quota in the amount corresponding to his subscription. The value of each quota may differ but can not be less than Esc20,000. Quotas can not be materialized in certificates, and evidence of their ownership is to be found in the by-laws and in the Commercial Registry.

Reporting requirements

The following information has to be filed with the Companies Registration Office: the composition of its Board of Directors in case of an SA, or the name, marital status and address of the managers in case of a LDA; the address of its registered offices, changes to any of the above, to its corporate name, scope of activity, share capital in case of an SA, or registered capital in the case of an LDA, or to any provision of the by-laws, the annual reports and accounts.

Directors' liability

Directors have the fiduciary duty to act in good faith in the best interests of the company, and, therefore, are liable for damages caused to the company by their acts, omissions, or breach of their legal or contractual duties, unless they can prove that did not act negligently. Directors are also liable for damages caused to creditors of the company when, due to their negligent breach of legal or contractual rules established for the protection of creditors, the company's assets become insufficient to meet its debts. As regards damages to shareholders and third parties, directors are liable under the general terms of civil liability. Finally, directors are subsidiarily liable for tax and social security debts of the company relating to the period corresponding to their office, unless they can prove that it was not due to their acts or omissions that the company's assets became insufficient to meet tax debts. Directors' liability is joint and several.

Parent company liability

Since the branch office of a company does not have legal capacity, the parent company is always liable for all debts arising from its acts and omissions. As regards a subsidiary/affiliated company, and provided that the parent company holds more than 90 per cent of its registered capital, the parent company is liable for fulfilment of the subsidiary's obligations towards its creditors.

Annual cost of compliance

The administrative annual cost of ensuring that a company complies with the Portuguese Companies Code is not significant. From among the costs that can be incurred annually by the company we highlight the ones relating to the registration of the annual reports and accounts in the Commercial Registry and the mandatory publications in the Official Gazette and in a local newspaper.

Employment

Regulatory environment

The employment relationship between employers and employees is regulated by several different laws and regulations, which are very restrictive in view of the protection to be conferred to the employees and their rights. The main rules of Portuguese labour law are imperative and the respective rights of the employees may not be waived.

Labour contract

The contract does not require to be executed by means of a written document. However, employers have a general obligation to inform their employees, in writing, of the basic conditions of work. Exception to this rule is the execution of a fixed term contract (see below) whose validity depends also on its execution by means of a written document containing some mandatory points.

Fixed-term labour contract

Its execution is only allowed in the specific cases provided for in the law and may be only renewed twice to a maximum duration of two years. The termination of the contract at the end of one or any of its periods of validity does not have to be based on any unfulfilment of the employee but he must be informed in writing by the company with an eight-day prior notice of its intention not to renew the contract, failing which the contract shall be renewed for an identical period of time.

On termination employees shall be entitled to a compensation equivalent to two days of basic remuneration per each full month of duration of the same.

Dismissal

Employers are not allowed to terminate labour contracts with their employees without just cause, the general concept of which and the facts that may constitute major violation of the employees' duties are expressly specified in law.

In general, any behaviour of the employee that, by its relevance and consequences, actually and immediately makes the maintenance of the employment relationship impossible, shall constitute a just cause for dismissal, to be proved in a disciplinary procedure.

In case of unfair dismissal, the employee shall be entitled to receive all global remunerations since the dismissal and to an indemnity equivalent to one month of basic remuneration per each year of seniority, or his reinstatement, if he so elects.

Redundancy

Redundancy, individual or collective, may only occur as a result of economic, financial or technical difficulties suffered by the company and implying the elimination of the respective positions of work, such difficulties requiring to be proved within a mandatory procedure, under penalty of the redundancy being judicially declared null and void.

In any case, even if the redundancy is valid and effective, the employees involved shall always be entitled to a compensation equivalent to one month of basic remuneration per each year of seniority, but of no less than three months.

Working day/week

As from 1 December 1996, the maximum daily period of work is 8 hours and the maximum weekly period of work is 40 hours.

Overtime is permitted in specific cases provided that overtime is paid at a rate of 50 per cent above the remuneration for the first hour and 75 per cent for the following hours. The total overtime performed may not exceed 2 hours per day and 200 per year.

Holiday entitlement

Employees are entitled to 22 working days of paid holiday per year plus a holiday subsidy of an equivalent amount. On termination of the employment contract they are entitled to a holiday remuneration and respective subsidy calculated pro rata to the work performed during the year of termination.

Employees hired under fixed-term contracts whose duration does not exceed one year are entitled to paid holiday leave and a subsidy equivalent to two days of basic remuneration per each month of duration of the contract.

Minimum salary

In 1997, the general minimum salary is Esc56,700 and Esc51,450 for housekeeping activity.

Sick pay

In case of sickness the employee shall be entitled to a subsidy of 65 per cent of his remuneration paid by the Social Security Department up to a maximum period of 1,095 days.

Maternity leave

Women have the right to maternity leave of 98 days, during which they are entitled to receive a subsidy equivalent to 65 per cent of their remuneration paid by the Social Security Department. The dismissal of pregnant women, during their maternity leave or while breast feeding, is deemed to be unfair.

Paternity leave on the same terms is stipulated in the event of death, physical or mental disability of the woman, or should both parents so decide.

Cost of employment

Employers must subscribe and maintain a valid insurance policy covering all risks and damages caused to their employees resulting from work accidents.

A monthly contribution equivalent to 24.5 per cent of each employee's remuneration is due to be paid by the employer to the general social security system. The employee's monthly contribution is equivalent to 11 per cent of the remuneration.

Foreign employees

Non-EU nationals to be hired in Portugal require prior approval from the Ministry for Labour, or a simple work visa if the work period is expected not to exceed, in one year, three months per semester. Residence permits are required even for EU nationals, although the prior approval for their hiring is not required.

Employees' representation/ consultation

The Portuguese Constitution provides for the employees' rights in the relationship with their employers to be represented by work committees and/or by unions.

There is a general obligation of the employers, as required in several cases specified in the law, to inform the employee's representatives and to obtain their prior opinion regarding matters which may affect the employee's working conditions.

Income tax

The earnings of the employees are subject to income tax at a rate of 15 per cent (lower rate) up to Esc1,050,000 per year and to a rate of 40 per cent (higher rate) when exceeding Esc6,150,000 per year. Earnings below Esc793,800 per year are exempted from taxation.

In general, for tax purposes all earnings of employees domiciled in Portugal, regardless of their nationality, shall be subject to income tax in Portugal. Even the amounts earned abroad shall be subject to income tax unless exempted as a result of bilateral agreements between states to avoid double taxation.

Should the employee not be domiciled in Portugal for tax purposes, any amounts earned in the country shall be subject to income tax except in the event of exemption resulting from any bilateral agreement to avoid double taxation.

Marketing arrangements

Agents

In Portugal, agency agreements are ruled by Decree-Law 178/86 of 13 October and Decree-Law 118/93 of 13 April. Particular protection is given to agents.

With regard to termination of contracts, the "clients indemnity" aims at compensating the agent for the profits that his activity continues to provide to the other party after the termination of the contract. The termination of agency agreements is only envisaged for non-fixed term contracts. Minimum periods of notice are established.

Some specific circumstances allow the termination of agency agreements. The non-fulfilment of the contract's obligations entitles the non-defaulting party to compensation.

Distributorship

There are no specific Portuguese laws regarding distribution. Distribution agreements are regulated by the general competition provisions set forth in Decree-Law 371/93 of 29 October. It is worth noting that the provisions relating to anti-competitive agreements are drafted in a roughly similar way as Article 85 of the EC Treaty. Moreover, the Council for Competition – one of the Portuguese anti-trust authorities – has consistently held that the national provisions should be interpreted in a similar way as the correspondent Community provisions. Therefore, the EC regulations granting block exemptions to certain exclusive distribution and purchase agreements as well as to certain motor vehicle distribution agreements can provide valuable guidance to the compatibility of a distribution agreement with the relevant national rules.

Franchising

There are no specific Portuguese laws regarding franchising. The comments made above on distributorship fully apply to franchising, including EU block exemptions. Franchising agreements are regulated by the general competition provisions set forth in Decree-Law 371/93 of 29 October. It is worth noting that the provisions relating to anti-competitive agreements are drafted in a roughly similar way as Article 85 of the EC Treaty. Moreover, the Council for Competition has consistently held that the national provisions should be interpreted in a similar way as the correspondent Community provisions. Therefore, the EC regulation granting a block exemption to certain franchising agreements can provide valuable guidance to the compatibility of a franchising agreement with the relevant national rules.

Industrial property

Industrial property is basically governed by the Industrial Property Code (IPC) approved by Decree-Law 16/95 of 24 January and by several legislations in international law which seek to harmonize the existing legislation of the various subscribing countries in order to simplify, not only the means of protection of the different private rights but also to promote industrial investment and development. As regards industrial property we make special reference to patents and trademarks.

Patents

The Portuguese legal system has various provisions which are intended to protect patent rights, in particular:

- the Munich Convention of 5 October 1973, ratified by Portugal in October 1991, and which came into force on 1 January 1992;
- the Patent Cooperation Treaty (PCT), which came into force in January 1995; and
- the TRIPS Agreement, reached during the negotiations of the Uruguay Round, applicable to the Portuguese legal system since January 1996.

In order to comply with the period of protection for patents stipulated in TRIPS, the new Code increased this period from the previous 15 years (from the date of granting, as stipulated in the old Code) to 20 years from the date of the filing of the application.

A delicate problem was raised on the patents for which application had been filed prior to 1 June 1995 (the date on which the new Code came into force) and for which Article 3 of Decree-Law 16/95 of 24 January stipulated that they would be protected in accordance with the old Code, ie, only for 15 years from the date of granting. This contradicts the 20-year period from the date of application, as set out in Article 63 of the Munich Convention and Article 70 No. 2 of the TRIPS Agreement.

Confronted with an international reaction against the lack of implementation of this 20-year period, the National Institute of Industrial Property (NIIP) adopted the following rules:

(1) To implement the new period of 20 years as from the granting to the patents whose applications had been filed prior to the coming into force of the new Code, provided their expected duration, as from the date of granting, is less than 20 years from the date of the filing.

(2) Nevertheless, if the 15-year period from the date of granting leads to a duration exceeding 20 years from the date of the filing of the application, the 15-year period would prevail (this is in particular the case for patents that took many years to be granted).

In practical terms that position of NIIP corresponds, with certain "nuances", to the acceptance of the new and longer period of 20 years from the date of the filing of the applications.

Trademarks

In the Portuguese legal system, the regulations which govern trademarks are, in particular:

- Industrial Property Code – Decree-Law 16/95 of 24 January;
- Rule (EEC) No. 40/94 of 29 December 1993 relating to the Community trademark;
- Rule (EEC) No. 2868/95 of 13 December relating to the execution of Rule (EEC) No. 40/94 concerning the Community trademark;
- Madrid Agreement of 14 April 1891, revised in Stockholm on 14 June 1967 and altered on 2 October 1979, relating to the international trademark;
- Directive 89/104/EEC of 21 December 1988, which harmonizes the legislation of the EEC members in relation to trademarks;
- TRIPS Agreement;
- Paris Union Convention.

The new Code also permits the registering as trademarks of numbers or shapes of the products or their respective packages and even sounds and advertising slogans. Furthermore, the registration of descriptive generic signs as trademarks, which previously was not usually allowed, is now possible, as long as, in day-to-day commercial practice, they are capable of becoming effectively distinctive.

The new Code goes beyond the protection of well-known trademarks, by stipulating that the registration of a trademark can be refused if, despite it being meant for products or services different from those of a trademark that enjoys great prestige in Portugal or in the European Union, the intention of such registration is to take unfair advantage of this prestige.

In cases of alleged unfair competition, it is possible for the owner of a non-registered trademark (or of any other IP right) to take action against an infringer.

Copyright

In accordance with Article 1 of the Copyright Code (Código do Direito de Autor e Direitos Conexos) the intellectual creations of literary, scientific and artistic nature, expressed in any form, are considered works and are protected under the terms of this Code, which includes the protection of the authors' rights.

The copyright is forfeit 50 years after the death of the creator of the works.

Acquisitions

Regulatory environment

The first qualification to be made when considering the rules governing acquisitions of companies refers to ownership of the target company: whether it is privately owned or under state control.

Secondly, regulatory control will depend on the business of the target company and on whether a private acquisiton or a public acquisition is taking place.

Public acquisitions are highly regulated by the Securities Market Code (Código de Mercado de Valores Mobiliários).

Acquisiton of state-owned companies

Privatisation of state-owned companies is made through the sale of the shares representing the capital or the increase of the registered capital. As a rule, this sale or increase of the registered capital is made by means of a public tender, an offer on the stock exchange or a public underwriting. In particular circumstances, privatisation may be made by means of a limited tender or direct sale of the shares or direct underwriting of the shares representing the increase in capital.

Formalities for private acquisitons

Formalities for the acquisition of shares in an SA company will depend on the type of shares involved (nominative or in bearer form). The acquisiton of nominative and registered bearer shares in a target company requires the execution of "Modelos 5" (official form for transfer of shares), registration of the transfer in the share register book and endorsement on the respective shares certificate. Transfer of bearer shares (unless subject to registration requirements) may occur by simple delivery of the shares. It is normal, however, to have a sale and purchase agreement containing representations and warranties and indemnities.

Transfer of a participation in a LDA company must be recorded in a deed of assignment of "quotas" executed before a notary public, and will then have to be registered in the competent commercial registry.

Formalities for public acquisitions

Public takeovers are governed by the Securities Market Code (Código do Mercado de Valores Mobiliários) and by the regulations issued by the Securities and Exchange Commission (Comissão do Mercado de Valores Mobiliários). Takeover rules apply to public SA companies, defined by law as companies with part or all of their registered capital distributed among the public in general, either due to the fact that they were incorporated by means of an underwriting offer addressed to the public or increased their capital by means of such an offer or are listed on a stock exchange or were in the past the target of a public offer or sale on a stock exchange.

Takeover offers are governed in great detail in the Securities Market Code and the Securities and Exchange Commission regulations, containing extensive provisions regulating the conduct of a bid, covering, for example, the contents of the documents to be circulated and the bid timetable, and compliance therewith is under the supervision of the Securities and Exchange Commission.

Takeover procedures are governed by general principles such as freedom to make an offer without any prior administrative authorisation, equal treatment of shareholders in equal position, timely disclosure of adequate, accurate and updated information and simultaneous disclosure of the bid to the bearers of the securities covered by it.

Competition and anti-trust

General

The basic rules on competition law and policy were set forth in Article 81 (g) and (j) of the Constitution of the Portuguese Republic, enacted in 1976. These provisions were later modified in order to suppress their ideological content.

Article 81 (e), as amended in 1989, establishes that it is the state's duty to "eliminate and prevent the setting up of private monopolies and to oppose all economic power abuses, as well as any practices harmful to the general interest".

On the other hand, Article 81 (f), as amended in 1982, determines that the state should also "ensure a balanced competition between enterprises".

These declarations of principle were brought into force under the first Portuguese Competition Law, adopted in 1983 (Decree-Law 422/83 of 3 December). This law has been amended several times, most recently by Decree-Law 371/93 of 29 October, which introduced in the Portuguese legal order a set of rules very similar to the equivalent provisions of EU law.

Scope of Decree-Law 371/93

Article 1(2) of Decree-Law 371/93 establishes that "without prejudice to the international obligations of the Portuguese state, this Act applies to restrictions on competition which occur in the national territory or which may have an effect within it".

Anti-competitive agreements and concert practices

Pursuant to Article 2(1), "all agreements between enterprises, decisions by associations of enterprises and concerted practices, in whatever form, which have as their object or effect the prevention, distortion or restriction of competition in the national market or a part thereof are prohibited".

This provision, whose resemblance with Article 85(1) of the EU Treaty is evident, sets forth a large list of prohibited agreements and practices, including the following:

- directly or indirectly fixing purchase or selling prices or interfering with the setting of prices by the free market, leading to prices which are artificially high or low (Paragraph a);
- limiting or controlling production, distribution, technical development or investment (Paragraph c);
- sharing markets or sources of supply (Paragraph d); and
- applying, whether systematically or occasionally, dissimilar conditions, in respect of prices or otherwise, to equivalent transactions (Paragraph e).

Article 2(2) provides that "any agreements prohibited under this Article are void unless they are considered justified under the provisions of Article 5".

Paragraph 1 of this latter provision, whose function in the context of Portuguese competition law corresponds to that of Article 85(3) in the framework of EU competition law, determines that "restrictive practices on competition which contribute to improving the production or distribution of goods or services or to promoting technical or economic progress may be considered justified if:

(a) they allow consumers of those goods or services a fair share of the resulting benefits; and
(b) they do not impose on the enterprises concerned any restrictions which are not indispensable for the attainment of these objectives; and
(c) they do not afford the enterprises the possibility of eliminating competition in respect of a substantial part of the market of the goods and services in question".

In this context, Article 5(2) establishes that "practices provided for in Article 2 may be subject to prior evaluation by the Council for Competition [one of the Portuguese enforcement authorities], according to procedures to be established by Ministerial Order of the Minister for Trade".

Such ministerial order has, indeed, been enacted (Ministerial Order 1097/93 of 29 October). It provides the legal basis for the Council for Competition to grant negative clearances and individual exemptions to potentially anti-competitive agreements and practices.

It should be noted, in this context, that, much to the detriment of enterprises' legal certainty, Portuguese competition law does not provide for a system of block exemptions applicable to certain types of agreements and concerted practices, as is the case in EU law. Nevertheless, it should be stressed that the Council for Competition has consistently held that the national anti-trust rules must be interpreted in light of the EU anti-trust provisions – on which they are largely based – and bearing in mind the interpretation given to them by the European Commission and the European Courts.

In practice, this means that, if a certain agreement or concerted practice would theoretically fall under the scope of one of the EU block exemption regulations, it is very likely that it shall benefit from an individual exemption granted by the Council for Competition under Ministerial Order 1097/93.

Abuse of a dominant position

Article 3(1) of Decree-Law 371/93 establishes that "any abuse by one or more enterprises of a dominant position within the national market, or in a substantial part of it, which has as its object or effect the prevention, distortion or restriction of competition shall be prohibited".

Paragraph 2 moreover states that "a dominant market position for specific goods or services is constituted where:

(a) an enterprise operates in a market in which it is not exposed to significant competition or in which it has the predominant market share in relation to its competitors;
(b) two or more enterprises operate jointly in a market in which they are not exposed to significant competition or in which they have a predominant market share in relation to third parties".

Unlike Article 86 of the EU Treaty, Article 3(3) of Decree-Law 371/93 sets forth thresholds related to market share above which the existence of an individual or joint dominant position is to be presumed. The threshold is set at 30 per cent in the case of an enterprise acting individually and goes up to 50–65 per cent in the case of joint action by enterprises. Such presumption is, nevertheless, rebuttable by the consideration of "other factors affecting the enterprises and the market".

As to the actual existence of an abuse, Article 3(4) establishes that it "is deemed to have occured if any of the restrictive practices provided for in Article 2(1) occur".

Finally, it should be noted that Article 4 also forbids "the abuse, by one or more enterprises, of a position of economic dependence on that enterprise by a supplier or buyer as the result of the absence of an equivalent alternative, whereby the behaviour of the enterprise takes any of the forms provided for in Article 2(1)".

Mergers

The system of regulating mergers established by Decree-Law 371/93 follows the same principles as that of Council Regulation 4064/89.

Pursuant to Article 7, "prior notification is required where the proposed concentration fulfils one of the following conditions:

(a) the creation or strengthening, as a result of the concentration, of a share higher than 30 per cent of the national market in specific goods or services, or in a substantial part of it;
(b) the turnover in Portugal of the participating enterprises was more than Esc30 billion in the preceding financial year, after deduction of tax directly related to turnover".

Unlike as is established in Council Regulation 4064/89, "prior notification shall be given before the legal transactions putting the concentration into effect are concluded and before the announcement of any public bid" (Article 7(3)).

On the other hand, "any legal transaction establishing the concentration shall produce no legal effects until tacit or express authorisation is given" (Article 7(4)).

Pursuant to Article 34, decisions on merger operations shall be taken by the Minister for Trade alone, or jointly with the minister responsible for the economic activities affected by the merger.

It should finally be noted that the merger regulations do not apply to credit institutions, financial companies or insurance companies (Article 7(2)).

State aid

Pursuant to Article 11, "aid to enterprises granted by the state or any other public body must not restrict or have a significant effect on competition in the market or a part thereof".

Enforcement authorities

The enforcement of competition law rests with two authorities, the Directorate-General for Competition and Prices and the Council for Competition.

The Directorate-General for Competition and Prices, which is a governmental department, is the body entrusted with the powers to investigate prohibited practices and to undertake merger control.

The Council for Competition has the power to take decisions on alleged infringements to competition law and to impose fines on enterprises. Its members are appointed by the government.

It is noteworthy that there is no hierarchical relationship between the two authorities.

In cases relating to anti-competitive agreements, concerted practices or abuse of a dominant position, "an appeal against a decision of the Council for Competition lies with the Lisbon District Court" (Article 28(1)).

On the other hand, appeals against ministerial decisions taken in the context of mergers "shall be heard by the Supreme Administrative Court" (Article 35).

Conclusions

Overall, Portuguese competition law seems theoretically adequate to provide an effective protection to the functioning of markets.

Nevertheless, there are some problems at the level of implementation. Decisions on competition issues are not taken by independent authorities. In concentration and state aid cases, decisions are taken by members of the government, whereas in other cases such decisions rest with the Council for Competition, whose members are directly appointed by the government.

On the other hand, the system of judicial review established by Article 28(1) implies that a lengthy judicial process may often follow a decision by the Council for Competition. This provides firms holding dominant positions with a very strong bargaining position on competition issues, insofar as the threat of litigation over many years produces a deterrent effect on competing firms wishing to bring cases before the Directorate-General for Competition and Prices.

Product liability

The product liability Directive of 25 July 1985 implemented by national law – Decree-Law 383/89 of 6 November – plays a significant role in the protection of both health and safety and economic interests of consumers and is of major importance in this field.

Strict liability

The Directive makes the producer directly liable for damages caused by a defect in his product. Since there is no requirements to show evidence of fault, there is no need to prove a contractual relationship between the claimant and the producer. The Directive does not affect existing national laws of contractual or non contractual liability.

Producers

Producers include (i) the manufacturer of the finished product or a component part, the producer of any raw material and any person who by his trade mark presents himself as the producer (the so-called "own brander"), and (ii) the importer into the EU (any supplier of a defective product). The Directive does not affect existing national laws of non-contractual liability. Note that liability is strict, because the injured person needs not to prove fault, but not absolute since there are certain defences available.

Two or more persons liable for the same damage under the Directive are jointly and severally liable, although they may seek contribution from each other (Direito de Regresso)]. Thus, all individuals involved in the chain of production and supply of a product within the EU may be considered liable.

The term product covers all movables except agricultural products. Components, raw materials, electricity and new technology products are thus included.

A product is defective if it does not provide the safety which a person is entitled to expect, taking all circumstances into account, eg, the presentation of the product, its reasonably expected use and the time it was put into circulation.

The Directive expressly imposes on the claimant the requirement to prove the damage, the defect and the causal link between defect and damage.

Pursuant to Directive on general product safety of 29 June 1992 implemented by national law – Decree-Law 311/95 of 20 November – "a safe product" is deemed one that in a normal use or reasonably expected conditions, including duration, does not present any risks or presents reduced risks compatible with its use and it is considered acceptable according to a high level of health protection and safety, including without limitation:

- the characteristics of the product, in particular its composition;
- the effects on other products when it is reasonable to expect their joint use;
- the presentation, packaging, labelling, any instructions for use, assembly, preservation and elimination as well as any other indication or information of the producer; and
- those consumers experiencing more risks when using the product, specially children.

Limits of liability

The producer's liability is not reduced when the damage is caused both by a product's defect and by the act or omission of a third party. The producer's liability may, however, be reduced or even waived when the damage is caused both by a product's defect and by default of the injured person or someone for whom he is responsible. The producer's liability cannot be limited or excluded by a "provision", which may include notices as well as contractual terms.

The period for legal proceedings to recover damages under the Directive is prescribed in two ways: (i) it is limited to three years from the date on which the Claimant became aware or should have become aware of the damage, the defect or the identity of the producer (ii) rights granted by the Directive are extinguished after ten years from the date on which the producer placed in the market the actual product which caused the damage.

Legal proceedings must be started within both periods.

Monetary limit on total damages applying is Esc10 billion.

Dispute resolutions

The common forms of dispute resolution in Portugal are the recourse to judicial courts (litigation) and arbitration.

Litigation

The procedures for judicial disputes in matters of commercial nature are undergoing profound changes. Thus, like in many other European countries, commercial courts were to be created on 1 January 1997, where cases shall be decided by judges of specialized competencies.

The judicial proceedings are governed by a principle according to which the judge must rule on the basis of the stated facts and established evidence. Unlike, for example, the English system, in Portugal the parties are not obliged to disclose all the evidence they may have.

A case is started by the plaintiff presenting in written form all the relevant facts and an objective claim. All the defence arguments must be presented in the defendant's reply.

As court proceedings are slow by nature, the parties may resort to a summary and provisional regime for settlement of urgent issues, which remain dependent on the main lawsuit. This is called a *providência cautelar* (preventive injunction).

There are two degrees of appeal, and appeals are normally confined to questions of law.

The losing party bears the administrative costs of the court proceedings. There is no tradition in Portugal of the losing party having to pay for the successful party attorney's fees, unless this has been contractually provided for.

Arbitration

Portuguese law expressly provides for the recourse to arbitration as an alternative to the traditional judicial system. The Arbitration Court may decide according to the law or according to equity, as the parties may choose. Although usualy more expensive than the judicial system, there has been an increasing recourse to arbitration, as the law provides for a period of six months for the conclusion of a case.

The whole proceedings rest on two fundamental principles: that of equality between the parties, and the adversary system (a systematic obligation of hearing the opponent party).

Unless there is an express waiver by the parties, an arbitration award may be the object of appeal to the judicial court of second instance (Court of Appeal) and from there to the Supreme Court. However, even where the parties have waived the appeal, the losing party is given the right to request judicial annulment of the arbitration award, for formal reasons.

International disputes in Portugal are commonly submitted to arbitration according to the rules of the International Chamber of Commerce (ICC).

Arbitration awards can be enforced in the same manner as judicial sentences.

16

TAXATION

The Portuguese tax system is based on taxation of transactions and taxation of real increments in wealth. Wealth, once assembled, is not generally subject to tax.

Commercial transactions of goods and services are generally subject to Value Added Tax (VAT) under the harmonised rules of the European Council Directives. The most notable exceptions are commercial or private transactions on real estate, which attract Real Estate Transfer Tax (SISA) and Stamp Tax (SELO), and financial transactions, which attract various stamp taxes. Excise taxes apply on a variety of transactions of goods, such as automobiles, fuel, alcohol, spirits and tobacco.

Some transactions, particularly on real estate, are burdened by a hidden tax cost consisting of notarial and registration fees.

All forms of individual or personal income, including capital gains, are taxed under unified tax rules (IRS), which aggregate different income baskets to derive taxable income which is subject to progressive rates of tax. Collective entities are taxed on their net income at a flat corporation tax (IRC) rate.

Individuals and collective entities which are resident in Portugal are taxed on their worldwide income. Non-resident individuals and collective entities are taxed broadly on their Portuguese-source income.

Non-residents having no fixed installation or permanent establishment in Portugal are generally taxed on gross income at flat withholding tax rates. Otherwise, tax will generally apply on net income derived in Portugal.

Domestic tax rules are overridden by the rules of Treaties for the Avoidance of Double Taxation on Income (DTAs), which allocate the tax jurisdiction and provide for reduced withholding taxes for specific types of income derived in Portugal by residents of the following countries: Austria, Belgium, Bulgaria, Brazil, Finland, France, Germany, Ireland, Italy, Mozambique, Norway, Spain, Switzerland, UK and USA.

The impact of tax rules in general is mitigated by specific statutory exclusions, exemptions, reductions and deferrals (collectively, tax benefits). More permanent tax benefits are provided for under the code of a particular tax; less permanent tax benefits are grouped in the Tax Benefits Code (EBF); short-term tax benefits generally appear under specific statute.

Tax rules in general and tax benefits in particular tend to place a heavier tax burden on labour and business income than on passive investment income and capital gains.

Individual income tax (IRS)

An individual is deemed a resident when remaining in Portuguese territory more than 183 days in any given calendar year, or having the use of a dwelling in Portuguese territory at the end of any given calendar year which may imply his intention of using it as his habitual residence.

Resident individual persons are taxed on their worldwide household income. Taxable income is derived from the sum of the net income of all income baskets less personal allowances. Aggregate net income is taxed at progressive rates of tax, between 15 and 40 per cent. The higher tax bracket is reached at an income level of US$40,000.

Resident individuals may elect to be taxed on gross Portuguese-source investment income at flat rates of 20 per cent for interest on bank deposits and debt securities and 25 per cent for stock dividends.

Non-resident individuals are taxed on gross Portuguese-source income at the following domestic rates (rates in brackets provided under most DTAs):

dividend income	25% (10–15%)
interest income	20% (10–15%)
royalties	15% (5–10%)
labour, pension income	25%

Capital gains from disposal of real estate is 50 per cent excluded from tax; gains from disposal of financial assets are taxed at a flat rate of 10 per cent but are exempt from tax if assets have been held for more than 12 months. These rules apply to residents and non-residents alike.

Corporation tax (IRC)

Resident companies

Collective entities, including companies, having their registered office or effective place of management in Portugal are deemed resident for tax purposes.

Resident companies are taxed on their worldwide profits on an accruals basis. Taxable profits, including capital gains, are derived from accounting profits, with adjustments made for tax purposes. Tax losses are carried forward for six years.

Interest costs are generally deductible. Interest accrued to a foreign parent may be dissallowed if deemed to originate from thin capitalisation. A company is deemed thinly capitalised if foreign shareholder debt exceeds twice the foreign shareholder's equity.

The Tax Administration has wide-ranging powers to correct pricing between related entities which do not reflect arm's-length conditions. There is no body of rules or guidance on acceptable or established transfer pricing practice.

A resident company may be taxed on the undistributed earnings of an offshore subsidiary domiciled in a tax haven jurisdiction.

Profits, whether worldwide or branch profits (see below), are taxed at a flat corporation tax rate of 36 per cent. In most cases, a municipal (local) surcharge tax is levied on the amount of corporation tax assessed, at rates of up to 10 per cent, resulting in an aggregate tax burden of 39.6 per cent.

A participation exemption, consisting of a tax exclusion of 95 per cent of dividend income, applies to resident companies holding 25 per cent or more of a subsidiary resident in Portugal or in the EU and qualifying under the Parent-Subsidiary

Directive, if the participation is held for more than two years or since inception of the subsidiary. Companies incorporated as holding companies (SGPS) benefit from the participation exemption irrespective of the holding percentage or period.

Permanent Establishments (branches)

Non-resident companies having a permanent establishment (branch) in Portugal to which Portuguese-source income may be attributed will be taxed under most of the same rules and rates as resident companies, with the following particulars:

- Generally, attributable income is limited to income from Portuguese sources. Attributable costs may include a notional overhead allocation from head office.
- A branch may adopt the yearly accounting period of the foreign company for tax purposes. Where this period does not coincide with the calendar year, it can only be changed every five years.
- There is no tax on the repatriation of branch profits to the non-resident company's head office.

Non-residents with no permanent establishment

Non-resident companies with no permanent establishment in Portugal are taxed on Portuguese-source income at a general flat corporation tax rate of 25 per cent, except for certain types of income, which are taxed gross at the following domestic rates (rates in brackets provided under most DTAs):

dividend income	25% (10–15%)
interest income	20% (10–15%)
royalties	15–25% (5–10%)

Dividends from participations qualifying under the Parent-Subsidiary Directive are taxed at 10 per cent until 1999.

Interest derived from the financing of qualifying public interest projects may be exempt from tax.

Interest derived from certain government debt securities is exempt from tax.

Capital gains derived in Portugal are 50 per cent excluded from tax if derived from the disposal of real estate and totally exempt if derived from the disposal of Portuguese securities.

Madeira International Business Centre (MIBC)

Companies incorporated in the MIBC are resident in Portugal for all domestic tax purposes and for the purposes of most DTAs.

Under the Tax Benefits Code, MIBC companies, as well as MIBC branches of non-resident companies, are generally exempt from IRC on all foreign-source income.

Non-resident shareholders of MIBC companies are exempt from Portuguese tax on dividends and interest paid by those companies.

Non-resident persons are exempt from withholding tax on interest paid by an MIBC bank and on royalties paid by any MIBC entity.

Special tax on stock dividends

Dividends distributed by S.A. companies generally attract a substitute inheritance tax at the rate of 5 per cent. This tax is not reduced under any DTA nor under the Parent-Subsidiary Directive.

Payroll taxes

Dependent workers' salary attracts social security contributions at the rate of 11 per cent to the employee and 23.75 per cent to the employer.

Directors' pay attracts social security contributions at the rate of 10 per cent to the director and 21.25 per cent to the company.

Self-employed workers are subject to social security contributions on an elected income base.

Social security exemptions apply to foreign EU workers and directors seconded to Portugal and maintaining social security coverage in their country of origin.

Payroll taxes are tax deductible in determining taxable income for IRC and IRS purposes.

Real estate taxes

The acquisition of real estate for a consideration attracts Real Estate Transfer Tax (SISA) at the general rate of up to 10 per cent, as well as Stamp Tax (SELO) at the rate of 0.8 per cent and notarial and registration fees at marginal rates of 0.3 per cent each. The aggregate tax burden associated with the acquisition of real estate is therefore generally 11.4 per cent over the higher of purchase price or official tax value. Residential real estate as well as certain industrial sites benefit from reduced rates.

SISA will apply to the transfer of shares in a limited liability company (LDA) whose assets include real estate if 75 per cent of the share capital is concentrated in the hands of the acquiror. SISA will also apply in a merger or division of companies where real estate title passes from one company to another, and on contributions in real estate to the capital of a company. SISA will apply regardless of transfer of legal title, at the time of delivery of real estate.

SISA is due on the higher of the purchase price or consideration or official tax value.

The holding of real estate attracts Real Estate Holding Tax (CA) at rates varying according to location between 0.7 and 1.3 per cent per annum on the official tax value.

Real Estate Holding Tax is creditable against income tax due on real estate income.

Gift and inheritance tax

Gratuitous transfers of any goods or rights are subject to Gift and Inheritance Tax at progressive rates of tax. The notion of gratuitous transfer includes the write-off of debt. The transfer of shares by gift or inheritance is generally not liable to Gift and Inheritance Tax.

The marginal tax rate for transfers between unrelated persons is 50 per cent of the value of the transferred asset.

Gift and Inheritance Tax is borne by the beneficiary of the gift or inheritance.

Stamp taxes and capital duty

Stamp taxes apply on a myriad of transactions and documents, with particular emphasis on financial transactions and insurance premiums.

A selection of transactions and the respective rates include:

any loan or credit facility principal	0.5%
bank interest or commissions paid	4.0%
security and collateral	0.5%

Statutory capital is subject to a once-off capital duty equivalent at the marginal rate of 1.1 per cent.

Value Added Tax (VAT)

All commercial transactions of goods and services in general are subject to Value Added Tax (VAT). The general VAT rate is 17 per cent. Exports of goods, in general, are zero rated. Imports of goods suffer VAT on customs clearance. IntraEU supplies of goods are charged to VAT on arrival in Portugal through self-assessment by the acquirer on behalf of the supplier. Financial services and real estate transfers are VAT exempt.

17

PORTUGAL IN THE 1990S

It is fitting that Portugal, whose caravels led western Europe into a golden era of commercial and cultural expansion in the 15th century, should hold the last world fair of this century which opens in Lisbon on 22 May 1998. Expo '98 will mark the 500th anniversary of Vasco da Gama's discovery of the sea route to India and, appropriately, it will be dedicated to preserving the oceans that the country's navigators first explored. The fair can also be seen as a long-overdue recognition of the country's political and economic achievements since the downfall of the dictatorship in 1974. If all goes well, by the time the fair opens Portugal will be headed for the first division of European monetary union and riding on a wave of national self-confidence.

Expo should celebrate Portugal's role in establishing the first maritime contacts between Europe, Africa, Asia and Brazil.[1] The period between 1415, when the Portuguese conquered Ceuta on the northern Moroccan coast, and 1580, when Portugal was invaded by Philip II of Spain, was a crucial one in the formation of the modern world.

Expo '98

Reflecting the country's pragmatic and down to earth temperament, Expo '98 will be used to give part of Lisbon a major and much needed facelift. Unlike neighbouring Spain, which went over the top with its Expo '92 in Seville and planned to create a high-tech centre for Andalusia (the site today is something of a cathedral in the desert, and the hotels built for it are largely empty), Portugal's ambitions are less grandiose and more realistic. The Seville Expo made a massive loss amidst corruption allegations. Lisbon's model is Barcelona, which successfully used the 1992 Olympics to regenerate the city.

Expo '98 is transforming a derelict dockland area along a five-kilometre stretch of the Tagus in east Lisbon into a new residential and business hub, the construction of which will have a significant impact on the pace of Portugal's economic growth through investment and tourism receipts. The 10 million or so visitors expected are forecast to boost Portugal's tourism income by US$1.4 billion in 1998. A record 130–140 countries are expected to participate, though some, like New Zealand, had such a bad experience at Seville that its government – mistakenly seeing the Iberian peninsular as one unit – were hesitant about taking part.

[1] See Kenneth Maxwell's pamphlet, *Portuguese Travels and the Meeting of Civilisations* (Camoes Centre, 1991).

The government estimates that Expo and related developments will contribute an extra 3–6 per cent to GDP growth over the 1997–2010 period. The new 12 kilometre Vasco da Gama bridge across the Tagus will be completed before the opening, the Oriente station (designed by the same Spanish architect, Santiago Calatrava, who produced one of Seville's Expo bridges) will provide metro, railway, bus and taxi services, a direct link with the nearby airport, a car park and a shopping centre.

Financial dependence on the government for the Expo project is minimal. By the end of 1996 the state had granted US$3 million of the total US$1.5 billion investment cost, most of the land, which belonged to the port authority, and rights to build on it and sell plots. Borrowings enjoy the guarantee of the Republic and government-owned land on the site has been incorporated as equity for Expo Urbe, the company responsible for the project. More than 20 per cent of the land under its domain had been sold by the middle of 1996. Short-term borrowings have been used to build up debt, which was then consolidated with medium-term borrowings. These have funded expropriations, site preparation and development. In order to enhance the role of equity in the project and also to attract private sector funds, sub-projects, with attractive cash flow potentials, have been identified and used to create subsidiary companies with external partners. These companies also help to ensure post-Expo prosperity for the area.

As a large portion of Expo revenues will be received in a very short period of time – and not until 1998 – market borrowings are limited to a maturity in 1999 when a major consolidation borrowing programme is planned to take account of the final costs and revenues.

Expo's aquarium, the biggest in Europe which recreates the ecosystems of Antarctica, the coral reef of the Indian Ocean, the Atlantic and the Pacific, displaying 25,000 fish, birds and animals, will be kept as an attraction. The Utopia pavilion, dedicated to the myths and legends of the sea from Atlantis to Jules Verne, will be turned into a multi-purpose centre for cultural and sports events. The halls of the international area will become an exhibition centre. Unlike Seville, countries will not build their own pavilions and then face problems disposing of them but will be given space for their displays, which will then be removed.

Like Rome, Lisbon is a city built on hills; it then developed down towards the Tagus. The first area to gain importance was Belém, to the west, and the 18th-century downtown section. The city then turned its back on the river and developed northwards to create new service areas. As Lisbon was transformed into a metropolitan area, the oldest and noblest areas rapidly became congested and lost their indigenous residents. The city councillor responsible for traffic policy claimed in 1990 that Lisbon was a city of one million with the traffic problems of a metropolis of five million. Expo will adjust the urban balance, creating a new eastern area. Housing, a new business centre and shops are being built, as well as restaurants, schools, neighbourhood services and an 80-hectare park. By 2009 it is estimated that 18,000 people will be living in the Expo village and other residential areas on the site.

Prospects

The Portuguese economy is growing at a faster pace than the EU average, due to the upturn in consumption and investment. The country stands a good chance of meeting the Maastricht requirements and entering Emu from the outset, unless it is excluded for political reasons. The government conservatively forecasts growth of 3.3 per cent in 1997 and 3.5 per cent in 1998 (see Exhibit 17.1). Growth is being sustained by several big projects, most notably Ford and Volkswagen's joint production plant, the new Tagus road bridge and 1998's Expo, which alone was expected to provide 1–1.5 per cent of GDP growth in 1997 and 1998. The impact of these projects, however, will be considerably diminished by the end of the century and Portugal will then face tougher times; central European entrants to an enlarged EU which are poorer than Portugal will be repeating the claims on EU solidarity that Lisbon made when it joined the EU, and the country's traditional sectors such as textiles, clothing and shoes, which are big employers, will feel the full brunt of trade liberalisation.

As living standards continue to rise so Portugal's relatively cheap labour costs will cease to be the economy's main competitive advantage. This means that greater efforts are still needed to boost productivity and improve the quality of education. Once it is in Emu the Salazar policy of being "proudly alone" (less than three decades ago) will seem light years away.

Exhibit 17.1

Government's economic forecasts, 1997–2000 (%)

	1997	*1998*	*1999*	*2000*
Real GDP growth	3.3	3.5	3.3	3.3
Gross fixed capital investment growth	7.4	6.3	6.2	6.1
Domestic demand growth	3.5	3.3	3.2	3.2
Export growth	8.4	9.9	8.8	8.8
Import growth	8.0	8.4	7.7	7.7
Inflation	2.5	2.3	2.0	1.8
Budget deficit (% of GDP)	2.9	2.5	2.0	1.8
Public debt (% of GDP)	64.0	62.5	61.0	59.4

Source: Ministry of Finance.

THE CO-PUBLISHERS

Banco Espírito Santo's overview

Banco Espírito Santo e Comercial de Lisboa (BES) traces its origins back to the second half of the 19th century, when José Maria Espírito Santo Silva established a foreign exchange brokerage firm. This company was transformed into Banco Espírito Santo in March 1920.

Banco Espírito Santo grew rapidly and soon strengthened its roots on a nationwide scale. During the subsequent years, its branch network spread out all over Portugal, its share capital doubled and the assets rose to ten times the initial figure.

In October 1937, Banco Espírito Santo merged with Banco Comercial de Lisboa and the new institution was named Banco Espírito Santo e Comercial de Lisboa, SARL and was presided over by the banker Ricardo Ribeiro Espírito Santo Silva.

The course of political events which took place in Portugal in 1974 produced serious changes in the legal-economic structure of the main economic sectors. In March 1975, BES, like all other credit institutions, was nationalised and transformed into a state-owned company.

Within the more favourable political and economic environment of the 1980s, BES's activities regained dynamism and between 1980 and 1990, the number of branches rose from 110 to 171. The Bank's capital was raised from Esc1.2 billion to Esc40 billion and its assets increased from Esc156 to Esc1.197 billion.

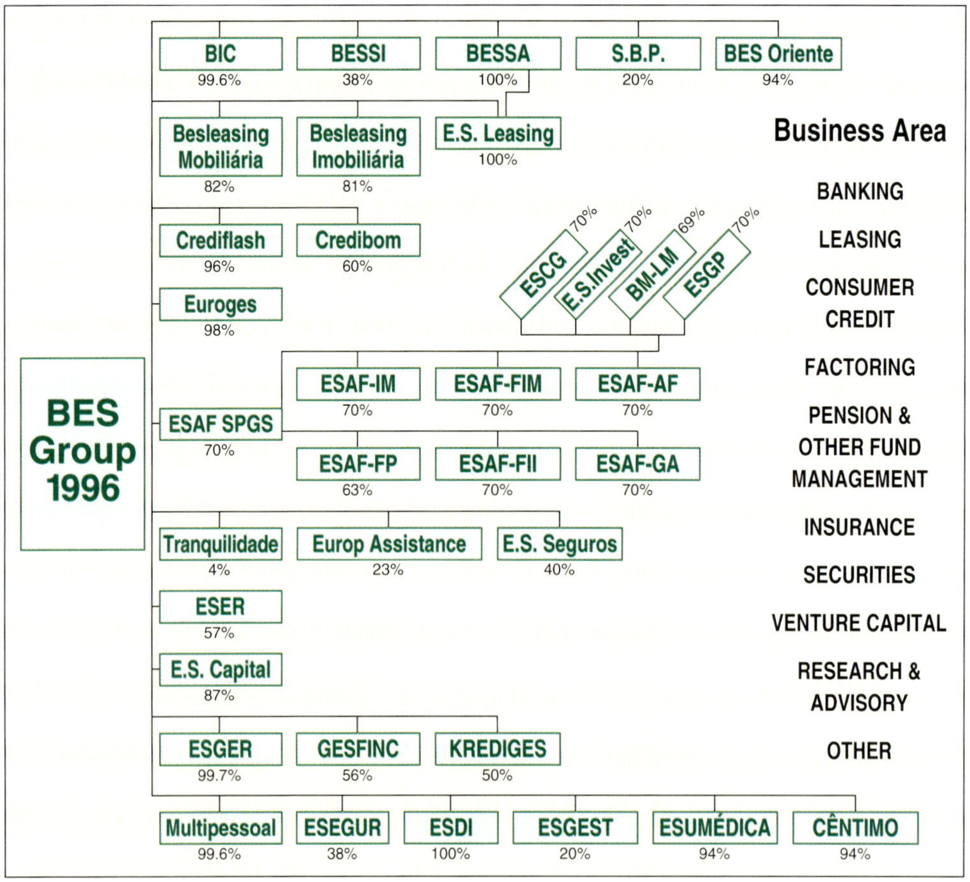

Reprivatisation - scope and mission

Since its reprivatisation in 1992, BES has consolidated its position at the centre of the BES Group, a global financial group offering an extensive range of quality services.

Whereas recent strategic developments in the Portuguese banking sector have led to increasing consolidation through acquisitions, the BES Group has decided to follow an organic growth strategy. This strategy enables it to achieve consolidated growth accompanied by appropriate levels of capitalisation and profitability.

The unique franchise of the Group, based on over 100 years of experience in the Portuguese economic and financial sectors, has enabled it to increase market share and secure good returns. Furthermore, since 1992 the BES Group has been able to build a consistent and well-balanced global financial group.

Retail banking

The Bank offers its retail customers more than a simple range of products and services; it seeks to provide a comprehensive service based on the cross-selling of products delivered by the various specialised financial companies of the BES Group.

The specific needs and profile of the Bank's high net worth individual customers urged BES to create a private banking department. The management structure responsible for this area of business operates alongside the traditional sales management structure, thus allowing an interchange of skills. Currently, the private banking network operates with 28 centres.

Mortgage loans and Personal Loans (upscale retail segment)	BIC
Life insurance, General accident insurance and Emergency assistance insurance	TRANQUILIDADE TRANQUILIDADE VIDA EUROP ASSISTANCE
Assets Management	ESAF
Credit Cards and Consumer Credit	CREDIFLASH CREDIBOM

Corporate banking

The highly professional and innovative approach that the Bank has adopted for the corporate sector has enhanced the Bank's positive image both among the major and the small and medium-sized corporations.

Emphasis on product quality is fundamental to BES's strategy, since it has enabled the Bank to foster customer loyalty and expand its customer base while allowing a fair reward for the value added to the services provided.

Due to the development of a global financial approach based on cross-selling, BES's corporate customers are able to find the best solution to their specific needs on a domestic or international level.

Commercial Banking	**BIC** BANCO ESPÍRITO SANTO (SPAIN) SOCIETÉ BANCAIRE DE PARIS (FRANCE) BES ORIENTE (MACAO)
Investment Banking and Project Finance	**BESSI**
Assets Management	**ESAF**
Leasing	**BESCLEASING** ESPIRITO SANTO LEASING (SPAIN)
Factoring	**EUROGES**
Brokerage	**ESER**
Outsourcing	**MULTIPESSOAL** **ESEGUR**
Research	**GESFINC**

Activity in 1996

The results achieved in 1996 are evidence of BES's competitive strategy.

Net profit surged to Esc23.6 billion – a 21 per cent increase relative to 1995. BES has posted the best financial performance, both in absolute and relative terms, among the publicly listed domestic banks.

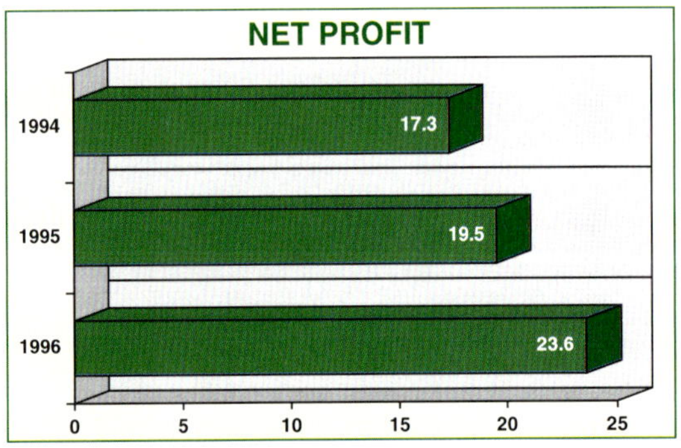

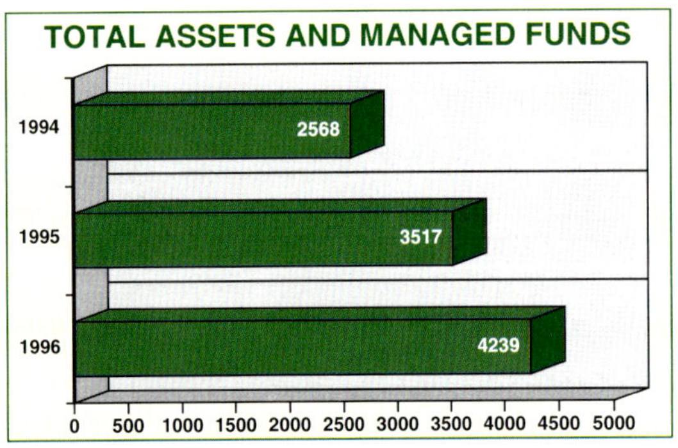

Profitability was clearly above the industry average, with the ROE reaching 18.6 per cent. Therefore, the BES Group remains among the most profitable European banks.

Consolidated net assets rose 19 per cent. As a result, the market share has increased by 1 p.p.

Together with business growth and high profitability, the BES Group has been able to improve its financial strength as well as asset quality.

At end-1996, the solvency ratio (BIS) was 11 per cent and overdue loans were equivalent to less than 3.4 per cent of the loan portfolio. In addition, BES has been consistently awarded the highest short- term and long-term ratings among Portuguese banks by Moody's and Standard and Poor's.

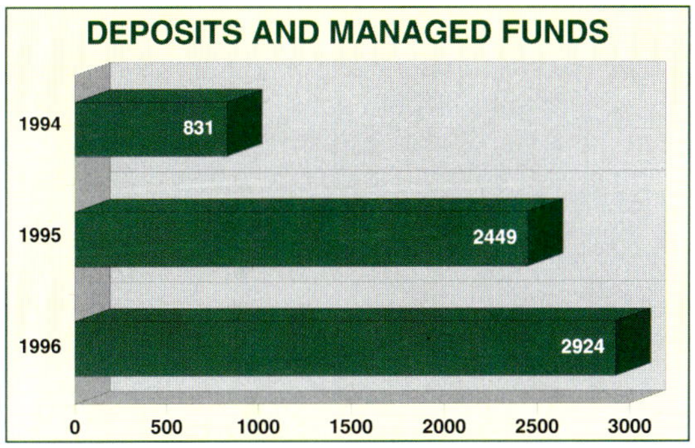

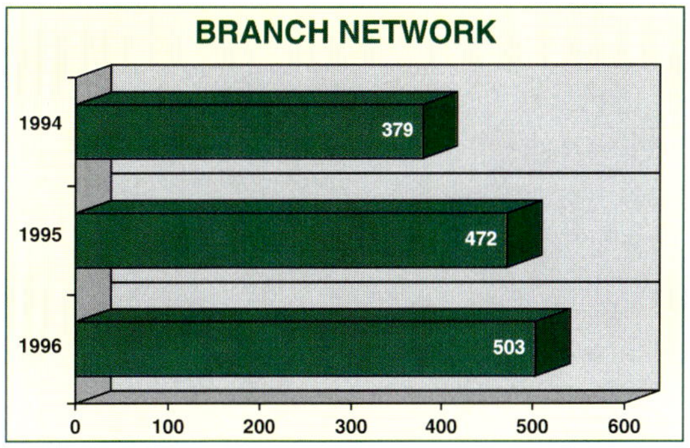

TRANQUILIDADE

Historical overview

Tranquilidade was founded in 1871, in Oporto under the name of "Companhia de Seguros Tranquilidade Portuense". The company was nationalised in 1975 and in December 1990 the company was reprivatised. (At that time Espírito Santo Group and Crédit Agricole took a majority stake through PARTRAN, a holding company.) Since then, the company has been consistently developing a competitive strategy which has enabled it to rank No.1 in global premium turnover (life and non-life) in the domestic market.

Strategic options

Since the reprivatisation, Tranquilidade has adopted a set of clear strategic guidelines:

• Repositioning of non-life business towards profitability rather than volume.

• Increased efficiency both in distribution and operations.

• Entrance into the life insurance market. This objective was accomplished through the creation in March 1994 of the life insurance company "Companhia de Seguros Tranquilidade Vida, s.a.".

• Increased cross-selling within the BES branch network. In order to promote cross-selling, a specialised company – Espírito Santo Seguros, s.a. – was created in March 1996 for non-life insurance products which aims to sell standardised products through the BES branch network.

• Internationalisation of activities. In October 1996, the Spanish life and non-life branch network of "Tranquilidade, s.a." and "Tranquilidade Vida, s.a." was launched.

Competitive position

The results achieved so far are encouraging:

• Tranquilidade ranks No.1 in the Portuguese insurance sector with a market share of 13 per cent.

• The company's outstanding results in the bank assurance business enabled it to achieve a market share of 17 per cent in the life insurance business.

• Net profit has grown steadily since 1992. In 1996, net profit rose by 24.7 per cent to Esc2.549 billion.

• Return on equity rose from 1.5 per cent in 1992 to 10 per cent in 1996.

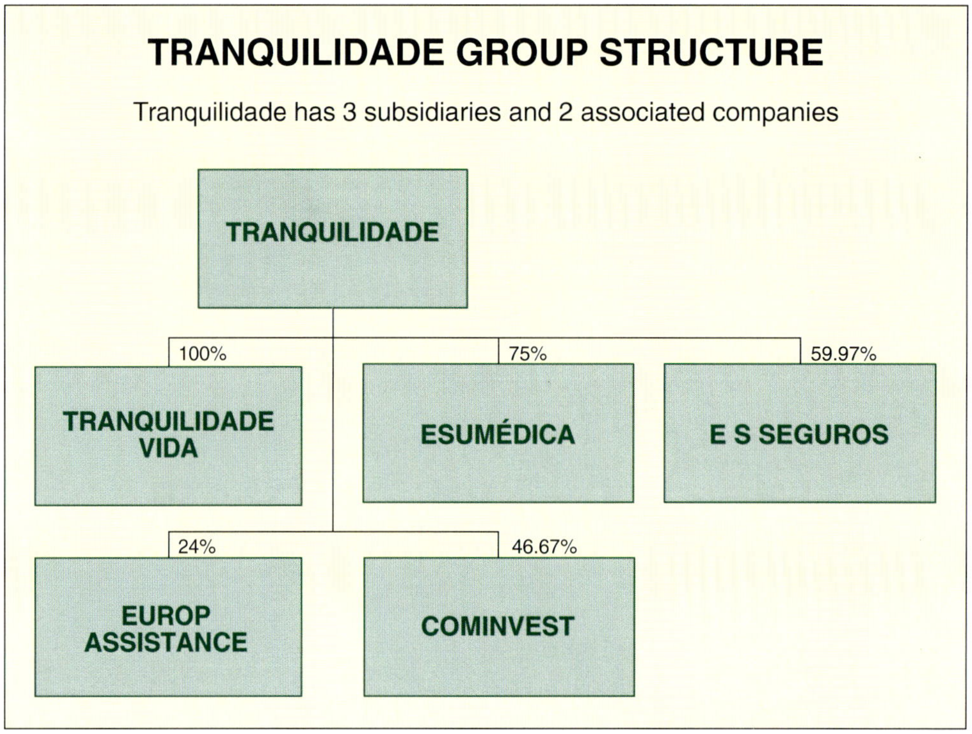

Banco ESSI is the investment banking arm of Grupo Banco Espírito Santo. Its main shareholders are Banco Espírito Santo, Espírito Santo Financial Holding, Banco Espírito Santo International and Compagnie Financière Espírito Santo. Other shareholders include Union Bank of Switzerland and Kredietbank Luxembourgeoise.

The Bank enjoys a leading position among the Portuguese investment banking and financial services sector. In 1995, Banco ESSI won the award for the Best Investment Bank in Portugal in the annual *Euromoney* Awards for Excellence.

From its Lisbon headquarters, Banco ESSI provides its clients with a wide range of investment banking services and products in capital markets, corporate finance, advisory and project finance.

The Bank's capital markets activity is split into two separate departments: debt and equity.

Debt

This department specialises in debt instruments including, the pricing of securities, swaps and derivatives, syndication, trading and distribution activities and the management of the Bank's treasury, proprietary debt accounts and foreign exchange business. The Bank has distinguished itself as a customer-driven unit of the larger Grupo Banco Espírito Santo, relying solely on its expertise and market understanding to fulfill the needs of its clients. Banco ESSI has strategically positioned itself to offer value-added products and ideas, namely, in the diversification of credit risk and interest rate arbitrage.

Equity

The department that focuses on equity manages the Bank's proprietary stock positions and also covers both primary and secondary market activities concerning equity transactions and instruments. Banco ESSI has actively participated in all major equity issues undertaken in Portugal and is now positioning itself to increase its power of placing European issues with domestic investors. Through its commitment to innovation and expansion of equity investment alternatives, Banco ESSI has consolidated a very solid relationship with its widespread domestic and international client base with dedicated sales and research teams that focus on providing updated high-quality research.

Banco ESSI's leadership in the primary market, with a 60 per cent market share and its outstanding performance in the BVL, where it holds a commanding market share of 20 per cent, highlights the Bank's placing power and trading capabilities for Portuguese equities.

Corporate finance

Mergers and acquisitions, leveraged buyouts, financial advisory, company valuations and project finance are the business of the corporate finance department.

Privatisation-driven business has assumed a key role in this unit's activity: this includes not only valuations and advice to the government and to the privatising companies but also to potential buyers. Project finance activity has focused on infrastructure, transport and energy projects.

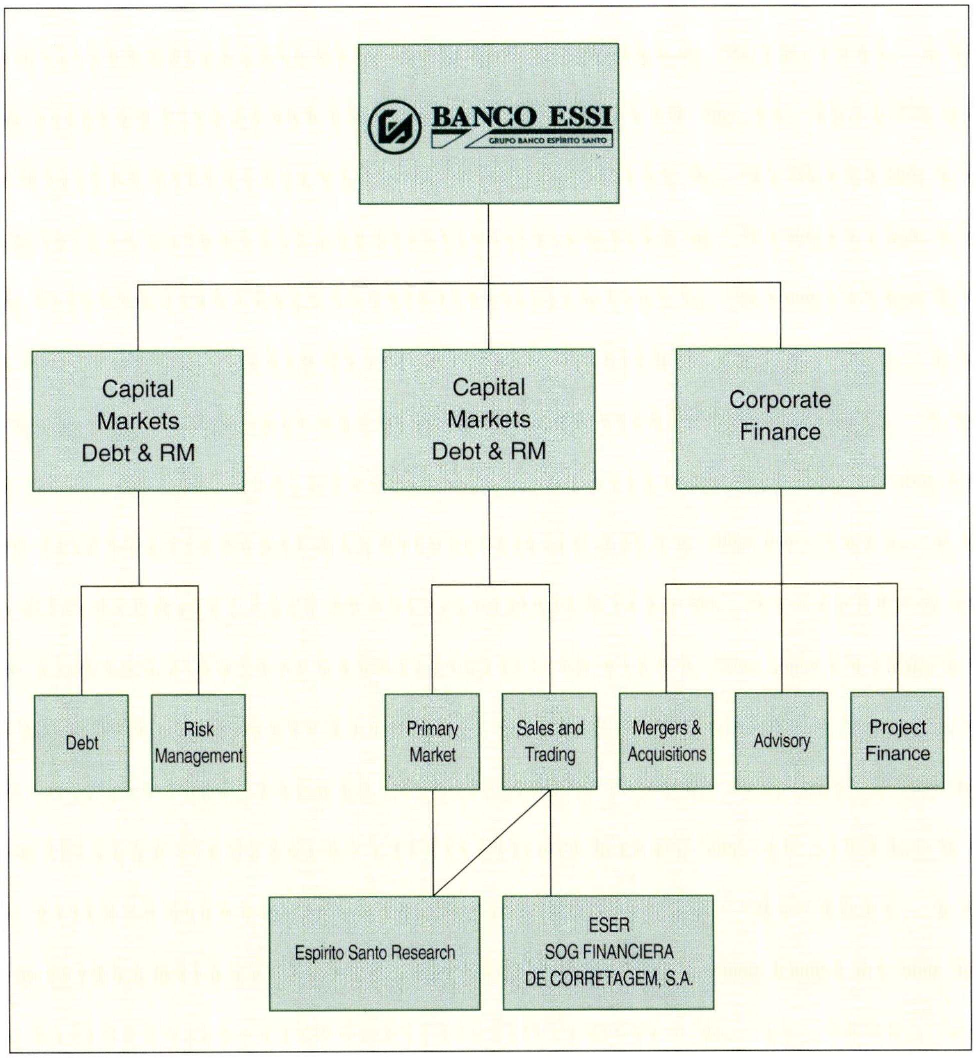

BOLSA
DE VALORES DE LISBOA

Historical background

Commemorating its 225th anniversary in 1994, the Lisbon Stock Exchange – BVL – moved into a new building in the new quarter of the town in order to accommodate the physical requirements demanded by the fast development of the securities market in Portugal.

European Union

This development is contemporaneous with the accession of the country to the European Union, in January 1986, and with the complete abolition of any restrictions on capital movements, both to residents and to non-residents. According to the present Securities Act, the stock exchange is a non-profit civil association whose members are the 11 dealers and the 9 brokers incorporated in Portugal.

A broker company can only intermediate orders in the market and has to maintain a minimum capital of Esc50 million. Dealers add to that capacity the possibility of being principal in an exchange transaction.They are required to have a minimum capital base of Esc500 million. Orders in the market have to be executed by one or more of these members.

Trading

Besides equities the bond market is also very active on the Lisbon exchange, particularly in the Treasury bond segment. Other listed securities are participation bonds and investment trust units.

In order to cope with the different financial capacities of local corporations, the exchange offers three listing categories: the market with official quotations, where the largest, most liquid and oldest companies have their securities listed; the second market to meet the special requirements of small and medium-sized companies; and the market without quotations for special situations and for trading rights issues and other similar securities.

The clear majority of transactions are executed electronically in a continuous process. For a very small slice of the market, orders are traded in a roll-call system with three daily automatic fixings. Although both are order-driven trading systems, it is possible to establish contracts with a member to improve the liquidity of an issue. Short selling (margin account operations) is allowed, according to the regulations issued by the Securities Market Commission, for a selected list of shares and T-bonds.

Clearing and settlement (C&S)

Both the trading and the C&S systems are integrated in a single electronic platform, which is run by an affiliated association of BVL called Interbolsa. This association is also the national Central Securities Depository and the official entity responsible for the ISIN codification of the Portuguese securities market.

Most securities are fully dematerialised. Settlement of exchange transactions is completed on a T+4 and DVP basis. No legal possession of the securities purchased is possible until payment is cleared by the central bank.

Share indices

The prices of the shares listed in the main segment – the market with official quotations – are shown by a share index called BVL-General, introduced on 5 January 1988 and computed daily taking the closing quotations of all listed shares.

Most industries included in that segment also have their own sectoral indices, although these have a more recent base date of 2 January 1991.

Finally, for the blue chips there is the BVL-30 index, which averages the 30 most liquid shares of that segment. The base date is 4 January 1993 and the sample is readjusted every quarter.

All these indices follow the same mathematical methodology: a capitalisation-weighted average of the share prices adjusted for every event, such as cash dividends, rights issues, bonus shares etc, and a base value of 1,000.

Guarantee Fund

The Guarantee Fund is aimed at ensuring the fulfilment of all commitments and duties of the BVL members towards their clients in relation to exchange transactions. However, only small orders issued by individual investors and by companies not included in a specific list are covered by the fund.

Listed companies disclosure requirements

Listed companies have to make public at least the following information:

- annual and first half reports;
- list of entities holding over 10% of the voting rights (2% for banks);
- transactions of large blocks of shares leading to voting rights crossing the following thresholds: 10%; 20%; 33%; 50%; 2/3;
- members of the board of directors; and
- share issues, dividends etc.

Costs

Trading in securities on the BVL involves costs due to the intermediaries (brokers, dealers and banks) and to the exchange. The intermediaries' commissions are negotiable. The stock exchange trading fee is collected both from the buyer and from the seller; fees range from 0.004% to 0.05% according to the type of security. There is no stamp duty.

The main provisions of the taxation system applicable to investment in securities are that:

- both residents and non-residents are taxed on income and on capital gains;
- for companies, both income and net capital gains are included in their P&L accounts and taxed accordingly;
- for individuals, capital gains are taxed at a lower rate than cash income;
- capital gains from bonds or shares held for more than 12 months are not taxed;
- for shares held for more than 12 months, the tax is 10%;
- income from securities is paid net of 20% withholding tax, except for non-residents investing in some particular issues of Treasury bonds, where it is paid gross;
- dividends from listed companies are subject to only 12.5% of income tax (withheld) plus 5% gift and inheritance tax;
- investment funds receive net profits from their investment portfolios as if they were individual investors, then pay gross profits to their investor units; and
- there are several double taxation treaties with other countries allowing for a reduction of the taxes paid in Portugal and deducted in the investor's country of origin.

Privatisations

The Portuguese government has decided to make use of the exchange market to sell the majority of shares of privatised corporations. From the beginning of the programme until the end of 1995, there were 52 special sessions in which all or part of the equity shares of 40 companies were sold to the general public (residents and non-residents).

A significant part of the capital sold is now listed on the BVL, contributing significantly to the capitalisation of the exchange market and to the annual trading volumes. At the end of 1996, 45.65% of the capitalisation of the market with official quotations was due to privatised companies.

Sources of information

The main sources of information on the BVL market and on the Portuguese capital market are:

- BVL publications: Monthly Digest; Securities Market Analysis (quarterly); Annual Report; annual fact sheet covering key market issues and indices over the last 11 years;
- Infobolsa: provides real-time information on the trading session, financial markets, news, listed companies' accounts, indices and other relevant information on the market;
- BVL Data: a computer database for Windows with monthly updates(floppy disc); and
- Vendors: Reuters, Telekurs, Bloomberg, Dow Jones Telerate, Datastream, FT EXTEL.

Lisbon Stock Exchange
Rua Soeiro Pereira Gomes
Edificio de Bolsa
1600 Lisboa
Portugal

Tel: (351) 1 790 0000/9904
Fax: (351) 1 795 2024/2022
http://www.bvl.pt/

ICEP

Investimentos, Comércio e Turismo de Portugal

What is ICEP?

ICEP – Investments, trade and tourism of Portugal – is the government agency responsible for promoting Portugal's economic activities worldwide.

ICEP's mission

It is ICEP's mission to inform and support all companies and business entities, to facilitate proactive business strategies, and to foster a business environment that is favourable to Portugal's international activities in areas such as foreign investment, trade and tourism.

ICEP encourages development

The key role of ICEP is to promote Portugal as an attractive location for investment and tourism as well as to act as a provider of export-related services and expertise to Portuguese companies looking for international opportunities.

ICEP promotes and develops Portugal's business image worldwide with particular emphasis on the following four major areas of activity:

- the export of Portuguese goods and services;
- foreign direct investment in Portugal;
- Portuguese investment abroad;
- tourism.

ICEP supports and assists

With its headquarters in Lisbon, ICEP has six regional offices and 46 offices around the world. Through the collection and distribution of information, corporate development programmes and marketing activities, ICEP strives to meet the needs of:

- Portuguese companies and business leaders with activities outside Portugal;
- corporations seeking to locate in Portugal;
- companies looking for joint venture partners;
- individual tourists and tour operators;
- trade and business press.

Whether in Portugal or abroad, ICEP has the capability and technical expertise to provide companies with relevant information about the Portuguese economy, its sectors and companies, laws and regulations.

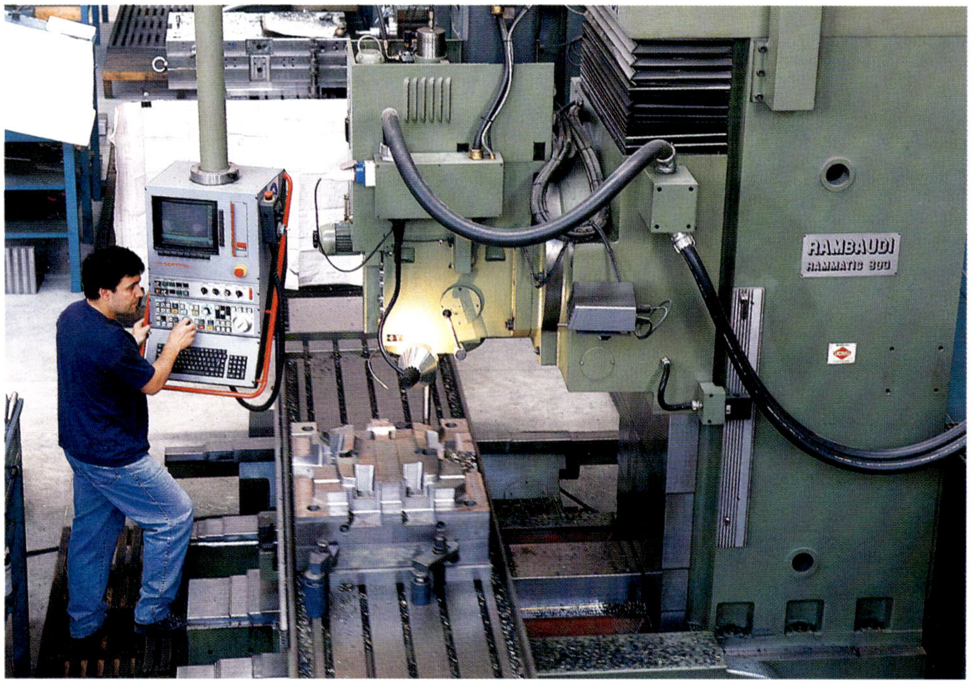

Through its databases, ICEP can also provide details on investment areas and plant sites and can identify joint venture partners and the most suitable suppliers of specific goods and services in Portugal.

Tourist information on leisure programmes, conferences, sports and cultural facilities, itineraries and accommodation can also be accessed through ICEP.

In addition, the agency plans and implements projects in targeted markets such as international advertising campaigns, Portuguese participation in international fairs and exhibitions, trade and business missions and visits to Portugal for traders. It arranges seminars and produces promotional videos and publications.

ICEP advises on investment projects

ICEP's foreign investment promotion programmes provide advice and information on investment decisions, as a first step towards implementing direct investment or entrepreneurial partnership projects in Portugal.

On request, ICEP will select sites and potential suppliers, prepare meetings with the Portuguese business community, public bodies, banks and other financial institutions.

The agency coordinates negotiations with Portuguese officials for major investment projects and provides updates on incentive schemes offered by the Portuguese government.

ICEP also administers a support programme for the internationalisation of Portuguese companies, helping them to develop international investment strategies and making incentives available.

How to contact ICEP

Headquarters: (Lisbon, Portugal)

Av. 5 de Outubro, n°101 - 1050 Lisboa

Tel. (351) 1 7930103

Fax. (351) 1 793 5028

Internet http://www.portugal.org

Portugal

A. M. PEREIRA, SÁRAGGA LEAL, OLIVEIRA MARTINS, JÚDICE E ASSOCIADOS

SOCIEDADE DE ADVOGADOS

Historical background

The firm, which is the largest in Portugal, was founded in 1968 and now has more than 80 qualified lawyers practising full time in various fields of law. The firm's traditional and main area of activity is business law.

It has achieved international standards of expertise in a wide range of related areas of law, in particular foreign investment, corporate law, banking and finance law, capital markets, privatisations, mergers & acquisitions, insolvency, employment law, EU and competition law, tax law, consumer protection, intellectual property (copyright, registration of patents and trademarks), commercial law, administrative law, public tenders, real estate

and construction law, environmental law, commercial and civil litigation and arbitration.

Corporate law

As far as this area is concerned, the firm has pursued numerous studies in corporate planning and organising of groups of companies, especially in mergers and acquisitions. Being the leading Portuguese law firm in terms of M&A and take-overs, A.M.Pereira...

have participated in the most important hostile take-overs to take place in Portugal. The firm has also provided assistance in the context of due diligence procedures, in negotiating and setting up consortia intending to participate in public tenders and it is also very experienced in advising on the responsibilities of directors in corporate management. Insolvency and liquidation of assets are also areas in which the firm has extensive experience.

Banking, finance and privatisations

Since it was founded the firm has specialised in banking law. Some partners, associates and other fee-earners specialise in this area. After Portugal joined the European Community in 1986, there was a boom in the Portuguese banking market, previously dominated by public companies. As a result, foreign banks started to come into the Portuguese market, having been advised by the firm. The firm also provided legal support in the privatisation of state-owned banks and other companies, both financial and non-financial.

The firm has extensive experience in project finance and corporate finance and has been involved in the major Portuguese projects of the last 15 years.

In addition, the firm provides support in the procurement of international loans and has given legal opinions to international lenders.

Tax law

The firm has several associates and fee-earners who specialise solely in tax law, concentrating mainly in the area of fiscal planning. With regard to both direct and indirect taxes, the firm has also practised extensively in contested tax debt cases. Some members of the firm have been contacted by the Portuguese Administration to give comments and advise on the drafting of bills and statutes in the fiscal area.

Intellectual property, trademarks and unfair competition

The firm attends to several matters in connection with industrial property, defence of brands and trademarks registrations and has extensive experience in contracts involving industrial property and intellectual property, having a number of associates who specialise in these areas.

Real estate

The firm has provided numerous services in the real estate area, namely by supporting investment projects in tourism developments (especially in the Algarve and Madeira regions) and industrial construction projects such as the implementation of some of the most important EC projects. Traditionally the firm also provides all the legal support to the biggest development projects in Portugal, covering the legal and fiscal planning of the investment, support in the area of construction law, and following up the whole legal process for transfer and registration of ownership. The firm also has considerable experience in mortgage, lease matters and procurement and public tender law.

Media and communications

The firm represents both domestic and foreign companies in the field of advertising, especially in connection with the preparation and launching of juridical and media restructuring projects.

A considerable amount of work has been done in the field of telecommunications. The firm provides regular legal support to the largest Portuguese telecommunications companies in connection with the development of contractual relations with third parties, as well as in connection with litigation.

EC law

The firm has extensive experience in the field of EC law, particularly with regard to EC competition law, intellectual property, economic law and litigation before the European Court of Justice. Associates of the firm have been deeply involved in EC law work, as post-graduate students, lecturers and practitioners.

The expertise of the firm in this field allows it to expand easily into new areas of EC law and to give clients the advantage of benefiting from the most recent trends of the European Court of Justice jurisprudence, for instance in the domain of deregulation and state-granted monopolies.

Litigation and arbitration

The firm takes care of all legal proceedings on behalf of clients. Numerous lawsuits are currently under way in judicial, administrative and fiscal courts. Several public and private companies are represented by our firm. Some of the most important and complex Portuguese lawsuits have been instituted and followed up by the firm in various jurisdictions.

As far as arbitration is concerned, several suits are proceeding or being prepared, some under ICC rules, others in accordance with the Portuguese arbitration regime.

Services offered

Whenever appropriate, professional services are provided in the various fields of law in close cooperation with other professionals and advisers such as auditors, accountants, brokers and financial institutions.

The firm has developed its own network of correspondent offices with domestic and international law firms and has a multilingual staff. Among the firm's clients receiving legal assistance are some of the major Portuguese and international companies operating in Portugal.

Languages: Portuguese, English, French, German and Spanish.

Contacts: António Maria Pereira, Luis Sáragga Leal, Francisco Oliveira Martins, José Miguel Júdice, Fernando Campos Ferreira, Victor Réfega Fernandes, Pedro Sáragga Leal, Dulce Franco, João Silva Herdeiro, José Luis Cruz Vilaça, Nuno Libano Monteiro, Gabriela Rodrigues Martins

Address: Rua Silva Carvalho, 234, 1250 Lisboa, Portugal;
Tel: (351) (1) 3800700,
Fax: (351) (1) 3877180; 3871728; 3882176; 3833771; 3873353; 3833841

Petróleos de Portugal

Petrogal, s.a.

Towards the next millennium

With turnover exceeding US$5.3 billion in 1996, Portugal's number one company, Petrogal, is now top of the Portuguese exports league. On 1 April 1976, Portugal's only oil refining company, Petrogal E.P., became a public company through the merger of four companies: Sonap, Sacor, Cidla and Petrosul.

Founded in 1933, Sonap had been operating as a distributor within Portugal and certain former colonies; Sacor owned the only two refineries in Portugal at Lisbon (Cabo Ruivo) and Oporto; Cidla, a subsidiary of Sacor, was formed to market and distribute butane and propane; Petrosul was awarded the contract for the largest refinery in Portugal (Sines), coming on-stream in 1979.

In 1989, the government decided that Petrogal should become a public limited company with the state remaining as sole shareholder. In 1991 the privatisation process began, the state retaining a 75 per cent holding and the remaining 25 per cent being sold to private shareholders under the umbrella of Petrocontrol.

During 1995 Petrogal's share capital increased to more than US$19 million with a redistribution of capital so that the state retained 55 per cent and Petrocontrol's holding increased to 45 per cent. Under the chairmanship of Eng. Manuel Ferreira de Oliveira, the present board of directors was elected and comprises Eng. Antonio Salvador Pinheiro, Dr Raul Sant'Anna Coelho, Dr Antonio Chalmique Chagas and Eng. Carlos Correa da Silva.

Market deregulation and privatisation have led Petrogal to embark on a programme of reorganisation and modernisation. With its updated network of service stations and upgraded refining facilities, Petrogal has already brought about significant improvements in competitive performance.

Petrogal 2000

Acknowledging the problems faced within the industry worldwide in terms of poor refining margins and over-supply, Petrogal has already launched an ambitious project, Petrogal 2000, which aims to bring the company's financial position within industry parameters by the end of the century. This decisive action is seen as the route to raising shareholder value while upgrading customer services and motivating personnel to further achievement.

The Priorities of the new strategy are:

- operational improvements that translate into reduced costs and increased productivity;
- strategic repositioning in relation to refining, with the production of hydrocarbons and greater commitment to natural gas; and
- financial optimisation achieved by management improvements and debt restructuring.

Prospecting and production

Petrogal is stepping up oil and natural gas exploitation and prospecting in order to access its own supply sources. As well as consolidating its position in Angola, particularly in the Cabinda region, Petrogal intends to acquire interests in crude oil production. Petrogal is Portugal's only refining company, with a distillation capacity of over 15.5 million tons per year.

The Sines refinery is the largest of the two currently operating and occupies an area of more than 320 hectares. Its distillation capacity is around 11 million tons per year and it has a total storage capacity of almost 3 million cubic metres, half of which is for crude oil. The Sines industrial complex was recently renovated and its refining facilities have been updated with the addition of new units: a modern conversion system, catalytic cracking, visbreaking, a new vacuum distillation unit and an alkylation unit. The refinery also includes a gasoline complex with recent investment in a gas oil de-sulphuration scheme permitting a reduction in gas oil sulphur content.

Refining

The Oporto refinery occupies an area of 290 hectares and has two atmospheric distillation units with a distillation capacity of almost 5 million tons per year. The refinery's total storage capacity is 1,600,000 cubic metres with the capacity to store up to 900,000 cubic metres of crude oil. The industrial complex also includes plants for fuels, base oils and lubricants, hydrocarbons, aromatics and solvents, all of which have quality approval. The aromatics and solvents plant has a storage capacity of 33,000 cubic metres and its reformate treatment capacity is 21,000 cubic metres.

Petrogal's terminals and tank farms are its main facilities for receiving, forwarding and storage and their most important port terminals are in Liexoes (Oporto), Lisbon and Sines. Petrogal's storage capacity for crude and other products is approximately 90 per cent of Portugal's total. In addition to the Boa Nova (Oporto) and Sines tank farms, Petrogal operates other storage facilities for liquid fuels in mainland Portugal, Madeira and the Azores.

Logistics

The Porto Brandão tank farm near Lisbon is the largest of the storage facilities supplying diesel, JP8 and fuel oil. The Aveiro tank farm is the second largest in terms of storing diesel and is the only storage unit for petrochemicals. In the Algarve, Petrogal's liquid fuel tank farm in Faro stores gasoline, diesel and aviation fuel. Petrogal has storage facilities in the Azores at Angra do Heroismo, Horta, Lajes and Porto Santo. Liquefied petroleum gases (LPGs) are stored at the Rosarinho tank farm, near Moita do Ribatejo, south of Lisbon, the Perafita tank farm near Oporto, and at the Oilivais tank farm near Lisbon.

Petrogal has formed a new company, CLC – Companhia Logistica de Combustiveis, to concentrate specifically on fuel logistics. CLC built a fuels storage and filling tank at Aveiras de Cima and a pipeline that connects this complex to the Sines refinery to supply central Portugal and the greater Lisbon area.

Commercial activities

Petrogal's activities span the following separate businesses:

- Galp Trading supplies the Petrogal Group with raw materials and products as well as selling refined products to the competition, to major Portuguese customers, the international markets and within the Group itself;
- Galp Fuels is responsible for the marketing and distribution of liquid fuels to be retailed within mainland Portugal; through the Galp brand, Petrogal owns a network of 1,190 filling stations;
- Galp Bunkers and Industry sells liquid fuels to the aviation and marine bunkers market as well as supplying the industrial sector;
- Galp Chemicals is responsible for managing and marketing chemical products, both produced by the aromatics plant and imported;
- Galp Special Products markets and distributes special products, lubricants, bitumens and asphalts, where the technical element is a major selling factor;
- Galp Gas markets and distributes Petrogal's gas fuels, bulk and bottled butane and propane. This operation has developed a distribution network of over 1,000 dealers and more than 2,000 direct customers;
- Galp Island and International's main role is to manage and coordinate the companies located outside mainland Portugal.

The Petrogal distribution network

One of the company's most profitable areas is the distribution of oil products. Petrogal leads the domestic market with a share of more than 55 per cent.

The company distributes a wide range of products direct to the end-user, including liquid fuels, liquefied petroleum gases, base oils, lubricants and chemicals as well as bitumens, chemical naphtha, waxes, paraffins, sulphur, for example.

Petrogal operates Portugal's largest distribution network consisting of 1,190 filling stations (of which 14 are motorway service stations), 800 outlets on the premises of major consumers, 11,000 bottled gas dealers as well as 2,000 industrial users. Via the Marine Bunkers service, Petrogal supplies the Portuguese naval and merchant fleets as well as domestic and foreign fishing industries. The company uses tank trucks, barges and tankers that are loaded straight through terminal pipelines. Civil and military requirements are dealt with by specialist staff from the Air Bunkers service based at Portugal's main airports.

Petrogal abroad

Petrogal is also very active abroad due to its excellent reputation among other international operators. The company's source of raw materials is safeguarded by a variety of markets dominated by the Middle East and supported by West and North Africa, Europe and Latin America. In 1996, exports had climbed to more than US$658.6 million – an indication of the substantial volume of Petrogal's overseas business.

International policy

Petrogal's international strategy aims at boosting Group sales in areas of the world that can offer competitive advantages. Ease of market penetration is another factor to consider along with the criteria of profitability and risk analysis defined for each area. Petrogal is also concentrating on the Spanish and African markets. One of Spain's largest foreign companies, with a network of more than 160 filling stations, Petrogal Española markets and distributes liquid fuels, lubricants and gases and is the company's representative in Spain. The strategy is to increase market share to 5 per cent.

Petrogal has a strong presence in Africa, particularly in Angola, Mozambique and the islands of Cape Verde and São Tomé Principe, where the company's aim is to reinforce that presence. The close relationship with Africa's Portuguese-speaking countries is to their mutual benefit, with the transfer of technology, vocational training and the provision of technical back-up. Naturally these markets can rely on the consistently high quality of Petrogal's products and services. The company's African operations are channelled through its associated or affiliated companies and contracts for supply and technical back-up services are held with local companies.

It is in Angola that Petrogal is most active, concentrating on prospecting and exploration through Galp Africa. The distribution of fuels is operated by Sonangalp with whom the company also holds a lubes contract. In Angola, Petrogal also owns Angran, a company which produces and distributes chemicals for agricultural, public health and home use.

Petrogal has a major interest in Mozambique's only gas distributor, Moçacor, which has two storage parks. In Guinea-Bissau, Petrogal's company Petromar distributes fuels and lubricants as well as marine bunker supplies. Petromar also operates a network of filling stations under the Galp brand. Petrogal is the supplier of lubricants in and around the islands of Cape Verde and São Tomé, and has technical back-up contracts with the local oil companies, Enacol and Enco.

The Petrogal Group

The mission of the Petrogal Group is to adopt common values that will lead to improved coordination and harmony between the various companies so that they can all contribute more to the Group's trading results. The Group comprises 17 subsidiaries and a similar number of associated and partly owned companies.

Human resources

One of the Group's leading companies in Portugal is the newly formed CLC – Companhia Logistica de Combustiveis which will manage the Aveiras park, supplying fuel to the whole of central Portugal. Other major players within the Group include the shipping company, Sacor Marine; Galpgeste, involved in service area managment within the Galp network; and Petrogas, the holding company of the natural gas business.

Human resources are the company's most valuable asset. Over 3,519 people are employed and Petrogal considers each one as being essential for the success of its mission. The company is striving to achieve the highest levels of professionalism and motivation by placing a high value on improving individual and team performance. The efficient administration of salaries, training, mobility and recruitment are the prime objectives in this area.

Communication

Petrogal is aware of the fundamental role played by employee loyalty, public opinion, economic viability and effective communication to ensure a company's success and to reinforce and enhance its image of credibility both inside and outside the company.

There is a strong commitment to ensure that the Petrogal name is associated with the Galp brand which, in turn, must be synonymous with an image of a company that is at the forefront of technology and offers a high-quality service.

Environment, quality and safety

Petrogal takes an active role in environmental protection and it is the company's aim to ensure global environmental awareness. Petrogal's approach to environmental issues, quality control and safety is in line with Portuguese and European Union legislation. Petrogal is seeking to increase its involvement with legislative and standards authorities in order to avoid accidents, protect people's health and safeguard the environment.

Image and ethics

It is essential that a consensus exists between all employees, on the basis of clearly defined work ethics set out in a code that serves as a reference for all those working in the Group. The code of ethics must govern all working relationships both within the company and when representing it. Being well-known in Portugal is not sufficient for Petrogal – what really matters is to create an image of quality to ensure total confidence outside the company.

Outlook for the Year 2000

On the basis of the parameters underpinning the Petrogal 2000 project, operational optimisation, strategic repositioning and financial restructuring, Petrogal is set to become a profitable company that will continue to be worthy of customer confidence as well as successfully raising shareholder value. Strategies have been well-defined and throughout 1996 there were signs that the desired changes had been taking place on the challenging route to the new Petrogal, providing the company with the means to fulfill its stated mission. The route to the next millennium and beyond promises to be an exciting and rewarding one for Petrogal.

SONAE as an innovative and leading company

SONAE is Portugal's leading company in the retail-related segments of the economy. In the last ten years, it has led the modernisation of retailing in this country through the introduction of the first hypermarkets stores and the development of state-of-the-art shopping centres.

A combination of vision, leadership, accelerated growth and profitability has made SONAE an innovative and renowned company with a dominant business influence in modern Portugal.

Historical background

Founded in 1959, in the Oporto area, the company's roots were curiously to be found not in retailing but in the high-pressure laminates industry. SONAE pioneered the production of decorative laminates and grew as a small company. The 1980s saw the beginning of a period of growth and expansion for SONAE. The Portuguese economy began to change and develop rapidly influenced by the country's entry into the European Community. Recognising this as an era of great business opportunities, SONAE started the expansion of its operations in new areas. In the 1980s, the company entered into the retailing sector, first acquiring the Modelo supermarket chain and then launching the first hypermarket in Portugal (a Continente store in Oporto). Forming SONAE Imobiliária was a natural step by which it began developing shopping malls adjacent to SONAE retail stores. CascaiShopping, Portugal's premier shopping centres, opened in the Lisbon region in 1991. At the same time the company invested in many other areas including communications, information technology, leisure and tourism.

The beginning of the 1990s brought new competitive challenges for businesses in Europe. To meet these challenges the holding company reorganised its core businesses into four areas:

- SONAE Indústria SGPS as an international manufacturing and marketing network of wood-based products with a global strategic focus and several industrial platforms based around Portugal, Spain, the UK, Canada, Brazil and South Africa;
- SONAE Distribuição SGPS as the leading retailer in Portugal in terms of market share, growth and profitability, with plans to expand its activities outside the country;
- SONAE Imobiliária SGPS, growing as the leader of shopping centre development levering the retail business;
- All other businesses, regarded as non-strategic activities, were grouped into Pargeste, the sub-holding responsible for new ventures.

In 1996, anticipating the new challenges of and international expansion of its different businesses, and the need to focus management resources on its development, it was decided that the business held by SONAE Indústria and Pargeste should be demerged from SONAE Investimentos SGPS.

As a result SONAE Investimentos SGPS is now the holding company solely dedicated to all retail-related businesses and a new holding company, Inparsa SGPS, was formed to concentrate on the wood-based business (SONAE Indústria SGPS) and all other activities in the Pargeste portfolio.

A demerger aimed at international growth

Following the demerger, SONAE Investimentos SGPS, a company listed on the Lisbon Stock Exchange, is now fully focused on retail-related businesses, and its portfolio and organisational structure are divided into four domains:

- **General retail – hypermarkets and supermarkets,** through Modelo Continente in Portugal and Modelo Investimentos in Brazil;
- **Specialised retail**, under the newly established sub-holding company SONAE Retalho Especializado SGPS;
- **Retailing real estate – shopping centres**, through SONAE Imobiliária SGPS;
- **Retailing of financial products**, by the companies grouped under SONAE Participações Financeiras SGPS.

Facts about the new focused SONAE

In 1996, SONAE profits after tax and minority interests were US$133 million and the consolidated turnover, related to the above sectors which remain in SONAE Investimentos SGPS portfolio after demerger, amounted to US$2.4 billion. SONAE's personnel numbered over 19,345, of which 3,931 were employed by CRD in Brazil.

Hypermarkets and supermarkets

The SONAE leadership in retailing is based on its continuous marketing innovation, the use of modern logistics and information technology systems and a strong programme of store expansion in all differents formats.

Today the company is clearly the leading Portuguese retailer with a market share of 40 per cent in the modern distribution sector but less then 10 per cent in terms of the total consumer market, which means that, despite its leading position, compared to similar companies in other countries, SONAE still has substantial growth potential ahead. In 1996 all different store chains showed a high rate of openings, particularly Modelo (a medium hypermarket store) that expanded by 14 stores, now numbering a total of 36. The new Modalfa (specialists in the textile range) and Worten (appliances and electronic goods) had, respectively, a total of 17 and 9 stores by the end of the year. Continente (the hypermarket chain), which is going to open the largest store in Portugal in 1997, now has 8 stores located in the large Portuguese cities.

The Brazilian operation, which was acquired in 1995, has confirmed the company strategy of international expansion, achieving a turnover of US$460 million and with its two flagships, Big hypermarkets and Real supermarkets, contributed to SONAE's results for the first time.

Specialised retailing

With regards to specialised retailing, the next step is to roll out the Max-Mat chain, the SONAE construction materials retailer, after fine-tuning carried out during 1996. The SONAE Quelle catalogue achieved its expected results for the second year of its operation. Other segments were evaluated last year through market research and as a result, a programme of expansion at prime locations in major cities will be carried out in new product areas as diverse as computers and sports goods.

Shopping centres

SONAE is actively involved in the promotion of new shopping centres. The first Portuguese modern out-of-town shopping mall was designed and opened in 1991 by SONAE in Cascais, near Lisbon. Today accounting for more than half of the market with its 176,000m of GLA (with more than 280,000m under construction), SONAE's goal is to reinforce its leadership. Relevant to this strategy is Colombo, the biggest shopping centre in the Iberian Peninsula, which is due to open in early autumn 1997 and other large ventures like Vasco da Gama at the EXPO '98 site and NorteShopping in Oporto.

Location, concept, tenant-mix and quality management have been instrumental in the success of SONAE's shopping centres business strategy which has attracted a significant number of well known, modern international retail chains to Portugal. In addition to development, SONAE Imobiliária portfolio includes a shopping centre and car park management business and more recently has started to extend its expertise to support a new housing development business.

Grosvenor, a leading British real estate company, has recently taken a 25 per cent stake in SONAE Imobiliária which, as a strategic partner, will make an important contribution to the development of activities outside Portugal.

Retailing of financial products

The success in financial products ventures, consumer credit since 1992 and the Visa Universo credit card launched in 1995, has led SONAE to widen the scope of its retailing activities. In March 1997, SONAE opened 43 financial shops in its hypermarkets and supermarkets, which will be complemented by a telephone service to sell savings, consumer credit, mortgages and insurance products. This initiative was seen as a good way to increase customer loyalty and to benefit from the SONAE customer base of 1.2 million families, a third of the Portuguese population.

An exciting future

The company strategy is to improve the rate of innovation and growth in retail-related businesses. Portugal, Spain and Brazil are the main countries in which SONAE is seeking either to consolidate its leadership or to secure a significant stake of the market.

Its workforce of 16,500 and its management team believe in an exciting future with a new world of retail opportunities. As the president of SONAE, Belmiro de Azevedo, used to say, quoting a well-known poet, "Wanderer, there is no path. The path is made by walking through".